A Homeopathic Guide to

partnership

and

compatibility

A Homeopathic Guide to

partnership

and

compatibility

Understanding Your Type
and Finding Love

Liz Lalor

North Atlantic Books
Berkeley, California

Published by
North Atlantic Books
P.O. Box 12327
Berkeley, California 94712

and
Homeopathic Educational Services
2124 Kittredge Street
Berkeley, California 94704

Cover and book design by Maxine Ressler
Printed in the United States of America
Distributed to the book trade by Publishers Group West

A Homeopathic Guide to Partnership and Compatibility: Understanding Your Type and Finding Love is sponsored by the Society for the Study of Native Arts and Sciences, a nonprofit educational corporation whose goals are to develop an educational and crosscultural perspective linking various scientific, social, and artistic fields; to nurture a holistic view of arts, sciences, humanities, and healing; and to publish and distribute literature on the relationship of mind, body, and nature.

North Atlantic Books' publications are available through most bookstores. For further information, call 800-337-2665 or visit our website at www.northatlanticbooks.com.

Substantial discounts on bulk quantities are available to corporations, professional associations, and other organizations. For details and discount information, contact our special sales department.

Library of Congress Cataloging-in-Publication Data

Lalor, Liz, 1956 –
A homeopathic guide to partnership and compatibility : understanding your type and finding love / by Liz Lalor.
  p. cm.
Includes bibliographical references and index.
  ISBN 1-55643-528-2 (pbk.)
  1. Typology (Psychology) 2. Homeopathy – Miscellanea. 3. Mate selection. 4. Love. I. Title.
  BF698.3.L35 2004
  155.2´6 – dc22   2004014219

1 2 3 4 5 6 7 8 9   DATA   09 08 07 06 05 04

*This book is dedicated to my son Emil.
Through the successful treatment of his illness
I was able to learn the unique healing quality
of homeopathic medicines.*

Contents

Foreword by Dr. Philip M. Bailey   xi

Introduction   1

    Understanding Partnerships with Homeopathy   2

    What Does a Homeopath Look For?   3

    What Is a Homeopathic Constitutional Remedy?   4

    What Is a Homeopathic Remedy?   7

    Which Constitution Am I? – How to Use the Summaries   11

The Constitutional Summaries   15

    Arsenicum Album   16

    Calcarea Carbonica   19

    Carcinosin   23

    Causticum   27

    Graphites   30

    Ignatia   33

    Lachesis   36

    Lycopodium   40

    Magnesium Carbonica   44

Medorrhinum 47

Mercurius 51

Natrum Muriaticum 55

Nux Vomica 59

Phosphorus 62

Pulsatilla 65

Sepia 68

Silicea 72

Staphisagria 75

Sulphur 79

The Partnership Combinations 83

Carcinosin Partnerships 84

    Carcinosin and Ignatia 92

    Carcinosin and Mercurius 98

    Carcinosin and Silicea 104

Lycopodium Partnerships 109

    Lycopodium and Calcarea Carbonica 119

    Lycopodium Man and a Lachesis Woman 124

    Lycopodium and Natrum Muriaticum 128

    Lycopodium and Pulsatilla 132

    Lycopodium and Silicea 140

Natrum Muriaticum Partnerships 148

    Natrum Muriaticum and Arsenicum Album 155

    Natrum Muriaticum and Causticum 162

    Natrum Muriaticum and Natrum Muriaticum 167

    Natrum Muriaticum and Phosphorus 172

Natrum Muriaticum and Sepia   179

Sepia Partnerships – The Sepia Woman   184

    Sepia Woman and a Lycopodium Man   188

    Sepia Woman and Medorrhinum   192

    Sepia Woman and Nux Vomica   201

Staphisagria Partnerships   209

    Staphisagria and Graphites   216

    Staphisagria and Mercurius   221

Sulphur Partnerships   226

    Sulphur and Lachesis   234

    Sulphur and Magnesium Carbonica   238

Bibliography   246

About the Author   247

Acknowledgments   248

Index of Film and Literature References   250

Endnotes   253

Index   269

Foreword by
Dr. Philip M. Bailey

This is a book that I have often thought of writing myself, but Liz Lalor has beaten me to it, and done a thoroughly good job. Out of the hundred or so homeopathic personality types that I have learned to recognize over the past twenty years, I have noticed that some naturally go well with others as couples. Just as Pisces people get on well with Taureans, so Nux Vomica gets on well with Ignatia. It is one thing to occasionally notice common combinations of types, but quite another to give serious thought to why this should be so, and to come up with sound reasons. Liz has done a remarkable job in describing common personality types in a manner that is easily comprehensible, yet also covers the essence of each type with enough subtlety to satisfy the serious reader. Secondly, she has analyzed the interpersonal dynamics of each combination with the help of a wealth of original insights. The result is, to my knowledge, the first book of its kind. A serious and entertaining exposition of how homeopathic types interact in relationships.

Human relationships are complicated systems, and yet certain personality types are attracted to each other, creating noticeable patterns which we can study. An example of this is the martyr type who is attracted to rescuing a victim type, which could be seen when a Carcinosin personality takes care of a Phosphorus in distress. Homeopathic types are especially well-suited to this kind of study, since they contain within their pictures profound essences, which can say more about a person's true nature than an exhaustive analysis of individual traits. However, in order to attempt such a study, the homeopath must first have sufficient skill and experience to be able to correctly identify constitutional types, and second, must have the psychological sensitivity to be able to observe and identify subtle interpersonal dynamics within couples. It is no wonder then that such a study has been so long coming, and I commend Liz for succeeding where most would fear to tread.

Ms. Lalor's work confirms the old adage that like attracts like, as illustrated by her chapter on the combination of two fiery creative types, Sulphur and Lachesis. These two types are easily confused by homeopaths, and it is to the author's credit that she is able to clearly show their differences, as well as their similarities. It also confirms the opposite adage that opposites attract. Few partners could be more dissimilar than Lycopodium and Pulsatilla, yet Liz provides us with a rich and realistic picture of why they would want to be together, and what each can give to the other. In doing so, she sheds light on all our relationships, and why they are worth the trouble they entail.

PHILIP M. BAILEY, M.D. is the author of *Homeopathic Psychology,* published by North Atlantic Books in 1995.

introduction

Understanding Partnerships with Homeopathy

Admittedly, a homeopathic guide to help you choose the right partner could be seen as unusual, since most people think homeopathy covers the treatment of physical illness. Health food stores now stock homeopathic remedies for all sorts of complaints, from travel sickness to hay fever. It is logical to think that if you are suffering from hay fever you might consult a homeopath, but you would be extremely unlikely to think of consulting a homeopath if you were having trouble with your relationship. What you will discover in this book is that homeopathy can be used to cure ailments of the heart as well as for cures of physical ailments. *A Homeopathic Guide to Partnership and Compatibility* is a modern-day guide that extends the realm of homeopathy into the sphere of relationships.

Have you ever wanted to know why you keep having the same fights with your partner? Do you have trouble finding someone who is able to understand what your needs are? Have you been in several unsuccessful partnerships, or are you in a difficult relationship now? We don't just become unhealthy when we get physically sick; we can also become unhealthy when we get embroiled in a relationship that is not compatible with our needs or sensitivities as a person. The main inspiration behind this book was to use homeopathic analysis to provide insights into your relationship patterns. Reading this book will not only help you understand what sort of person you are; it will provide understanding between yourself and your partner, so that both of you can arrive at a workable compromise. Understanding is the first step in learning to love yourself and others, and the insights gained from this book will also prove invaluable in all of your future relationships.

What Does a Homeopath Look For?

Let me give you a brief description of how a homeopathic consultation works. I usually start a consultation with a discussion of all the physical complaints, or presenting issues, you have. (If you have come for help with emotional issues, I start with those instead, because they are the presenting issues.) I then move on to the type of person sitting before me, and what concerns me most in thinking about the person before me (you) is why the stresses or experiences in your life are expressed in a particular way. In a homeopathic consultation I try to find the one event or set of circumstances which caused or contributed to making you unwell; it is labeled as the "never-well-since" symptom. If you have been sick ever since a particular traumatic event, or an unsuccessful relationship, this is obviously significant because a relationship that does not meet your needs and sensitivities is eventually going to cause you a lot of stress, and contribute to your failed health.

While there may be many self-help and how-to books that explore relationships, homeopathic analysis of relationship compatibility is unique because it can explain the psychology of relationships through the process of truly understanding your emotional needs. The homeopathic understanding I offer in this book is not a list of positive-thinking mantras that help you in your partnership for one month; it is a permanent framework of health that is concerned with helping you understand more about yourself, and what sort of relationship will be compatible with your personality. In homeopathy, the *constitutional remedies* provide the analytical structure needed to explore how you work, and how your relationships work.

What Is a Homeopathic *Constitutional Remedy?*
· ·

You do not need any knowledge of homeopathy to use this book, and although it is written in language that every reader can understand, there are phrases and terminology specific to homeopathy that need to be explained before going any further. The term *homeopathic constitution* encompasses all of the characteristics of a person — it defines the connecting relationship between the physical, emotional, and mental characteristics. Constitutional analysis is inclusive of the whole person and is based on the assumption that it is a state of being the person moves into as a result of emotional trauma. A *constitution* is not a personality type or individual, nor is it a set or permanent state that is predetermined for life. A person moves into a constitutional state and can stay in that constitution for a short or long time. Homeopathic constitutional analysis is based on matching the person's state to a *homeopathic remedy.* Each remedy picture described in this book is analyzed in relation to how each constitutional type behaves in love and relationships. Through an understanding of the personality of each constitutional type, we can get an idea of our own personality and, consequently, those with whom we would be compatible.

In this book I use characters in films and literature as examples of different constitutional types in relationships. I selected films for reference on the basis that the characters portray the full meaning and nature of a constitutional picture, and they range from golden oldies such as *The African Queen* to the modern-day film *American Splendor.* (The list of films and books is at the end of this book for your reference.) It is not crucial to know the films or books used in order to understand the constitutional pictures described because a constitutional personality picture is not the character in the film as such; it is a state that is inclusive of the core essence of the personality of the character and the discussion will be enough to help you understand the gist of each constitution. I also continually refer to the *theme* running through a constitutional type. The theme is the connecting link between the physical, emotional, and mental characteristics of a constitutional picture. In assessing constitutional pictures, do not concentrate on the character or form a stereotype of the personality picture; concentrate on the theme, which motivates the person's feelings, and the emotional themes acted out within the relationships that are indicative of the constitutional picture.

The constitutional types I have chosen to discuss in this book are some of the most common types that I see every day in my clinical practice. The partnership combinations I have chosen to discuss are based on my clinical experience counseling couples; these are also the most common combinations that I have observed in film and literature. If you do not find your particular relationship combination, you should be able to work out the potential positives and potential negatives from the discussions of your constitution with other combinations.

Throughout this book, unless the discussion is specific to male or female issues, I avoid gender references in descriptions of constitutions or the role of partners. If there is no gender reference in a heading, the discussion of a relationship is neutral, and whether the partner is a man or woman is irrelevant to the issue of compatibility. In some chapters in the relationship section, the discussion is gender-specific, and in those chapters it is important to the understanding of the relationship combination to discuss from a male or female perspective. The films discussed are predominantly heterosexual in nature, simply because the majority of romance films are centered on traditional male-female roles. I tried, however, to include as many non-biased films to illuminate the constitutional types portrayed by characters. I use plural pronouns in the discussions of constitutional types to imply that the discussion is inclusive of both "she" and "he." Because homeopathic constitutional analysis is inclusive of the whole person and is based on the assumption that a person moves into a state of being, there is no benefit in analyzing gender differences relative to emotional themes and motivations, unless of course, it is crucial to the emotional trauma or development of the person or constitution.

Each constitutional type responds differently to the same trauma, and a homeopath tries to find out why and how you as an individual get stressed by an event in your life. Homeopathic constitutional analysis is always concerned with the underlying presenting themes and emotional causes of illness or emotional discord. Homeopathy does not look at the emergence of disease as simplistically as, for example, cancer being caused by negative thought patterns; rather, homeopathy treats each individual's response to trauma within his or her life. Each constitutional analysis will have what can appear to be a list of positive and negative feelings, or "healthy" and "unhealthy" phases. Homeopathy is not about trying to impose concepts of what are the positive sides of a constitution. It is not relevant or applicable to judge aspects of a constitution in those terms. Homeopathy is not based on negative or positive constructs, but instead on the premise that when people go against their true selves they will move into their unhealthy phase. It is therefore crucial that you identify within yourself the tendency to have both the healthy and unhealthy presentations of your particular constitutional personality. Homeopathic understanding is also based on the premise that a particular event in someone's life has the ability to throw that person into an unhealthy phase. In homeopathic analysis an unhealthy phase could last for one day or a week or twenty years, depending on what causes it.

I spent years counseling patients before I studied homeopathy. During twenty-four years as a natural therapist treating back pain sufferers with various forms of alternative therapy, I found the recurring, underlying theme of their back tension always originated in the difficult issues within their relationships. It was clear to me early on that I needed to understand somatic psychotherapy. Homeopathy is the only health-based therapy that gives form and definition to the true meaning of somatic, which implies that the expression of mental and emotional conditions runs through the physical body. Even though I might be treating a patient with a simple case of hay fever, it is essential that I also treat the whole personality of the patient. Including the whole person in treatment is what is wonderfully unique to the practice of homeopathy. A constitutional analysis encompasses who you are, how you operate in the world, how you interact with people, and, most important for this book, what you are like in your relationships. In my work as a homeopath the same issues still exist; behind all the presenting stressors of my patients I continually see a lot of angst coming from miscommunication in their relationships. This finding is what led me to write this book. No other homeopathic study has looked at the issues of compatibility and at the psychology of relationships through the eyes of homeopathy. If you are a homeopath and you have never thought about analyzing your patients by what they are like in relationships, then this book will provide useful insight.

All relationships have the potential to be successful, and homeopathic constitutional analysis can provide a framework for that success. Love and understanding, of yourself and your partner, is possible when you understand the emotional motivations behind constitutional remedies. A true partnership will reflect the depth that is gained from understanding and finding your true self within your constitutional homeopathic personality.

What Is a Homeopathic Remedy?

Homeopathy is based on the practice of a substance being used as a medicine that is *like* the disease that needs to be cured. The founder of homeopathy, Samuel Hahnemann, called this the theory of "like cures like." He discovered the theory of homeopathy by testing *Cinchona officinalis*. *Cinchona officinalis* comes from what is commonly known as the quinine tree because its main product or ingredient is quinine. Herbalists had previously considered *Cinchona officinalis* to be an excellent medicine for feverish states because it provided relief from fever by promoting gentle perspiration. Because Hahnemann was a leading eighteenth-century German chemist and physician he was already familiar with the clinical use of quinine as a treatment for malaria. Hahnemann experimented by ingesting small amounts of quinine bark and discovered that the crude substance produced the same symptoms as the disease malaria. To reduce the toxicity of the crude substance, quinine, Hahnemann experimented with diluting a tincture of *Cinchona officinalis*.

Hahnemann discovered by diluting *Cinchona officinalis*, he was able to reduce the toxicity of the crude or raw substance quinine bark. He also found when he diluted and had vigorously shaken the dilution, known as *potentizing,* he was able to increase the effectiveness or potency of the solution as a medicine. It was this process of both diluting and potentizing that enabled him to discover that the effects grew stronger the more he diluted and potentized the substance. The process of infinitely diluting and potentizing medicines has always been criticized by the scientific world. Homeopathic remedies are diluted and potentized by taking one drop of a solution and adding that one drop to 99 drops of water ad infinitum; up to 6, or 30, or 200, or even a million dilutions. From a conventional chemist's point of view, a dilution past 12, known as "Avogadro's number," or the point of infinity, would have none of the original solution left in the substance. For example, this means that when chemists examine the homeopathic dilution of *Arsenicum,* derived from the poison arsenic, they will find no trace of the original poison arsenic. Homeopathic remedies are diluted beyond the point of containing any of the original source or substance − for arsenic, then, the important aspect of dilution is when a homeopathic remedy is made from arsenic, it is no longer arsenic.

The magazine *New Scientist*[1] recently reported an amazing discovery in support of the original findings of Hahnemann and the experience of homeopaths for centuries. The article is based on the findings of two Korean chemists who discovered in the process of diluting solutions in water that the molecules behaved the opposite to the belief systems that conventional chemistry has always had. Dissolved molecules are assumed to spread farther apart in the dilution process. The two chemists discovered that they do the opposite. Because the molecules do in fact clump together, it throws light on the belief that homeopaths have always had that the water has a memory of the original substance and the solution does indeed become more potent the higher the dilution is. This book is not intended to prove the foundation of homeopathy; rather, it is enough to note that new scientific and medical discoveries are always being made, and skeptics who have easily dismissed homeopathy on the basis that the remedy dilutions are too extreme to have any effect or potency as a medicine must now confront their own skepticism.

The remedy prescribed in a homeopathic consultation is one that matches, or is most "like," the mental and emotional characteristics, as well as the physical characteristics, of the patient. All the symptoms that a patient describes in a homeopathic consultation are cross-checked and confirmed in a homeopathic book known as the *repertory*. A repertory has been compiled from what is referred to in homeopathy as *provings*. The first proving was when Hahnemann discovered that *Cinchona officinalis* as a diluted substance produced symptoms in a healthy person that matched the disease malaria. The repertory contains case notes and observations of hundreds of homeopaths over two centuries of practice. Homeopaths believe that the effect of the homeopathic remedy mirrors the effect of a crude overdosing or poisoning. Because it is important to understand the crude substances that are used for homeopathic medicines, the repertory also contains extensive clinical toxicological reports that can be used for reference material on toxicology. The process of adding to the repertory is an ongoing study based on clinical observations of provings by homeopaths of today.

The most simple of dilutions in my practice that confirm the theory of "like cures like" is the homeopathic use of the remedy *Allium cepa*, a dilution of red onion. This is a common homeopathic medicine used for the symptoms of hay fever and runny eyes caused by various allergic reactions. The effects of cutting an onion are most like the symptoms of the hay fever sufferer. I prescribe the homeopathic remedy *Allium cepa* on the basis of matching the symptoms to the effect of cutting an onion in a healthy person. This is an example of a simple case of a proving. The provings of homeopathic medicines are based on historical recordings that prove efficacy – in this case, if onion cutting causes the eyes to water in a healthy person, as a diluted and potentized substance it will cure the unhealthy person of the same watery eyes. It is easy to understand this process as being similar in theory, although it is dissimilar in practice, to the effects or process involved in conventional allopathic vaccination. It is the diluting and potentizing of substances that distinguishes homeopathy from the conventional medical application and effects of allopathic vaccination.

The original substances that homeopathic remedies were made from were varied. Remedies were made from plants, minerals, animals, chemicals, and even diseased tissues. In the constitutional summaries section of this book, the description of each constitutional type begins with the origins of the remedy. This section is very interesting and important to read because it will give you an understanding of the substance the homeopathic remedy is derived from. Homeopathic constitutional understanding is based on understanding the nature and characteristics of the substance that was used to make the remedy.

Homeopathy is unique in the sense that the nature of the person must also match the action and nature of the substance from which the remedy was derived; this is why the repertory also contains toxicology reports. Understanding the source of a homeopathic remedy can help you understand more about yourself because your constitutional personality will mirror the actions of the original substance that was diluted. Running through the personality picture of each constitution is a theme that also connects to the nature of the original substance, as well as connecting the physical, emotional, and mental characteristics. For example, the personality traits of the constitutional type Sepia, when stressed, match, and mirror the personality traits of the source of the remedy *Sepia,* which is made from a dilution of ink produced by the cuttlefish. Sepias behave the same way when cornered in life as the cuttlefish behaves when cornered in the sea.

The distinction a homeopath makes is that the person also has the physical ailments that are consistent with the personality. A constitution cannot be described as purely a personality type because your constitution is your personality as well as your particular physical tendency to suffer from particular ailments. The mental and emotional personality or characteristics of the Lachesis constitution mirror and are most "like" the personality and behavior of the bushmaster snake from whose venom the homeopathic remedy is derived. The physical complaints of the person needing *Lachesis* also mirror and are most "like" the physical hemorrhagic tissue destruction of poisoning from the bushmaster snake. Homeopathy prescribes *Lachesis* for people in a "like"-Lachesis state. The Lachesis state mirrors and carries the theme of the original source the homeopathic remedy was derived from. In this book I use the venomous film character of Margo, played by the actor Bette Davis in the film *All About Eve*. The character Margo is not a Lachesis personality or a Lachesis individual; the character is in a Lachesis-"like" state that is matched by the homeopathic remedy *Lachesis*. In prescribing *Lachesis* the remedy, it is proven within homeopathic understanding that the person will move to the more healthy aspects of Lachesis or out of the Lachesis state.

Homeopathic constitutional prescribing is inclusive of the somatic theme running through the person's physical, emotional and mental characteristics, and the original substance from which the homeopathic medicine was derived. Constitutional therapy has a unique advantage over conventional forms of counseling, because it is concerned with understanding and affirming individuality. It is not an ideologically based therapy or series of thinking processes that force everyone to have the same approach. A homeopath is able to understand the needs of each individual constitutional type. It is this side of homeopathy that I explore in this book.

Homeopathic constitutional analysis is based on the assumption that when you know who you are, you also know what fulfills you emotionally. After reading this book you will understand the needs you have as a person, and what you are like in relationships.

Which Constitution Am I? – How to Use the Summaries

The first section contains the summaries of each constitution. For each constitution the summary first describes the origins of the remedy. This is followed by a list of key mental and emotional characteristics, and then a list of key physical characteristics. These brief checklists in bullet-point form can be used as a guide and introduction to the different constitutions. The summaries are not a definitive diagnosis of your constitution; you have to then read the relevant chapters to expand that diagnosis in greater depth. It should be noted that you will not have *all* of the mental and emotional characteristics or suffer from *all* of the physical characteristics. You must, however, have the tendency to suffer from some of the physical characteristics. And you must have the main theme and the tendency to think and feel the majority of the feelings listed under the mental and emotional characteristics. Each constitution has to be assessed across all aspects.

The main theme of a constitution is understanding the crossover, or connection, between the mental and emotional, and physical characteristics. There has to be compatibility between how each person behaves mentally and emotionally, and the particular types of physical complaints that they have a tendency to suffer from. The theme in Calcarea carbonica of being mentally conservative, emotionally fearful, and resistant to change is transferred to the physical plane as congestive and stagnant circulation problems that cause constipation. Therefore, it is not going to be possible to be a Calcarea carbonica constitution if you love change, even though you might suffer from constipation problems. The Calcarea carbonica homeopathic remedy is derived from the inner lining of an oyster shell. The theme of tentativeness and needing to hide is the theme that mirrors the relationship between the source of the remedy and the mental, emotional, and physical characteristics. A Calcarea carbonica is not a person or individual. Homeopathy is based on the principles of "like cures like"; therefore, Calcarea carbonica is prescribed on the basis that the person has moved into a Calcarea carbonica-like state that is "like" a fearful oyster shell clamping shut.

All women to some degree suffer emotionally and physically from premenstrual tension. Homeopathic analysis does not stop at a diagnosis of premenstrual tension. Each constitution responds differently, and this is what distinguishes homeopathic understanding from any other form of therapy. A homeopath looking at a person will look behind and underneath physical illnesses to discover the real personality of the person. A homeopath will want to know how a woman operates in life, and in her relationships. How she feels emotionally before her menses is what distinguishes her from someone else. Before menses, is she hypersensitive to being hurt, angry, and guarded, or revengeful like a Natrum muriaticum, or hard to please and petulant like a Pulsatilla, or does she sink into depression and need to run away like Sepia? A homeopath looks deeper into her emotional nature to see what distinguishes the symptoms of a complaint like premenstrual tension from those of the next woman. It is the answers to these questions that indicate your constitution. This is also the picture that you need to construct to arrive at the correct choice of constitutional remedy.

The

constitutional
summaries

Arsenicum Album

Origins of Arsenicum Album

The homeopathic remedy *Arsenicum album* (shortened to Arsenicum) is derived from a dilution of the poison arsenic. It is important to note the relationship between Arsenicum the constitution and the toxic effect of the poison arsenic. The crucial feature of the physical ailments of the constitution Arsenicum is the speed to which Arsenicums are overcome with weakness and prostration. The speed matches the destructive nature of arsenic. Arsenicums are intensely aware of the fragility of health and the potential for any illness to overwhelm. Gustave Flaubert wrote a graphic account of death by arsenic poisoning in his novel *Madam Bovary*. What is most fascinating in this account, from a homeopathic point of view, is the speedy decay of the body. The body needed to be sealed in three coffins by the next morning because the decay was so rapid that mourners were overcome by the stench. Arsenic as a poison is chaotic and threatening in its speedy destruction. Arsenicums carry the threat of destruction as a theme deep within their constitutional psyche.

Arsenicums perceive the world as threatening and potentially dangerous; it is this feeling of weakness that causes Arsenicums to be constantly anxious about health, and it is this threat of destruction that drives Arsenicums to relentless obsession about health. Arsenicums' sense of inner weakness and fragility is protected by an exacting personality. The need to be efficient and perfect in all that they attempt highlights their inner vulnerability, and reflects their need to protect themselves from the threat of the world.

Key Mental and Emotional Characteristics

- High achieving.
- Fastidious.
- Perfectionist.
- Cannot tolerate incompetence and hypercritical of all inefficiency.
- A strong need to set high standards.
- A strong need to create order and precision in their lives.
- Very critical of inefficiency or the lack of logic in others' decision-making processes.
- Can perceive confusion or disorder as threatening.
- Immaculate appearance, especially for work.
- Very fearful of disease.
- Very fearful of being out of control.
- Tendency to worry about recovery from illness.
- Fearful of death but, ironically, are suicidal if they believe there is no cure for their illness.
- A strong fear of poverty or loss of income.
- Can suffer from anxiety attacks about their health or their family's health.
- Extreme restlessness when anxious, especially between midnight and 2 A.M.
- Place high importance on security of family and relationships.
- Fearful when alone.
- A strong need to surround themselves with *objets d'art* or with beauty.
- Possessive and protective of family and possessions.

Key Physical Characteristics

The crucial physical feature of Arsenicum is the intense debility that is associated with all of the physical ailments.

- Fevers and colds characterized by feeling chilly with burning temperatures.
- Feel emotionally better from heat and are fearful of cold when sick.
- Hay fever with burning eyes and swelling of the eyes and lids.
- Headaches that come periodically and often with a specific emotional reason behind their cyclic nature.
- Painful stomach ulcers and gastritis that burn, often relieved by sipping cold water.
- Burning, acrid, and offensive diarrhea.
- Dry, itching, and burning eczema.
- Vomiting that is often associated with feeling fearful and restless.
- Asthma that is worse between midnight and 2 A.M., and is relieved by sitting up.
- Offensive, acrid perspiration that is associated with anxiety at night.
- Cold, deathly face covered in sweat, associated with extreme fear and anxiety.
- Cystitis and burning urination with blood and pus. Paralysis of the bladder in the elderly.
- Exhaustion and debility after exertion.
- Degeneration and slow loss of weight, with impaired nutrition.
- Destructive diseases and complaints with acrid discharges.

Calcarea Carbonica

Origins of Calcarea Carbonica

The homeopathic remedy *Calcarea carbonica* (shortened to *Calc-carb*) is derived from a dilution of carbonate of calcium, prepared from the inner layer of an oyster shell. The most obvious function of the oyster shell is to provide protection for the soft oyster inside. Calc-carbs carry the same theme of needing protection of a soft, inner emotional being. The problem is Calc-carbs do not have the protection of the oyster shell; consequently, they seek outward protection in the world. Because Calc-carbs struggle with issues of security and protection in the world, they will obviously change a lot depending on how secure they feel. Calc-carbs will be a lot more fearful in a relationship with a constitution that does not take into consideration how potentially threatened they feel being in the world without a shell to protect them.

The most important thing to ask yourself, if you think you are Calc-carb, is how do you feel about being in the world by yourself? Do you think you would cope if you did not have the support of family? If you feel that financial stability, a secure home, and a supportive partnership, are absolutely crucial to your health, then it is more than likely that you are Calc-carb. The oyster is the slowest creature in the ocean. This same tentativeness and lack of surety is a theme within Calc-carb. Calc-carbs know that the partner they choose in life must be able to protect and look after them.

Key Mental and Emotional Characteristics

- Very happy to stay at home and care for the family.
- Strong emotional need for the structure of family.
- Do not like a lot of any sort of pressure or responsibility.[2]
- A strong sense of duty and responsibility toward the family.
- Can be overly conscientious at work and will personally take on the worries of the business.
- Can often be very religious. (Calc-carbs emotionally like the idea of others or God having responsibility.)
- Lots of fears and insecurities, with a quite specific fear of heights.
- Excessive worry about the health of themselves or the family.
- Lots of fears about financial loss.
- Sensitive to what others say.
- Often very afraid of and resistant to change.
- More comfortable working in a big company; very unlikely to set up their own business and be able to cope.
- Slow to make decisions.
- Stubborn, especially if they are feeling insecure.
- Lacking emotional stamina to deal with conflict.
- Slow and steady but very responsible and reliable.
- Content and happy when not overextending themselves.

Key Physical Characteristics

The *Calc-carb* homeopathic remedy is derived from a dilution that contains a high percentage of the mineral calcium; the types of problems that affect Calc-carbs physically have to do with nutrition and structure of their body. People suffering from a calcium deficiency have bone malformations, muscle cramps, and a range of nervous afflictions, including heart palpitations. People suffering from hypercalcemia, or too much calcium, have bones that are overcalcified and brittle. Calcium is needed by the body for both protection and stability of muscles and bones; too much calcium, and the bones become brittle. Both deficiency and excess are themes that are seen in the need Calc-carbs have to overprotect and find protection.

- Circulation problems.
- Liable to get chills very easily.
- Can suffer from excessive perspiration on the head and the head usually feels cold.
- Cold, damp feet.
- Suffer from obstinate constipation. The most interesting aspect of Calc-carbs' constipation is that they do not suffer any ill effects from being constipated, even if they have not had a bowel movement for a week. (The homeopathic remedy *Calc-carb* is often used for children and babies suffering from constipation.)
- Babies and children are totally dependent and in constant need of love and support from their parents. Calc-carbs emotionally reflect the same somatic feeling of needing support as a theme throughout their entire physical being.
- Chalky, claylike stools, especially in children (with the stools often resembling those of hypercalcemia, a disease of too much calcium in the blood).
- Milk allergies. (*Calc-carb* is a remedy that is often used for babies suffering from sour vomiting and diarrhea from not being able to digest milk.)
- Sleep that is often disturbed by worry or unpleasant dreams.
- Delayed development of teeth.
- Crave sweets.
- Because circulation is affected Calc-carbs often have the tendency to put on weight easily.
- Lacking in physical stamina.
- Early menses as a result of emotional trauma or physical exertion.
- Often suffer premature ejaculation and exhaustion from the exertion of sex.
- Slow healing of skin.

- Nails that crack easily and cracked skin.
- Arthritis and weak limbs, especially from exertion or climbing stairs. (Calc-carb is often used for children who are slow to walk.)

Carcinosin

Origins of Carcinosin

The homeopathic remedy *Carcinosin* is derived from a dilution of cancerous breast tumor. Admittedly, it could be an uncomfortable thought to consider that homeopathy has medicine derived from a breast carcinoma — any association with cancer is terrifying. It could also be disconcerting if you can identify with the description of the Carcinosin constitution, just as it is disconcerting having the persona or energy of the bushmaster snake that Lachesis is derived from. But a constitutional Lachesis is not a snake and Carcinosin is not cancer. A homeopathic remedy is prescribed as a constitutional on the basis of being "like" the presenting picture of the personality of the person. The personality of the person must match the nature of the original substance that the homeopathic remedy is derived from. A homeopathic remedy does not have within it any of the original substance; it carries the memory or imprint of the characteristics of the behavioral patterns or theme of the original substance. The person is not matched to the substance or to the toxicology of the substance; the personality is matched to the action and nature of the substance. The personality of the constitution Carcinosin behaves "like" the behavior and progression of the disease cancer. Carcinosins are not cancerous, nor will they get cancer.

The relevant homeopathic concept in choosing the right remedy to match your personality is "like cures like." Cancer arises from the abnormal and uncontrolled division, and overgrowth of undifferentiated, or poorly differentiated cells. The undifferentiated cells divide and duplicate quickly without controls. Initially, the malignant cells invade surrounding tissues; as the cancer grows it expands, and begins to compete with the surrounding tissues and organs for space. Eventually the tumor metastasizes and invades the surrounding body cavities, entering lymph or blood systems; this enables the cancer cells to travel unchecked and uncontrolled throughout the body. The reason I have outlined the above pathophysiology is that it is crucial to the understanding of the constitution Carcinosin. The image that comes to mind is one of an ungrounded or undifferentiated energy that is expanding and desperately pushing on all that surrounds it, in the attempt to find definition or containment. Carcinosins do not know their personal boundaries. The description of the pathology of cancerous growth mirrors and is "like" the personality of the constitution Carcinosin. Carcinosins are on a journey of self-discovery. Carcinosins are not sure of themselves; they need to push very hard in life to be able to find definition. Consequently they are always expanding and pushing limits and boundaries to find out who they are. If you are content with yourself you are not Carcinosin, and if you know who you are you are not Carcinosin.

Key Mental and Emotional Characteristics

- Strong, overdeveloped sense of duty and commitment.
- High expectations of themselves; obsessive and perfectionist need to achieve.
- Find it very hard to get in touch with their feelings; can appear to be numb. Often have a "shut down" look in their eyes.
- Suppress feelings, and consequently struggle with depression.
- Family history of suppression, especially of grief and sadness.
- Warm, caring, empathic, and sensitive to others' feelings.

(This is also based on their sense of duty and commitment.)

- A strong need for physical expression through exercise; this can be quite varied in expression – cross-country racing, long-distance running, dance, yoga, and so on.
- Sympathy for the suffering of others, especially animals.
- Suffer anticipatory anxiety.
- Overly serious, especially when confronted with making decisions.
- Sensitive to being punished or reprimanded.
- Struggle with standing up for themselves, especially in relationships.
- Have a passionate need to find and define themselves.
- Restless need to leave home so they can discover who they are, but often struggle with feelings of guilt about leaving their family to fend for themselves. (This is also based on their sense of duty and commitment.)
- Feeling of having to live up to others' expectations. Carcinosins feel a pressure to grow up too soon.
- Rebellious as children, often rebelling against authority.
- Feelings of not being wanted in childhood.[3] Childhood for Carcinosins is experienced as prolonged fear and unhappiness.
- A very strong fear of cancer. This fear has to be quite marked as the majority of people can say they fear cancer.
- Unable to sleep if worried.
- Love travel and adventure.
- Excited in thunderstorms.

Key Physical Characteristics

The fact that the list does not contain many distinguishing physical symptoms is significant. The lack of distinguishing physical characteristics mirror and match the nature and progression of the disease cancer. It is completely logical that Carcinosins will present with very few distinctive physical characteristics, as the nature of the disease cancer often escapes being noticed until it is too late. One of the most disturbing aspects of cancer is that cancer sufferers often have no idea that they have the disease until the tumor is so large it pushes on the surrounding tissues or organs. The homeopathic remedy *Carcinosin* is prescribed because the personality mirrors the patterning or theme of the pathology or behavioral patterns of the disease. It is not prescribed because the person has the disease cancer.

- Family history or personal history of cancer, or family history of diabetes.[4]
- Strong health history of repeated examples of the breakdown of the immune system, such as repeated bouts of tonsillitis or recurring bronchitis.
- Numerous dark moles on skin.
- Warm[5]-blooded.
- Feel emotionally good at the seaside. This can match the need on the mental and emotional level for expanse.
- Sleep curved and bent over, with the knees touching the elbows.[6]
- Crave fats and chocolate. Both of these foods are sensually very satisfying, so it is not that hard to understand the emotional need that Carcinosins have for them; however, a lot of other constitutions also crave fats and chocolate, so it is not distinctive enough to prescribe on this basis alone.
- The eyes can often have a bluish sclera.[7]
- Twitching eye muscles.
- Prolonged history of insomnia, especially in childhood.
- Constipation with inactivity of the bowel, often relieved by pressure or bending forward.
- Strong need to masturbate[8] and strong sexual drive. This is not exclusive to Carcinosins, so confirmation of constitutional type must be based on other factors.

Causticum

Origins of Causticum

The homeopathic remedy *Causticum* is derived from a diluted tincture of potassium hydrate. The following descriptions of potassium deficiency mirror the constitutional picture and nature of Causticum. Potassium is an essential mineral necessary for the maintenance of normal growth; it is used by the body to stimulate nerve impulses for muscle contractions, and to regulate distribution of fluids within cell walls. Severe potassium deficiency (hypokalemia) causes muscle weakness and paralysis. Deficiency impairs the balance of fluids; symptoms include constipation, paralysis of the rectum, and irregular or slow heartbeat (cardiac dysrhythmias). A potassium deficiency also interferes with glucose metabolism, which results in various nervous disorders such as anxiousness, restlessness, and insomnia. The opposing themes of paralysis and overstimulation run through the psyche of Causticum across all levels.

Causticum is excitable, stimulating, and restless. Causticum is also, conversely, stuck, paralyzed, and anxious. Causticums are an interesting mix of emotional sensitivity, empathic reactivity, and mental and emotional stagnation. The more overstimulated Causticums are, the more likely they are to shut down emotionally. In my practice I have used *Causticum,* the remedy, when patients' response to a deep loss or grief has been so totally overwhelming or paralyzing that they literally cannot get on with their own life, even after what would be seen as an acceptable mourning period.[9] Causticums have such a strong mindset that they are completely obsessed. The most extreme picture of this type of person is a religious fundamentalist terrorist, while the not-so-extreme picture might be a vegetarian activist. Obviously, the manifestation of the passionate views of Causticum can be varied. Most commonly, the picture I see of Causticums in my practice are those who are so committed to a particular cause that they cannot "loosen up" emotionally. This is the unhealthy, contracted picture of Causticum.

Key Mental and Emotional Characteristics

- Intensely serious and idealistic.
- Extremely moralistic and responsible.
- Can be incensed by what is seen as injustice. This anger often means that Causticums can become obsessed with a particular cause or underprivileged group.
- Can appear self-righteous or dictatorial.
- Emotively sensitive and empathic toward the suffering of others or intensely reactive to another's feelings.
- Can become overcome by other people's grief.
- Excitable and restless.
- Extremely overstimulated mind.
- Causticums embrace everything they do with intensity and purpose.
- Causticums find it hard to let go[10] of depression and grief, often because they see the cause of the grief as so worthy.

Key Physical Characteristics

The tendency to be paralyzed or stuck in a particular mindset is so strong that it crosses over to the physical more intensely in Causticum than in any other homeopathic constitution. Consequently, *Causticum,* the remedy, is good to use for paralysis of nerves, contraction of muscles and tendons, and paralysis of bodily functions such as constipation and bladder incontinence. Causticums who have not been able to bring about ideological change are noticeably physically aged before their time and disillusioned with the world they have not been able to change.

- Arthritis and rheumatism of the fingers and hands where the muscles and tendons have contracted.
- Legs or feet cramping at night, or the more extreme symptom, ataxia, the inability to lift the foot when walking.
- Constant need to clear the throat with a feeling that the mucus is stuck or trapped. *Causticum* is a good remedy for weak chest muscles that are struggling to expel mucus in elderly patients with emphysema or pneumonia.
- Facial neuralgia that comes on from exposure to cold wind.
- All conditions and contractions are made worse by cold weather.
- Conversely, facial twitching or hysterical convulsions are made better by sipping cold water.
- Stammering caused by the inability to relax contracted facial muscles.
- Constipation so extreme it feels like the rectum is paralyzed and the person feels the need for help from gravity to be able to pass the stool; consequently, the need to stand up.
- Bladder incontinence or retention.[11]
- Convulsions or tremors that occur after fright or grief.
- Chest pains or spasms and heart palpitations.
- Raw, burning[12] skin conditions.

Graphites

Origins of Graphites

The homeopathic remedy *Graphites* is derived from a dilution of the mineral graphite, a carbon containing a small amount of iron. The sphere of action that *Graphites* affects the most is nutrition and circulation. Graphite the mineral is used in machinery to help resolve[13] friction. Graphites' emotive sensitivity has the same theme, reflecting the sensitivity that allows graphite to resolve the friction of machinery parts. People who are the constitutional type Graphites are extremely sensitive and finely tuned to react to conflict and disharmony. When you spill the mineral graphite on the floor the small particles clump together. The same desire to clump together is part of the psyche of Graphites. People of this constitutional type are very happy when surrounded by family and friends.

Calc-carb is often confused with Graphites because Calc-carb is also home and family oriented. The difference is in the emotional excitability and purpose of Graphites. The character of Debbie in the North American production of the television program *Queer As Folk* is a wonderful example of an emotional Graphites, and conversely, the character of Ted in *Queer As Folk* is Calc-carb. The difference between the Calc-carb Ted and the Graphites Debbie is that Ted is conservative and more stable and far less likely to get excited or overtly emotional. Calc-carb is stagnant and Graphites is excitable, like the spilled particles of graphite that rush madly around forming clumps. For Graphites, the purpose in life is to live through family and friends, while Calc-carb uses family and the security of home and money as protection.

Key Mental and Emotional Characteristics

- Easygoing and happy.
- Warm and supportive with family and friends.
- Home-oriented and welcoming.
- Career is not as important as family.
- Sensitive to conflict or arguments, especially in relationships or family.
- Can often feel unsure of oneself.
- Often find it hard to make decisions, especially if there is a conflict.
- Sad and despondent, especially if they feel alone.
- Tearful if upset and often need to cry and immediately share how they feel.
- Excitable and sensitive, especially to music.
- Emotionally restless when trying to concentrate mentally.
- Can often anticipate problems, and suffer from anxiety about the future.
- Fretful and impatient over little things.
- Can often remember[14] sad memories from childhood.

Key Physical Characteristics

Graphites often has a tendency to put on weight easily because of the problems with circulation and nutrition. Graphites' skin is also sensitive. The tendency for every aspect of Graphites' skin to crack or fester is simply a reflection of a sensitive nature. Calc-carb also suffers from circulation problems that are reflected in the tendency to gain weight and the tendency for skin to crack. If there is confusion between the two constitutions, the distinguishing physical characteristic can be made on the basis of temperature aggravation: Calc-carb is aggravated[15] by cold, while Graphites is aggravated by warmth.

- Tendency to be overweight and often feel worse when hungry.
- Circulation problems that cause skin problems such as eczema and psoriasis. Skin that cracks easily, itches to the point of bleeding, and heals slowly. Skin eruptions that ooze a honeylike discharge.
- Skin that cracks in winter. Skin that is often worse at night from the heat in bed.
- Cracks in the corner of mouth or lips.
- Thickened nails.
- Sweaty and offensive foot perspiration.
- Light sensitivity.
- Eye discharges.
- Dry ears.
- Sensitive fluid retention in the legs.
- Late menses that are often too pale or too light.
- Males can often lose erection during sex; whether this is as a result of circulation problems or emotional sensitivity is debatable.
- Flatulence and often feel uncomfortable in tight clothes.
- Often suffering from nausea during menses.
- Difficult constipation, often causing hemorrhoids and fissures.

Ignatia

Origins of Ignatia

The homeopathic remedy *Ignatia* is derived from a dilution of the seeds of a St. Ignatius bean. The seeds contain a high level of the poisons strychnine and brucine. Strychnine is also an ingredient in the homeopathic remedy *Nux vomica*. As with *Nux vomica*, *Ignatia* produces a characteristic excessive sensibility of the senses and a tendency to produce convulsive spasms. The levels of strychnine are far stronger in *Ignatia* and the result is a far more destructive picture than with *Nux vomica*. The destructiveness is manifested in the more extreme, unstable emotionalism of Ignatia in comparison to the emotional control of Nux vomica. The constitution Ignatia mirrors the nature of strychnine in the sense that mental, emotional, and physical sensations are cramped inside and struggle for expression. Because the emotions are more aggravated in Ignatia, pressure often builds to the point of being hysterical. Ignatia has the theme of needing to be free emotionally to express the excessive build-up of feelings.

Key Mental and Emotional Characteristics

- Idealistically romantic with a strong desire to find the perfect relationship.
- Strong drive to achieve goals.
- High expectations of everyone and easily disappointed.
- Emotionally very expressive, very passionate, and

emotively explosive.
- A strong need to have their emotional idealistic needs matched by intense emotional engagement with the world.
- Ignatia will often create a drama emotionally in order to vent built-up emotions.
- Very sensitive, and easily upset or hurt.
- Volatile in relationships, and prone to be very jealous.
- Hysterical, often moving from anger to tears very quickly.
- Inner conflict over expressing feelings and will often feel guilty after hysterical outbursts.
- Brooding, characterized by continual sighing, especially if hurt or grieving.
- Hysterical grief.

Key Physical Characteristics

The theme of excessive passionate emotions finding and needing an outlet is expressed physically in Ignatias as strange, contradictory, hysterical, and paradoxical physical peculiarities. Strychnine, because it is such a strong poison, interferes with the coordination of physical function. The destruction of the nervous system causes irregular and erratic pains and spasms, which come and go or shift location. The erratic, contradictory emotional nature of Ignatia and the nature of the poison are particularly evident in Ignatias' painful joints, which feel relieved from moving.
- Inflamed painful joints that paradoxically feel relieved from pressure and massage.
- Cramps in the stomach, with a lot of flatulence, that paradoxically are relieved by eating acidic, hard-to-digest foods and feel worse by eating bland, soothing foods.
- Hysterical paralysis or anesthesia.
- Spasms of muscles around the eyes, mouth, face, or limbs, and especially the back.
- Have the feeling of a lump in the throat as if they cannot swallow.[16]

- Sinking, empty feeling in stomach that is relieved by breathing deeply.
- Jerking of the limbs when trying to go to sleep.
- Nervous, spasmodic coughs with no sign of illness.
- Pains in muscles that are improved by exercise or travel.
- Heavy menses with pains that come on quickly and then disappear.
- Headaches that are relieved by yawning or vomiting.
- Perspiration only on the face.
- Insomnia from grief.
- Headaches from grief with intense pain.
- Diarrhea brought on by grief.
- Menses and excessive bleeding brought on by grief.
- Suppression of sexual desire due to grief.
- Tendency to overeat as a way of holding grief in and down.

Lachesis

Origins of Lachesis

The homeopathic remedy *Lachesis* is derived from a dilution of the poison of the Surukuku snake of South America, commonly known as the bushmaster. As the name implies, this snake is the master of its territory and has a reputation when disturbed of chasing its victim and attacking. It is known as one of the most poisonous and vicious snakes purely because the majority of snakes will choose to run rather than fight. The dilution of bushmaster snake venom was first made by the famous homeopath Hering, whose first experiments with the remedy were made when working in the Amazon as a zoologist. The poison was so toxic that just in the process of physically preparing the homeopathic remedy it was potent enough to throw Hering into a coma-like state with delirium and fever. Because homeopathy is based on the principle of "like cures like," the personality of a Lachesis constitution has to match the personality of the bushmaster snake. Lachesis has the ability to disarm, charm, entice, and seduce victims. Lachesis is a personality state that has the same stunning and disabling qualities of the bushmaster poison and a theme that is reflective of the hyper-vigilance of the bushmaster snake. Across all levels Lachesis does not like restriction or control. Lachesis does not relax; even when charming and enticing, Lachesis is continually aware of any sort of perceived competition or threat to autonomy or territory.

Key Mental and Emotional Characteristics

- Charismatic, charming, and enchanting.
- Sharp-tongued and loquacious, but can also be very entertaining and charming.
- Witty, with a good sense of humor.
- Passionately opinionated and can often appear arrogant.
- Fearful of relationships[17] or commitment because they do not want to be restricted.
- Critical if anyone gets too close and demands anything of them.
- Very possessive about their territory or possessions.
- Competitive; need to be in a favorable position to relax.
- Angry and aggressive if they feel imposed upon.
- Vengeful if they feel imposed upon.
- Suspicious and paranoid of feeling imposed upon.
- Often do not want to go to work because they react to being constrained by commitment to work or by expectations from management.
- Sarcastic if upset.
- Strong-minded and intolerant of social conventions or restrictions.
- Often very religious.
- Quick-thinking, with a sharp ability to assess situations.
- Often deliriously ramble on from one subject to another and find it hard to collect thoughts.
- Intense nervous irritability and restlessness.
- Often fearful of going to sleep in case their heart stops.[18]
- Often need drugs to be able to calm mental hyperactivity and emotional hypervigilance and paranoia at night.
- Strong sexual drive.
- Strong fears of poisons and snakes. Everyone can express fear of snakes to varying degrees, but the fears Lachesis suffers are quite marked.

Key Physical Characteristics

The same emotional intensity is also present in the physical. The physical characteristics of Lachesis are one of the strongest indicators of this constitution. The theme of the physical characteristics of Lachesis is "like" the death from snake poison. *Lachesis* is a hemorrhagic remedy. When Lachesis is sick the picture that often presents is reflective of the edematous or fluid swelling and congestion that matches the effect of the poisonous venom. Snake poison decomposes the blood and constricts the heart muscle, causing circulation to cease and damaging nerves. The speed and intensity of the onset of the physical complaints as well as emotional aggravation and the degree of destruction across all levels will often indicate the remedy *Lachesis*. All the physical conditions that Lachesis suffers come on with extreme intensity and pain. The headaches throb intensely, the hemorrhoids form thromboses quickly, and all the fevers are reflective of the picture of the original "proving" by the homeopath Hering.

- Rapid onset of diseases with extreme pain and exhaustion.
- Restlessness at night with nightmares and sleep apnea; often waking fearful of suffocation and not being able to breathe.
- Asthma aggravated by intense emotional excitement, fear, or panic.
- Chest palpitations and fear of going to sleep in case they have a heart attack.
- Constipation with the feeling that the anus feels tight and constricted.
- Hemorrhoids that can become constricted and hemorrhagic.
- A sensation that the throat is being constricted[19] and they cannot swallow.
- Headaches from heat and the sun.
- Headaches before menses or during menopause.[20]
- Trembling of the whole body, especially the tongue.
- Extreme sensitivity to physical touch.

- Shifting, throbbing neuralgic pains.
- Cramps and pains in the legs that are aggravated by constriction but also by motion.
- Hypertension, often aggravated by alcohol.
- Hot flushes.
- Excessive sweating and hot perspiration, especially at night.
- Skin lesions that have a bluish, hemorrhagic appearance.
- Pains often start on the left side and move to the right side.
- Suppression of discharges; for example, aggravated before the menstrual flow and then feeling relieved with the onset of menses.
- Aggravated if sexual desires are suppressed.
- Cannot stand tight clothes around the neck or waist. (This is reflective of their intolerance of any sort of constriction or constraint.)

Lycopodium

Origins of Lycopodium

Dr. Samuel Hahnemann, the founder of homeopathy, listed some interesting dichotomies in the personality description of Lycopodium. The personality traits listed ranged from "great timidity" to "cannot bear the least contradiction ..." to "... breaking out in envy, pretensions and ordering others about." (Hahnemann, pp. 863–864). These personality contradictions run the whole way through the constitutional picture of Lycopodium. It is an interesting dilemma for Lycopodium to one minute feel a lack of confidence and, with the next breath, brim with enough bragging arrogance to be able to win over an entire roomful of people. The thread that ties the two sides of Lycopodium together is a desperate need to remain on top and survive. The only way Lycopodium can see to remain on top is to be very big and very important. The theme that ties the two parts together is explainable in the evolutional history of the plant from which *Lycopodium* the remedy is derived: *Lycopodium clavatum*. The underlying psychodynamic trauma of Lycopodium is that *Lycopodium clavatum* was, thousands of years ago, a large tree, and now it is a small club moss. Lycopodiums carry this existential threat to their largeness in their psyche. The crisis of size is the theme of Lycopodium. Lycopodiums are fearful of any threat to their potency and importance in this world.

Lycopodium as a substance was traditionally used as a coating agent for allopathic medicines. Its natural coating quality meant that the tablets did not stick together and, as it had no known allopathic side effects, it was also safe to use. The fact that *Lycopodium* was used to resolve friction and stop tablets from sticking is interesting; this quality reflects the need that Lycopodiums have to avoid conflict and confrontation. *Lycopodium* as a substance was also used externally on skin to stop rubbing and friction. The ability to soothe and charm as well as the ability to coat the bitter pills of life, and to make sure that at the end of the day they float and do not sink, is the essence and theme of Lycopodium. *Lycopodium* as a substance has the ability to float on liquids without being dissolved and is without taste or smell. Lycopodiums also carry the same chameleon theme in their nature. Lycopodiums do not want to "stick" or be involved emotionally in case it threatens their position in the world.

Key Mental and Emotional Characteristics

- Warm and charming.
- Good at climbing the social ladder.
- Love feeling socially important and powerful.
- Bombastic, egotistical, and bragging.
- Fear not being needed.
- Need family and the support of society.
- More comfortable in a relationship where the other person needs them.
- Fear of impotency. (This is true for the female as much as for the male Lycopodium.)
- Supportive of family and loved ones.
- Lycopodiums can also fear their dependency on family and the responsibility of looking after the family.
- Work hard to maintain financial security in the world.
- Intelligent and financially prudent assessment of financial risks.
- Streetwise.
- Fear taking on new ventures.
- Lack of self-confidence.

- Fear losing.
- Dictatorial, especially with their family.
- Depressed if they feel like they have failed.
- Anxious if they think they could be sick and anxious if they are sick.
- Promiscuous and, even when loyal in a relationship, will flirt and charm because it reinforces their potency.

Key Physical Characteristics

Underlying Lycopodiums' physical weaknesses is continual anxiety that they will fail or suffer from loss. Lycopodiums have to work so hard at survival that they are slowly worn down, and all the physical illnesses are either brought about by anxiety or are exasperated by anxiety. The need for security in the world is reflected in the struggle that Lycopodiums have with trying to control food intake. The same emotional dichotomy or contradiction exists in the fact that Lycopodiums are virile[21] but they can also be impotent. The weak areas are ailments having to do with the loss of function, in particular the loss of function in the urinary system.

- Heartburn after anger or anxiety.
- A need to eat until full; conversely, eating only a small amount can feel like too much.
- Bulimia (the pattern of overeating and forcing oneself to vomit and purge).
- Painful flatulence that is worse in the afternoon from 4 to 8 P.M.
- Bloating and flatulence after anxiety.
- Wake frequently at night to eat, especially if feeling insecure.
- Often need to eat for energy to avoid headaches; conversely, can also suffer from headaches as a result of overeating.
- Crave sugar if feeling nervous.
- Frequent urination at night.

- Sexual promiscuity and sexual impotency.
- Premature ejaculation.
- Often have a worried or furrowed brow.
- Prematurely gray hair.
- Right-sided complaints that often shift to the left side.
- Aggravated by cold but also crave open air.
- Dry skin, especially on the nose and aggravated at night.
- Dry throat, especially when nervous.
- Wake frequently from bad dreams.

Magnesium Carbonica

Origins of Magnesium Carbonica

The homeopathic remedy *Magnesium carbonica* (shortened to *Mag-carb* for both remedy and constitutional type) is derived from a dilution of carbonate of magnesia, which contains the mineral magnesium. A tissue salt deficiency of magnesium results in loss of nervous system function. A person suffering from a physical magnesium deficiency will experience muscle cramping and tremors, as well as emotional apprehensiveness, confusion, and disorientation. The theme of a person who is suffering from nerve fiber contraction is reflected in the emotional and physical action and nature of Mag-carb. Mag-carbs literally shut down feelings to avoid feeling anxious. Mag-carbs[22] experience a sense of underlying apprehension and anxiety that they then experience as fear of rejection and abandonment. This is reflected in the need that Mag-carbs have to protect themselves from conflict or disharmony. Often the effort of dealing with anxiety and the effort of holding down feelings of apprehensiveness result in Mag-carbs suffering from depression. The anxiety that Mag-carbs suffer is so intense that they end up suppressing it just to be able to function. When Mag-carbs suppress their emotional feelings they often then experience the effects of the suppression physically, in muscular cramps and neuralgic pains that reflect magnesium deficiency.

Key Mental and Emotional Characteristics

- Strong feelings of emotional abandonment.
- Fearful that something bad will happen, either to themselves or their loved ones.
- Fearful that they will be deserted by their partner. Mag-carbs can often have strong co-dependency issues in relationships.
- Strong need to hold the family unit together; they are often viewed as the family peacemaker.
- Family or support from a relationship is crucial to feeling secure.
- Comforted by working in large supportive groups. It will be the Mag-carbs working within an organization who will seek to create harmony and cooperation among the members.
- Do not like conflicts or arguments, especially among family members.
- Feel anxious during the day, and often feel emotionally safer at night in bed.
- Work hard to provide strong financial security.
- Do not like to travel far from their bed or home.
- History of suppressing their feelings; and a strong history of depression.
- Often use dreams to work out what they are feeling.
- Have a recurring dream of being lost in their own home.
- Can appear monotone and depressed.
- Do not like to talk, especially in the morning.
- Look as if they are worn out and that every step they take is an effort.
- Often have strong dependency issues to do with food.

Key Physical Characteristics

The types of physical complaints that Mag-carbs suffer are brought about with stress of emotional disharmony or discord within family and relationships. The theme of suppressing anxiety also crosses over to the physical, and it is impossible to ever reject the emotional cause when considering the physical complaints of Mag-carb. If Mag-carbs ever feel threatened on any level they will internalize all anxiety and it will be expressed as muscular aches and pains or be reflected in a sensitive stomach.[23] Mag-carbs often suffer from constipation when they are avoiding making decisions. The opposite of this is also experienced, in that Mag-carbs also suffer from diarrhea when they have anxiety or conflicts. Mag-carbs have a characteristic physical theme: they suffer from sour perspiration, sour diarrhea, sour vomit, and a sour temper when they are sick.

- Gastrointestinal complaints resulting from anxiety.
- Either extreme constipation after mental strain, or watery diarrhea after conflict or anxiety.
- Neuralgic muscular pains and cramps that are aggravated in bed at night.
- Restless at night, often needing to get up and move around. (Note, that Mag-carbs emotionally feel better when in bed, but worse physically.)
- Often suffer from tired and exhausted legs that feel relieved by walking outside in fresh warm air, but they will feel worse from any slight cold wind.
- Often wake tired in the morning.
- Suffer from restless sleep, and are often troubled by dreams.
- Physically sensitive to touch, especially when upset.
- Sensitive to noise and all discord.
- Menses flow at night in bed but slow down during the day.
- Cyclically worse before menses; every month Mag-carbs will feel very tired or suffer with sore throats (even if they are menopausal).

Medorrhinum

Origins of Medorrhinum

A homeopathic remedy does not have within it any of the original substance; it carries the *memory* or imprint of the characteristics of the original substance. The homeopathic remedy *Medorrhinum* is derived from the microorganism *Neisseria gonorrhoaea*, which causes the disease gonorrhea. A homeopathic remedy is diluted past the point of having any of the original substance, therefore Medorrhinums are not the disease gonorrhea; they instead contain within their personality qualities "like" the presentation of the disease state. I know that it might seem bizarre to ever consider making a medicinal remedy out of a disease state, but a homeopathic remedy is able to contain the essence of the manifestation of disease. A homeopathic constitution is an energy state that reflects, across all levels – emotionally, mentally, and physically – the nature of the substance from which it was derived.

The extremes of the personality Medorrhinum match and are "like" the intensity of the disease. The presentation of the disease state of gonorrhea is intense and spontaneous, and eruptive with profuse physical discharges. If gonorrhea is left untreated there is a risk of disseminated gonococcal infection (DGI), which means the disease state moves inward, making clinical detection difficult until the person presents with severe pathology. The same progression is visible in the constitution Medorrhinum. The way Medorrhinums tackle everything is reflective of the intense, eruptive nature of the presentation of the disease gonorrhea. Medorrhinums also have a reflective personality introversion that borders on extreme paranoia, mirroring the disease state of gonorrhea DGI, if left untreated.

If you identify yourself as Medorrhinum, the most important theme is the alternating polarities of behavior accompanied by an intense desire to push the boundaries of experience. The character Brian in the television series *Queer As Folk* is a wonderful portrayal of Medorrhinum. Brian is intensely passionate and extreme in his drive and desire to experience life. He is paranoid, hypercritical, and hypervigilant of societal expectations or personal constraints. He also balances on an unpredictable edge of love or hate, as well as passion or aggression. The Calc-carb character in the show, Ted, constantly remarks and laments on the unpredictability of Brian's character. Unpredictability and the theme of alternating polarities of behavior are the energy of Medorrhinum.

Key Mental and Emotional Characteristics

- Alternates between extroversion and introversion.
- Can appear hypervigilant or even paranoid about all perceived controls and restrictions.
- Can alternate between feeling passionate love or passionate hate.
- Can alternate between being workaholic or lazy.
- Avoid responsibility and societal conventions or expectations.
- Intensely need to inflict violence for wrongs done to them; intensely intolerant of criticism.
- Passionate or aggressive.
- Shy or very open and energetic.
- Intense passion for living.
- Desire to experiment with and experience everything; often party all night — "sex, drugs, and rock and roll" — and then crash for days.
- Periodically need to escape by either traveling or by escaping into drugs or stimulants.

- Can suffer from claustrophobia.
- Have fears about their sanity.
- Fear the dark.
- Can feel alienated from the world.
- Extremely hypervigilant about any restrictions. Very fearful of being contained in prison or trapped in relationships (love partnerships or friendships).

Key Physical Characteristics

The emotional intensity of Medorrhinums is matched on the physical plane by the discharges and the extreme inflammatory nature of all the health issues that commonly affect Medorrhinums.

- Prone to infected, pus-filled discharges when sick regardless of the condition; such discharges are reflective of the purulent nature of gonorrhea.
- Acrid and offensive discharges.
- Tendency to be prone to inflammatory conditions such as cystitis (inflammation of the bladder), urethritis (inflammation of the urethra), vaginitis, prostatitis(inflammation of the prostate), and ovarian cysts and tumors.
- Skin inflammation, with redness, swelling, and pus.
- All sorts of skin conditions such as herpes, warts, cysts, moles, eczema, and rashes.
- Frequent colds and influenza, all with blocked nose, ears, and throat with chronic, excessive mucus.
- Complications from colds that progress to chest infections.
- Bronchitis and asthma, usually from early childhood.
- Extremely restless feet in bed at night; matching the mental and emotional restlessness.
- Medorrhinums are "night owls"; they do not want to go to sleep.
- Sleep in an unusual position, on their stomach with knees tucked under.
- Arthritis and rheumatism and swollen joints – conditions

that reflect the systemic disease disseminated gonococcal infection, DGI.

- Personal or family history of gonorrhea.[24]
- Strong sexual drive.

Mercurius

Origins of Mercurius

The homeopathic remedy *Mercurius* is derived from the metal mercury, commonly referred to as quicksilver. In all metals except mercury, atoms are held closely together in orderly, regular rows and columns known as metallic lattice. This means that when metals are bent, beaten, or stretched, the rows of metal atoms move without losing their structure. This is not the case with mercury, which lacks a stable form and is constantly changing shape and reforming; mercury is not solid like other metals. Because mercury is not solid, it can evaporate and form odorless, colorless vapors. Liquid mercury is used in thermometers precisely because its inherent changeability makes it able to react to and register changes in temperature.

The fact that this is a metal that cannot retain structure is reflected in the psyche of Mercurius. Mercurius constantly reacts and responds to every stimulus as if "like" a thermometer. People who are this constitutional type are unable to maintain order or predictability; their mercurial mind is changeable, and their emotional nature is unstructured. Reactivity is the theme of Mercurius. Exposure to high levels of mercury is toxic; it causes nervous system damage, neurological tremors, and alterations in personality and mood.

Mercurius will not always feel emotionally unstable; it is only when stressed or feeling undermined and threatened that Mercurius will feel emotive or reactive. The underlying changeability and sensitivity of Mercurius creates a constitutional picture that is hypersensitive and hypervigilant to contradiction. Mercurius does not like to be contradicted, and will always interpret contradiction as a critical attack; Mercurius always reacts violently to being attacked. Mercurius fears exposure of emotional unpredictability, and the mercurial, impulsive reactivity continually undermines feelings of sanity. Depending on the strength of feeling, the reaction will be physical or verbal violence directed toward the person who is seen to have offended; violence toward oneself is also possible. The self-directed violence is a convoluted undermining of ego and self that result in Mercurius feeling confused and disintegrated. The Mercurius who is fatigued, confused, and unsure is the most common presentation of Mercurius in my practice. The most important emotional characteristic is how quickly Mercurius can feel overtaken or influenced by stronger personalities. The mercurial theme of thermometer reactivity is a good image to refer to in considering Mercurius as a constitution.

The above description is Mercurius when stressed; when unstressed, Mercurius is exciting, stimulating, creative, and innovative. Emotive reactivity has a healthy presentation, and in healthy Mercurius the reactivity becomes a channel for creative thought and action.

Key Mental and Emotional Characteristics

- Very exciting and creative intellect; stimulating and interesting.
- Very sharp, quick intellect, often self-taught; quick to adapt and pick things up.
- A common constitution among members of the acting profession, Mercurius can adapt and change form easily.
- Also a common constitution in creative jobs, such as the arts, advertising, or design.
- Very quick mind; often processing information so fast that they speak in a hurry.
- Able to adapt quickly to new environments.
- Constantly changing emotions; emotional reactivity and sensitivity.

- Introverted and emotionally intense; acutely aware they lack stability.
- Can initially appear closed and extremely cautious.
- Guarded and suspicious in case of attack.
- Easily influenced by stronger personalities.
- Obsessed with trying to create order in their lives.
- Very sensitive to discord or disharmony.
- Easily embarrassed.
- Sensitive to injustice.
- Often crave a very conservative life to try to balance out the feelings of insecurity inside.
- Thoughts are often presented in a disintegrated way.
- Often feel like their memory is weak.
- Always dissatisfied and always looking for new stimulus.
- Like changing routine and traveling; physically also very restless.
- Worry about losing their sanity.
- Dictatorial and egotistical.
- Even when emotionally healthy, do not like to be contradicted.
- Often feel they have to work hard at restraining their feelings.
- The more unhealthy Mercurius can suffer from violent desires to kill anyone who contradicts or criticizes.

Key Physical Characteristics

The homeopathic remedy *Mercurius* is often used for conditions that have a destructive,[25] debilitating nature. When considering *Mercurius* as a constitutional remedy you will not always see the full destructive nature of mercury; however, you have to be able to see the start of this process. The most common physical symptoms that present are restlessness, exhausting excessive sweating at night, mouth ulcers, and heartburn. The temperature sensitivity of mercury is reflected in physical sensitivity of Mercurius to changes in temperature.

- Constantly changing internal thermometer — cold, then hot, and then cold again.
- Very restless.
- Often feel weak, exhausted, and shaky, especially in the legs.
- Bone pains.
- Lots of problems from excessive perspiration, especially exhausting at night.
- Excessive saliva.
- Intensely thirsty.
- Sensitive digestion but with continual hunger.
- Skin conditions that ulcerate and are slow to heal — mouth ulcers, herpes that ulcerate and scar, and leg ulcers.
- Burning skin conditions with acrid discharges and fetid odors.
- Heartburn that is aggravated at night.

Natrum Muriaticum

Origins of Natrum Muriaticum

The homeopathic remedy *Natrum muriaticum* (shortened to *Nat-mur* for both remedy and constitutional type) is derived from a dilution of sodium chloride, which is common salt. The physical dietary side effect of too much salt is that it causes fluid retention; the emotional side effect is that Nat-murs retain their emotions. Nutritionally, *Natrum muriaticum* is used as a tissue salt to help distribute water throughout body tissues. The very nature of water is that it is meant to flow. Nat-murs are retentive; they do not flow. They are perfectionists, excelling at whatever they take on. Life is methodically and systematically sorted; everything has a place and everything is in its place.

The emotional identity of Nat-mur is immature and underdeveloped in contrast to an overdeveloped mental control. The emotional immaturity that Nat-murs carry stems from a family history of overcontrolling and overexacting parents. Nat-murs sink into emotional negation because their own identity and persona has been so contained and controlled that they have not matured enough to be able to know how to respond appropriately. Nat-murs walk a fine line between giving too much in relationships and needing too much emotional support. With the fluid balance being so tentative, it is easy for Nat-murs to perceive hurts where none were intended. Nat-murs are mentally sensible and controlled and mature beyond their years but emotional teenagers when it comes to love and relationships.

The emotional lessen in life for Nat-murs is to stop retaining and controlling the fluid nature of their emotional being. Nat-murs carry with them the theme of trying to contain and control their intense emotive reactions to life. Love and relationships are potentially anxiety producing; they do not know how "to do love," and because Nat-murs feel love so intensely, they feel vulnerable and threatened by their lack of emotional control. For Nat-murs in such an open state, hypersensitivity and hypervigilance to hurt[26] and rejection act as their best defense mechanism.

Key Mental and Emotional Characteristics

- Emotionally very emotive and empathic but also very guarded.
- Very strong need to control their environment.
- Perfectionist. "Type A" personality.
- Principled and moralistic.
- Sensitive to the needs of their partner — empathic, warm, and supportive. But a fine line exists between the role of "giver" and the role of "martyr" with Nat-murs.
- Do not give up easily; will often hang on to a relationship way past its "use-by date."
- Feel personally responsible for the welfare of family and the world.
- Can feel a lot of guilt if they have not lived up to family expectations.
- Like to feel they connect deeply with people and take love and friendship very seriously.
- Will seek revenge if hurt.
- Can be very guarded if hurt in previous relationships and will not be willing to commit to a new relationship.
- Very sensitive to being criticized and hang on to hurt or grief for a long time.
- Adverse to help or consolation; like to be alone and cry alone.

- May need alcohol or drugs to be able to relax.
- Premenstrual tension that emotionally manifests as irritation, anger, or sadness, or perceived and imagined hurts.

Key Physical Characteristics

Nat-murs control emotionally and physically. The crossover from emotional holding to physical holding is particularly clear in the various fluid-retention problems that Nat-murs suffer. Commonly, the Nat-mur battle of control manifests in intensely painful migraines, which eventually force Nat-murs to stop and rest. Pain is often the only thing that will allow Nat-murs to stop, to let go and rest. Nat-murs can also suffer intense menstrual pain and cramps because they struggle emotionally with letting go to their physical processes. The physical use of pain is a Nat-mur regulator that allows them to let go; this is also mirrored emotionally in the classic Nat-mur "martyr to the cause," syndrome. Emotional hurt and pain also allows them to rest; Nat-murs like to go off alone to brood and lick their wounds.

- Congestive headaches and migraines, often from sinus inflammation.
- Sinus troubles that alternate between a dry or constantly runny nose.
- Dry or difficult-to-pass stools, causing hemorrhoids, or stools that are runny and unformed; often alternating between the two extremes within the same stool motion.
- Often find it hard to let go enough to urinate in public toilets.
- Menses often late, and the flow is contracted and painful.
- Often suffer from a dry vagina and feeling adverse to sex — always after emotional hurt.
- Unable to sleep due to grief or upsets. Nat-murs also have an obsession there is a thief[27] in the house and they worry about being vulnerable.
- Sweating, especially on the face when eating.

- Crave salt.
- Fluid retention, especially pre-menses.
- Dry mucus membranes, especially the mouth and lips.
- Dry, cracked skin.
- Tight, contracted muscular back pain.
- Contracted hamstrings and ankles.
- Easily perspiring palms.
- Aggravated by all heat, especially the sun.

Nux Vomica

Origins of Nux Vomica

The homeopathic remedy *Nux vomica* is derived from a dilution of tincture taken from the seeds of a poison nut *strychnos nux vomica*. It was commonly referred to as the poison strychnine because the nut itself contained a high percentage of the poison. Strychnine poisoning creates a fanatical degree of spasms and severe cramps. A poisoning overdose affects the gut and travels to the blood and spinal cord; the eyes bulge, the muscles contract, and the whole body goes into convulsions. Death comes as the convulsions get more violent, and the respiratory muscle spasms cause the respiratory system to shut down.

Nux vomicas carry in their psyche the inner threat of possible annihilation. Nux vomicas are always on guard, and only relax when safely at home away from the world. The inability for Nux vomicas to relax and let down their guard against possible attack is mirrored in the types of physical strain and tension they suffer. Nux vomicas are fanatically intense[28] and driven to succeed; they need to secure their position in the world so they can ward off any possible annihilation or poisoning. The most important aspect to consider when determining if you are the constitution Nux vomica is the confidence that you have in your ability to fight and win. Nux vomicas never doubt they will win and, more important, they make sure they never relax enough to allow any thoughts or fears of failure to influence them. It is this degree of confidence and arrogance that distinguishes

Nux vomicas from Lycopodiums. Lycopodiums are equally arrogant and driven to survive, but they have fear and doubt; Nux vomicas are so driven they do not stop to consider failure.

Key Mental and Emotional Characteristics

- "Type A" personality.
- A strong need to win.
- Competitive in work and love.
- Jealous if feeling threatened.
- High achievers.
- Ambitious.
- Irritable and angry if contradicted.
- Workaholics.
- Compulsive.
- Irritable if impeded in their career.
- Fastidious.
- High sex drive.
- Violent if opposed; malicious and vindictive.
- Fear of humiliation.
- Tendency to collapse from overwork and exhaustion.
- A strong need to rest and be quiet.
- A strong need for stimulants like alcohol, drugs, or coffee.
- Zealous in all aspects of life.
- A strange delusion or paranoid fear that someone is sleeping in their bed. This is, of course, an extension of the energy or fear of having been misplaced or poisoned. This fear indicates how intensely Nux vomicas need to be the only one in control or the only one in their bed.

Key Physical Characteristics

The picture of poisoning with strychnine must be able to be identified in the types of constrictions, spasms, and marked sensitivity of the physical complaints.

- Tense feeling in muscles.
- Spasms and cramps.
- Intolerant of tight things around the waist, or pressure on the stomach.
- Irritability after meals.
- Gastrointestinal cramps and disturbances.
- Colic (spasms in the stomach).
- Gastritis from overeating or alcohol abuse.
- Constipation with cramps and ineffectual urging to pass stools.
- Cystitis (bladder infection or irritation), with constant urging.
- Back pain and cramps, which are worse at night.
- Sleep aggravations.
- Irritability in the morning.
- Waking at 3–4 A.M.
- Insomnia due to an overstimulated mind.
- Often feel better after short sleeps and cat naps.
- Craving for spices and coffee, and all stimulants; also crave alcohol and drugs. (Drugs are usually needed by Nux vomicas to try to slow down their mind at the end of the day.)
- Sinus irritations and hay-fever-like allergies.
- Chills and cramps from the cold.
- Convulsions.
- Heart palpitations from sudden excitement.
- All pains are relieved by heat.

Phosphorus

Origins of Phosphorus

Phosphorus is a mineral that plays a conductive role in every chemical reaction in the body. Physiologically, phosphorus enables cells to utilize carbohydrates, fats and proteins; phosphorus is also used for the maintenance and repair of cells, and for production of cellular energy. Phosphorus is a non-metallic element that is luminous in the dark and is unique because of its ability to produce light. Within the persona of the constitution Phosphorus is the essence of phosphoric conductivity and light. The phosphoric nature of the element phosphorus is reflected in the luminescent, sparkling ability to stimulate others and be stimulated by them. The conductive nature of phosphorus, the mineral, is reflected in phosphoric, enthusiastic involvement and ability to bubble and bob enthusiastically from one thing in life to another.

The theme of Phosphorus is conductive; Phosphorus needs to stimulate, enthuse, and receive. They need continual acknowledgment, excitement, and stimulation to be able to be healthy and shine. Phosphorus is a mineral that is essential for the production of cellular energy. A deficiency of phosphorus can cause rapid weight loss, mental and emotional fatigue, nervous disorders, and irregularities in breathing. The dark side or unhealthy side of Phosphorus is emotional anxiousness, overexcited nervousness, and mental indifference to everything in life. Phosphorous is affectionate, loving of self and others, joyful, carefree, and childlike – but only when receiving necessary affection and attention. In partnerships, Phosphorus needs to gravitate toward people who are going to give the most amount of attention.

Key Mental and Emotional Characteristics

- Childlike, open, and enthusiastic.
- Love new adventures, travel, and excitement.
- Fall in love very quickly, and love the excitement of new lovers.
- Warm, loving, and generous.
- Sympathetic to the plight of others.
- Dislike unpleasantness and are confused by suffering in the world.
- Sensitive to others' feelings.
- Very nervous and excitable.
- Easily overwhelmed emotionally; can become anxious or fearful.
- Somatic inner knowing they can be easily extinguished.
- Feel a lot better if there is someone around to protect them.
- Can be inconsolable if grieving.
- Very needy of company and hate being alone.
- Emotionally sensitive to weather changes, especially thunderstorms.
- Fear death, especially if alone at night.
- Hot flushes, especially on the face, particularly when feeling embarrassed or strongly about a particular subject.

Key Physical Characteristics

Physically, Phosphorus also needs attention. Phosphoric light can be extinguished very quickly; consequently, Phosphorus is a constitution that can get very sick, very quickly.

- Sensitivity to all external changes, especially the onset of cold weather.
- Fall ill very quickly.
- Chest infections and coughs that come on quickly as a result of exposure to cold.
- Infections that deteriorate and progress quickly into pneumonia.
- Injuries that easily hemorrhage or become serious infections.
- Tendency to suffer from bleeding gums after dental work, polyps that bleed easily, noses that bleed easily, hemorrhoids that bleed easily, or bleeding too heavily during menses.
- Sensitive to smells.
- Hypoglycemic – skipping a meal will cause fainting or sudden exhaustion.
- Vertigo or dizziness.
- Very sensitive stomach and bowels.
- Tendency to suffer from exhaustive diarrhea.
- Vomiting and nausea relieved by cold drinks, but followed soon after by vomiting.
- Sensitive, easily disturbed sleep.
- Too excited to go to sleep and always wake feeling tired.
- Joints that give way or inflame suddenly.
- Anxiety attacks and heart palpitations, with hot flushes.

Pulsatilla

Origins of Pulsatilla

The homeopathic remedy *Pulsatilla* is derived from the *Pulsatilla nigricans* plant, commonly called a wind flower. The delicate flower sits so precariously at the end of a very fine stem that it is constantly vulnerable to the environmental force of the wind. Just as the flower is constantly changing positions, the same is true for the emotional state of Pulsatilla. Pulsatilla will not easily be confused with too many other constitutional pictures. Emotional sensitivity, emotive changeability, and mental unpredictability are the Pulsatilla themes that connect the delicate flower to the constitutional personality. Pulsatilla reacts sympathetically and emotively, whether the issue is happy or sad. The most important aspect of the constitutional persona is that Pulsatillas feel comfortable with their changeability. They compensate for emotional unpredictability by feeling comfortable with knowing they need continual reassurance. Pulsatillas are not willing to let go of anything that makes them feel needed or secure; if they feel deprived at all, or if one thing is not right, they are very likely to be peeved and burst into tears. Pulsatillas are so susceptible to becoming overexcited that their tears will flow spontaneously from feeling sadness or joy. The petulant, hypercritical irrationality of Pulsatillas is usually rare; they have such an endearing nature, they usually are able to get what they need. The inner psyche of Pulsatillas knows that they need to be able to flow with the wind if they are going to protect their delicate flower.

Key Mental and Emotional Characteristics

- Sympathetic.
- Affectionate.
- Timid.
- Soft, effeminate, feminine persona; regardless of gender.
- Emotionally sensitive; tearful if upset.
- Feel sorry for themselves if they do not get what they want.
- Submissive and eager to please their partner; conversely, petulant if they do not get their own way.
- Will often be very happy to take on the beliefs and practices of their partner.
- Easily doubt themselves and feel discouraged.
- Very needy of sympathy and attention.
- Feel terrible if left alone, especially as children, but also as an adult if left alone by their partner.
- Emotional changeability and emotional unpredictability.
- Quick mood changes from weepy to irritable, especially when feeling unnoticed.
- Possessive and jealous of loved ones.
- Strong need for reassurance. (This is not only projected on to their partner; they also turn to religion for reassurance.)
- Shy and timid; often taking some time to trust strangers.
- Fearful of feeling insecure.
- Fearful at night if alone.
- Very emotional with all hormonal changes; likely to be irritable one minute and teary the next.
- Unlikely to sleep if overexcited or worried.

Key Physical Characteristics

Emotional sensitivity and emotive changeability is a Pulsatilla theme that is mirrored in the physical complaints. The theme of the physical sensitivity of the flower to wind is expressed uniquely in Pulsatilla as an exaggeration of all physiological processes. Pulsatilla is overly sensitive to allergens in the environment, overly sensitive to rich food, overly sensitive to stuffy rooms, overly sensitive to heat, and relieved by open air but overly sensitive to cold. All the emotive states of Pulsatilla express themselves in physical complaints. If Pulsatillas try to hold back their emotions they suffer physically; conversely, if Pulsatillas are suffering physically from suppression of, for example, the menses, they will be affected emotionally. The very nature of Pulsatilla is to be healthy only when allowed to be as changeable as the flower in the wind.

- Chilly, but unable to tolerate heat.
- Love walking in open air even though they feel the cold.
- Pains in limbs relieved from gentle walking.
- Pains in joints relieved by constantly changing position and location.
- Pains aggravated by heat at night and relieved by cold.
- Digestive sensitivity, especially to fatty, rich foods.
- Heartburn, burping, and flatulence after rich food.
- Crave cold drinks, and relieved by cold drinks, even though they are not thirsty.
- Dry mouth but not thirsty.
- Duration and presentation of menses is constantly changing – from irregular flow, to short duration, to excessive bleeding with clots, to menses with a light flow.
- Headaches from delayed menses, during menopause.
- Flushes easily.
- Sleeplessness when overexcited, with the same thoughts going over and over.
- Headaches from overwork or worry.
- Sensitivity and pain urinating, often from trying to delay urination.
- Sensitive to environmental allergens.
- Excessive, yellow-green mucus, with all colds or hay fever.
- Eczema, aggravated by rich food and by heat; itchy at night.
- Itching, sensitive eyes with excessive discharge.

Sepia

Origins of Sepia

The homeopathic remedy *Sepia* is derived from the ink that cuttle-fish squirt out when they sense that danger is present. If cuttlefish feel hemmed in or threatened they need to quickly create a subterfuge so they can escape. The Sepia theme of escape and subterfuge runs through the presentation of the emotional, mental, and physical complaints. Sepias need independence, freedom, and individuality, if they are to remain healthy. Sepia as a constitutional picture is unique in the sense that there is a stark difference between the healthy and unhealthy presentation.

The most common physical symptom Sepia will complain of is a complete lack of interest in sex. In the case of Sepia, this is not an isolated issue; it is a symptom of a much larger problem. Sepia in a relationship or family that does not allow space or freedom will always eventually arrive at the unhealthy, depressed version of Sepia. Sepias are not just disinterested in sex; they are emotively disinterested in constrictive relationships or constrictive roles. The typical presentation of the unhealthy Sepia is a mother or wife who feels overburdened by the demands of her husband, partner, or children. A Sepia man will react the same way as a Sepia woman, but societal permission has traditionally made it easier for a man to be independent, or free to walk away from family. It is rare to be a Sepia man who has moved into the unhealthy presentation of the constitutional picture. The extreme difference between the passionate Sepia and the unhealthy, depressed Sepia woman makes it imperative to discuss female Sepia. Sepia knows that if she doesn't walk away, she will lose herself. In deciding if you are Sepia, you need to determine whether you are feeling hemmed in by the constraints of family and children. Cuttlefish like to swim alone; they do not collect in groups; likewise, even when healthy, Sepia need to be able to find individuality and independence. This is the theme of Sepia.

Key Mental and Emotional Characteristics

- Healthy Sepias are nonconformist.
- Need to find meaning and purpose in life – through career, occupation, or creative outlet.
- Freedom is crucial to feeling happy and secure.
- The Sepia love of space and freedom is often expressed in a love of dance, movement, or exercise.
- Often feel better if they are busy and active; even feel better if they rush around and clean the house.
- Healthy Sepias are creative and passionate.
- Need physical and emotional space to be able to feel alive.
- All gender role expectations of wife and mother will threaten Sepia women.
- Unhealthy Sepias are irritable and defeated.
- When they feel distraught, can often present as typical nagging harridans.
- Unhealthy Sepias look and feel overburdened and exhausted.
- React to restrictions with anger.
- Feel emotionally disconnected if they feel overburdened.
- The cuttlefish need to create subterfuge has parallels in Sepias' feeling cut off and detached.
- Premenstrual tension, anger, and weepy depression are all worse if Sepias feel overburdened.
- Indifferent to everything when depressed and passionately creative when healthy.

- A Sepia woman who is able to walk away from family is healthy. Sepias often stay feeling overburdened out of a strong sense of duty; this is the type of self-suppression that will eventually lead the Sepia woman into crippling depression. It is, of course, far healthier for Sepia to know that some independence will prevent the need to walk away in the first place.

Key Physical Characteristics

The homeopathic remedy *Sepia* is good to use for post-natal depression; the new mother often feels emotionally like she needs to escape and this feeling is "like" the theme of Sepia. The theme of Sepia constitutionally has to always reflect the nature of the cuttlefish wanting to swim alone. The more space that Sepias have, the more likely they are to be healthy. Sepias suffer adversely from hormonal changes. When they are not feeling emotionally threatened, Sepias do not build up anywhere near the same degree of premenstrual tension. If they are active physically through dance or some form of exercise, Sepias do not have the same degree of tension. If Sepias are emotionally creative and independent, they also do not suffer from extreme premenstrual tension.

- Bloating and swelling before menses; premenstrual tension.
- Dry vagina and low libido.
- Irregular menses, often with profuse pain.
- Back pain during menses.
- Hormonal pimples.
- Hormonal headaches.
- Hot flushes at menopause.
- Infertility, miscarriages, prolapsed uterus, morning sickness during pregnancy.
- Stress incontinence after childbirth.
- Leucorrhoea (whitish or yellowish discharges) after sex.
- Lack of energy, especially in the morning and if depressed.

- Faint easily, especially with hormonal changes.
- Constipation, especially with hormonal changes or depression.
- Yellowy skin blotches.
- Feel sick cyclically, every 28 days, even if male or non-menstruating female.

Silicea

Origins of Silicea

The homeopathic remedy *Silicea* is derived from silica. A large amount of the surface of the earth is made from the components of silica. Silica supplies the strength or grit of the sand on the beach; silica is one of the main components of glass, and silicates are also deposited in the stems of plants giving them strength in their stems. Silica, as a mineral, is used nutritionally to strengthen hair, nails, and teeth. Silica is also used nutritionally for defects of connective tissue caused from poor metabolism and assimilation of minerals. Silica as a tissue salt is present in the connective structure of skin, hair, nails, and blood; it is also a constituent of mucous membranes, nerve sheaths, and bones.

Silicea as a constitution presents with the same theme of the vulnerability of shattered glass, but with a seemingly converse dichotomy of being strong enough to hold up the stem of a plant. The same theme of searching for connective structure is also visible in the psyche of Silicea. Siliceas suffer from shyness and lack of self-confidence, yet they overcome these by forming strong moral codes and by holding onto strong ideas and beliefs that help them find structure and inner strength. Siliceas are conscious of their assimilation faults, and are very conscientious about trying to eradicate them. Siliceas spend a lot of time creating a perfect outer image to try to reinforce their internal shakiness. This process creates a personality that is very refined and delicate, yet very exacting. This dichotomy of strong inner convictions juxtaposed with a seemingly delicate fragile outer presentation is the theme of Silicea. Siliceas are shy and appear outwardly as if they acquiesce because they do not argue or disagree; however, internally Siliceas never acquiesce and they never change their beliefs and morals

Key Mental and Emotional Characteristics

- Delicate, shy, timid personality.
- Refined appearance; never "loud" or outrageous.
- Outer appearance matches their inner moral refinement.
- Can appear to lack confidence, in stark contrast to their strong moralistic views.
- Inflexible.
- Have strong opinions, yet often feel the need to rely on the opinions of others.
- Nervous, anxious, and overly conscientious about making decisions.
- Sensitive to feeling upset or offended.
- Fear failing. (This fear is always unfounded because Siliceas' conscientiousness prevents them from making mistakes.)
- Struggle with change.
- Slow to develop relationships.
- Slow to decide on a choice of career. (Because their career has to live up to their strict moral codes, Siliceas will often have several career changes.)
- Headaches caused by worry and anticipation.
- Very discerning in choosing friends, and value them very highly.
- Do not like to be pushed, prodded,[29] or forced into situations; they like to feel they have taken their time to assess all new situations.
- Adolescence is a struggle for Silicea. (It is the time in life when Siliceas are confronted with needing to find enough inner grit and conviction to be able to stand up for what

they believe. Silicea teenagers can be inflexible, especially
if they do not respect their parents.)
- Particularly afraid of noises in the house at night.

Key Physical Characteristics

Siliceas struggle to find enough inner physical strength to cope with
the demands of living. Siliceas have to continually physically and
emotionally assess how to maintain their health and well-being. In
examining the constitution Silicea, you must be able to see continual conscientiousness over all the details of their life and especially
their health. Siliceas always need to assess the amount of energy
required for any given situation; even when healthy, a Silicea is not
going to present as a robust person who is able to take on high-
energy-requiring challenges.

- Can feel weak and fatigued, with low physical stamina.
- Frequent colds, chills, and flu resulting from physical or
  emotional overexertion.
- Headaches from overexertion.
- Need to wrap up very warmly to protect themselves
  from chills.
- Nutritional assimilation issues with bones, teeth, and hair.
- Struggle nutritionally with assimilation of minerals and
  nutrients.
- Tendency to suffer from scarring as a result of acne; all
  wounds heal slowly.
- Tendency to suffer from slow-healing abscesses and cysts.
- Often sick if they can't perspire.[30]
- Tendency to have profuse, offensive sweating of feet
  and head.
- Constipation, and difficulty finding enough energy to pass
  stools.
- Retain their menses to try to avoid the inevitable onset of pain.
- Typically suffer from acne that starts in the early twenties,
  which is much later than the usual teenage hormonal acne.
- Sensitive to pain, chills, overexertion, and noise or upsets.

Staphisagria

Origins of Staphisagria

The homeopathic remedy *Staphisagria* is derived from a dilution of the seeds of *Delphinium staphisagria*, commonly known as louse-wort. Dioscorides,[31] a Greek pharmacologist, discovered its use as a parasiticide, and it was applied externally in the Middle Ages to relieve itching from lice bites. *Delphinium staphisagria* is also a poison that was used by the Greeks and Romans. Poisoning causes violent vomiting and salivation, slowing of the pulse and respiration, and death from paralysis of the spinal cord and asphyxia. *Delphinium staphisagria* was also used to stop the contractive convulsions caused by strychnine poisoning. It was obviously not able to prevent death, but the suppressive nature of the poison was able to relieve the painful spasmodic convulsions associated with strychnine poisoning, by shutting down all spinal nerve responses.

The theme of suppression and repression has to be mirrored emotionally, mentally, and physically for the constitution to be Staphisagria. Homeopathy is based on the principles of "like cures like." The theme of Staphisagria is "like" the suppressive nature of the poison. If there is no history of emotional suppression, physical abuse, or mental abuse, it would be very unlikely that Staphisagria would be the right constitution. There are a lot of constitutions that suffer from abuse. Staphisagrias are unique in the sense that they turn the oppression and abuse on themselves in the form of suppression of their feelings. This suppression is as powerful as the suppressive nature of the poison *Delphinium staphisagria*. Nat-mur also has a history of emotional repression but Nat-mur is able to get angry and rebel. Staphisagrias suppress feelings by not allowing any expression of anger or rage; they are proud of the fact that they are able to remain nice and sweet. Staphisagrias have developed justifiable reasons for why they need to suppress their feelings; they are protecting a very painful history of some form of abuse. The theme of suppression and composure has healthy and unhealthy advantages, as well as disadvantages and consequences for Staphisagria. Staphisagrias eventually always lose control because their suppression is challenged by the equally powerful force of their anger and rage at being continually abused and repressed. When Staphisagria lose control they are abusive because the build-up of emotion is overwhelming. Staphisagrias then sink into remorseful self-abuse that mirrors their history of abuse. Within Staphisagria is the theme of abuse, out-of-control abuser, and the remorseful self abuser.

Key Mental and Emotional Characteristics

- Mild and gentle, very sweet and composed; Staphisagria do not provoke disagreements because it is below their dignity to get angry.
- Struggle with assertion, because they are overly sensitive to reprimands[32] or rejection.
- Pride on not feeling angry.
- Sensitive to arguments, and will get very insulted by conflict or rudeness.
- Sensitive to what others think about them.
- Often imagine and perceive insults that are not intended.
- Suppress their feelings so much that they are not able to control their rage and anger when it does finally explode.
- Fear losing control; they know they are usually violent.
- Suffer from remorseful guilt after feeling angry.
- Often unsure of what they feel because they suppress so much.
- Dwell on sexual feelings, often as a result of trying to suppress sexual feelings.

- Often remorseful, and self-abusive after sexual feelings.
- Abuse themselves emotionally and physically for being so disgusting.
- Feel self-righteous and good about not expressing "bad" sexual[33] or emotional feelings.
- Usually have some sort of addictive behavior they are trying to suppress.
- A history of abuse – sexual, emotional, or physical.

Key Physical Characteristics

There is a strong physical theme between the suppression of emotional anger and the expression of pain in the body. Staphisagria has the theme of cramping and suppression of muscular function, and the opposite sensation of extreme sensitivity and pain. All of these mirror the neuralgic damage caused from *Delphinium staphisagria* poisoning.

- Physical trembling caused by trying to control anger.
- Headaches caused by suppressed anger or suppressed sexual feelings.
- Muscular cramps and spasms, caused by tension.
- Stomach pains and colic, caused by suppressing anger.
- Painful cystitis (bladder infection), caused by retaining and suppressing the urge to urinate.
- Painful sex from trying to suppress sexual enjoyment.
- Eczema, psoriasis, and skin irritations, aggravated by feelings of remorse.
- Sensitive to being touched,[34] Staphisagria often trembles with any sort of contact. In homeopathic practice, the remedy is used after surgery to relieve extreme neuralgic pain. (Staphisagria suffer from extreme pain sensitivity and nerve neuralgia, especially facial neuralgia, which reflects the nature of spinal nerve damage from *Delphinium staphisagria* poisoning.)
- Itching[35] skin eruptions.
- Excess salivation.[36]

- Quite often are unable to stop yawning.[37]
- Sensitive teeth, aggravated by brushing.
- Frequent masturbation needed as a form of relaxation.
- Insomnia, from sexual thoughts, especially if repressing sexual desire.
- Strong desires for stimulants, especially tobacco, to help with relaxation and suppression.

Sulphur

Origins of Sulphur

The homeopathic remedy *Sulphur* is derived from the element sulfur. Sulfur is a yellow crystalline solid that is found underground and is only able to be mined and forced to the surface in molten form at extremely high temperatures of 115° Celsius.[38] The same degree of intense heat that is needed to extract sulfur is also able to be seen as the motivational theme in the psyche of the constitution Sulphur. The explosive, expansive heat needed to extract sulfur is matched by Sulphur constitutionally and mirrored by their reactive genius and creative self-absorption.

It is important to understand and know the core motivations behind each constitution. If you just look on the surface, it is possible to confuse Nux vomica with Lycopodium, or Lycopodium with Sulphur. All three constitutions are essentially egoistical, but the egotistical motivation of each is different. Nux vomica needs ego to eliminate possible threats, and builds ego to win. Lycopodium needs ego for survival and security, and builds ego for greatness. Sulphur's relationship with ego is distinctive. Sulphurs are altruistically inspired by a sense of greatness and need to inspire the rest of the world to see the beauty they see. Sulphur uses ego as fuel for an unfaltering, inspirational desire to light the fire of knowledge and creativity in humanity.

The psychodynamic force behind Sulphur's passion and intensity is the heat and power of the element sulfur. Sulphur has conjured up so much force behind the exploding volcano that to not be recognized is crippling. If the world is not inspired and Sulphur is ignored, Sulphur sinks into intensely acrid, cynical depression.

Key Mental and Emotional Characteristics

- The majority of creative geniuses are Sulphur. Sulphurs are either viewed as inspirational geniuses or grandiose, philosophers or full of hot air, depending on the viewer's perception.
- Tendency to boast and exaggerate; Sulphurs may be accused of having "delusions of grandeur," or can be viewed as innovative, again depending on the viewer's perception.
- Extroverted and fanciful.
- Absent-minded and completely absorbed by their own thought processes.
- Often want to be left alone to pursue their thought processes and creativity.
- Have a strong need to surround themselves with objects of inspiration and beauty.
- Passionate and enthusiastic about what interests them and very uninterested in what does not inspire them. Sulphurs will not even feign polite interest.
- Ambitious, with either a realistic or overexaggerated view of their abilities, again depending on the viewer's perception.
- Feel claustrophobic, if forced to conform to societal expectations.
- Social, especially if they are the center of attention or the social activity involves indulging in good food and wine.
- Can often by accused of being self-centered, especially by their partner.
- Adverse to the practicalities of life, Sulphurs are not interested in the day-to-day practicalities of earning money and going to work.

- Can suffer from obsessive, crippling hypochondria. Sulphurs especially fear losing their mind or intellectual capacity.
- Tendency to get caught up in fearful fancies about health, or potential rejection by the world.
- Acrid and cynical, if they have lost faith in being acknowledged.
- Become depressed and withdrawn if the world has failed to recognize their contribution.
- Sulphurs are crippled if they feel they have caused their own failure.
- Become physically sick if they have been embarrassed by failure.
- Spiritual and religious, but unconventional in their faith, even if they belong to an established religious institution.
- Can be completely disinterested in conforming to societal pressures about appearance.

Key Physical Characteristics

Sulphurs do not hold back from experiencing life, nor do they hold back from overindulging in all the good things in life. Sulphurs love to eat and drink; consequently, Sulphurs also spend a lot of time suffering from their indulgence in food and alcohol. Sulphurs also spend a lot of time worrying about their illnesses, which are all ironically caused by overindulgence. Sulphurs' intensity and explosiveness is also expressed in numerous skin conditions that are characteristic of the heat and burning of the element sulfur.

- Aggravated by heat.
- Skin afflictions, aggravated by internal and external heat.
- Eczema and itching skin at night, aggravated from becoming hot in bed.
- Sweat excessively, especially on the head and feet, often with a strong sulfur smell.
- Love to eat large meals and love to eat frequently.
- Feel faint if they have not eaten, especially around 11 A.M.

- Stomach complaints, aggravated by overeating, indigestion, frequent flatulence (often hot and sulfur-smelling flatus), hemorrhoids, and morning diarrhea.
- Wake up between 2 and 5 A.M., aggravated by either heat or digestion.
- Dream, talk, and twitch during sleep.
- Dry, burning, itching eyes.
- Aggravated in stuffy, warm rooms.
- Crave lots of stimulant foods – sweets, coffee, spices, and alcohol.
- Hot, flushed face after overindulging, especially in alcohol.
- Skin complaints such as acne rosacea, all aggravated by overindulgence in alcohol and sweets.
- Burning discomfort in joints.
- Stooped over and often feel like their back is unable to support.
- Headaches, aggravated by digestive complaints.
- Headaches that occur periodically, such as headaches that occur on the weekend.
- Frequent, urgent urination, especially at night; often aggravated by overindulging in alcohol.

The
partnership
combinations

Carcinosin Partnerships

The Theme of Carcinosin

A homeopathic remedy is prescribed as a constitutional on the basis of being "like" the original substance. The person is not matched to the substance; rather, the personality is matched to the action of the substance. The homeopathic remedy *Carcinosin* is derived from a dilution of cancerous breast tissue. Cancer arises from the abnormal, uncontrolled division and overgrowth of undifferentiated, or poorly differentiated cells. The undifferentiated cells divide and duplicate quickly without control. Initially, the malignant cells invade surrounding tissues; as the cancer grows it expands and begins to compete with the surrounding tissues and organs for space. Eventually the tumor metastasizes and invades the surrounding body cavities, entering lymph or blood systems where it is enabled to travel unchecked and uncontrolled throughout the entire body. The reason I have outlined the pathophysiology is that it is crucial to the understanding of the constitution Carcinosin. The image that comes to mind is one of an ungrounded or undifferentiated energy that is expanding and desperately pushing on all that surrounds in the attempt to find definition or containment. This description of the pathology of cancerous growth mirrors and is "like" the personality of the constitution Carcinosin. Carcinosin is on a journey of self-discovery.

The homeopathic cure and essence of the use of this remedy is its ability to ease the relentless pursuit that haunts Carcinosins to find solidity of personality so they can know a personal boundary. Carcinosins are definable by their lack of definition – this is their essence and it is a theme that you must be able to identify within yourself if your constitution is Carcinosin. Carcinosins are not sure of themselves; they need to push very hard in life to be able to find definition; consequently, they are always expanding and pushing limits and boundaries to find out who they are. If you are content with yourself you are not Carcinosin, if you know who you are you are not Carcinosin, and if you are not trying to continually improve or prove yourself you are not Carcinosin. Carcinosins need to gain form and differentiation on a cellular level so the endless search for definition is able to cease.

The essence of Carcinosin is someone who does not have ego. The *Concise Oxford Dictionary* defines ego as "conscious thinking subject; . . . part of the mind that reacts to reality and has sense of individuality; self-esteem." Carcinosins lack a sense of individuality; they have no sense of individual defining ego. If you are not looking for who you are you are not Carcinosin. The presenting personality pictures of Carcinosin can seem contradictory; if Carcinosin lacks definition and containment, the variables between control and loss of control are vast. Consequently, it is not easy to define the personality of Carcinosin.

The Emotional History behind Carcinosin

With Carcinosins it is not unusual to find a family history of excessive control by overexacting or needy parents. This family history can equally be applied to several constitutions – Sepias, Medorrhinums, Nat-murs, and Staphisagrias all contain in their history the effects of excessive domination. The aspect that distinguishes Carcinosins is that they have often been given too much responsibility, and too much is expected of them at an early unformed age. Carcinosins have not had time to find out who they are; they have quite often been so contained, or so overcontrolled, or are so overly conscientious that they are unsure of who they are, or what defines the limits of their personality.

If you control a child with the expectation that they grow up very quickly and assume responsibility, the opposite often happens to the child's feeling about themselves. It is very likely that such children are able to take responsibility for the household, but they will not have been given the time and freedom to explore growing up. The chance to explore this is an important part of adolescence. Teenagers slowly form a sense of who they are by reacting to constraints and defying the authority of parents and society. In the expanse of their personality they find their ego; if this process is bypassed, they do not have the opportunity to find themselves. It is not always the case in the development of Carcinosins that their parents have deliberately set out to control or expect too much. It might be that a parent has died, and the child is forced to grow up quickly and take responsibility for running the household, or maybe the parent is unable through illness or drug addiction to be able to parent effectively. The resulting dilemma for Carcinosins is they live up to the expectations of others and often feel like they have had to grow up so quickly it has not been possible for them to know who they are. Carcinosins are used to playing out their responsible side, but they feel uncertain and indecisive when they try to stop being so responsible.

The rigidity and high expectations in the upbringing of Carcinosins leave them with a heavy legacy. Every choice in life carries with it a life-or-death heaviness. Their overdeveloped sense of duty and commitment creates an overburdened seriousness that leads them to worry about every decision they make. It is as if they know in their psyche that they are essentially fighting within themselves a disease that has the potential to destroy their life. The crisis for Carcinosins often comes when they have to face failure for the first time.

The Emotional Legacy for Carcinosin

In my practice Carcinosins typically come for consultation at the point in their life when they have lost the ability to continue to make decisions. The effort to maintain order and definition in their life has overwhelmed them to the point they can no longer move forward; the effect of taking on too much at a young age catches up. Carcinosins will always carry the same patterning from their childhood into their adulthood; they will always set themselves up in situations that demand incredibly high standards. The goals that they set are often impossible to achieve so it can become a self-fulfilling prophesy of failure for Carcinosin. The goals they set are also the system of defining who they are, so it is impossible to see a Carcinosin who has not striven at some point in life for perfection, or who is not currently striving for perfection.

When other constitutions like Lycopodium, Nux vomica, or Sulphur fail, the angst and pain are visible to all around them. A lack of ego means Carcinosin gives no definition to grief. The process becomes the same as the pathology of the disease state that is present in cancer. Carcinosins silently accumulate all their sadness and grief within themselves. The grief of other constitutions is always visible if you scratch the surface; in contrast, Carcinosins expand their sadness deep within their cellular tissue to the point that they are so overwhelmed with tremendous anxiety, it is difficult to unravel. They are then crippled by the struggle to find enough definition of personality to make simple decisions in life.

Conversely, the other presenting picture of Carcinosin is the person who has outwardly pushed so hard in life to be now completely exhausted. The presenting underlying dilemma and conflict are the same. The essence of Carcinosin is a person who is desperate to find definition. The flip side of the anxious Carcinosin crippled by indecision and struggling with taking control is the Carcinosin so overcontrolled and obsessive in the pursuit of excellence to the point of carrying everything too far and not being able to stop. The underlying intensity of everything being a life-and-death situation is present in both presentations.

Carcinosin triathletes who turn up at my clinic with adrenal exhaustion from pushing their bodies to the extreme are the same constitution as the Carcinosins who turn up with such crippling depression they are unable to be motivated enough to get out of bed. The patients who have injured themselves running in races or skydiving off tall buildings are the same constitution as those who are so overanxious about making mistakes they are unable to achieve anything in their lives. The professional student who has not been able to leave university and is continually researching a doctoral thesis is the same constitution as the worker who feels trapped in an unchallenging job but lacks the self-esteem to achieve anything else. The vibrant dancer who has come to consult me for continual injuries is the same constitution as the Mount Everest climber who nearly died attempting to reach the summit. The warm and gentle animal shelter worker who suffers the effects of getting emotionally caught up in the work is the same constitution as the hard-nosed executive who suffers from the stress of making the right decision. An abused wife of an alcoholic who is so depressed she cannot find enough sense of herself to walk away is the same constitution as the busy mother who is so caught up in being a fantastic mother, wife, and employee; neither one has any idea who she is.

What exists in all the above expressions of Carcinosin is the need to expand. Neither presentation can be divided into the healthy or the unhealthy presentation of Carcinosin. The dilemma crosses into both presentations. It is not possible to say that the wife suffering depression in an abusive relationship is the unhealthy presentation of Carcinosin, or the climber who has reached the summit of Mount Everest is the healthy presentation. This is a dilemma that is quite unique to the psyche of Carcinosin; no other constitution has this dichotomy.

The Challenge for Carcinosin in Relationships

This lack of ego definition can become a real problem for Carcinosin, especially in the area of relationships. The essence of what is lacking is differentiation or boundaries. The only definition of healthy Carcinosins are the people on the journey to find their ego. Just as the immune system has lost the physiological defenses against advancing cancer cells, Carcinosins need to find their ego. Being potentially undifferentiated or undefined, Carcinosins will change dramatically from relationship to relationship. There will be no consistent picture in the following discussions of relationship combinations. This is in stark contrast to Nat-mur; a guarded Nat-mur will be consistent, regardless of which constitution they are in a relationship with. Changeable and reactive Mercurius will still possess a sense of who they are; emotive Pulsatilla will also still have a sense of who they are. Carcinosins do not have this; their lack of definition or lack of ego means that whether they are happy or unhappy, at peace or anxious, fulfilled or depressed, the personality of Carcinosin will always be shaped or determined by the other person's constitutional compatibility to Carcinosin. The state of Carcinosins will never solely be based on, or determined by, the persona or health of Carcinosin themselves. There are too many holes in their undeveloped immune systems for it to be any other way. Carcinosins will always be affected by the people around them. The positive side to this emotive and empathic sensitivity is seen in the ability Carcinosins have to acquiesce and give emotionally to another's feelings or suffering. The negative side is seen when Carcinosins lose themselves in the desire to please another.

Healthy Carcinosins are the people who are at peace with themselves. They will have a sense of no longer being suppressed and needing to obsessively push themselves to the limits of endurance to define who they are. They will no longer oscillate between the extremes of loss of control and the obsessive need for control. They will still be easygoing or happy to acquiesce to others' feelings, but they will not lose sight of themselves in the process. They will not be crippled by guilt or a sense of failure if they do not live up to the expectations of family or partner. They will not allow themselves to become the victim of either their own need to excel or of someone else's expectations to achieve. They will be far more accepting and aware of the process of expanding[39] emotions inside of themselves and will be willing to allow their partner in life to take some of the burden of their feelings. They will also be far more forgiving of themselves as well as being far less sensitive to the criticisms or expectations of others.

Examples of Carcinosin in Films

The film *Personal Velocity*, written and directed by Rebecca Miller, is the story of three different versions of Carcinosin. Each story is a reflection of the diversity of the constitution Carcinosin. In the first story Delia, played by actor Kyra Sedgwick, could easily be mistaken for Staphisagria. Delia is stuck in an abusive relationship with a husband who beats her. One night, after another beating, she decides to leave to save her three children. She escapes with the thought she wants to save her children, but she soon finds out she is escaping to save herself, so she can find a sense of self and her own sense of power. She is not Staphisagria. Staphisagria would stay within the boundaries of abuse and self-abuse, and delude herself by playing the role of the abuser. Delia's mother left Delia as a teenager; Delia was forced to take over the responsibility for her upbringing and her father. Delia found her definition and power as a teenager by pushing the limits of her sexual experience. After escaping her husband she is once again on the same journey of defining herself through her sexual power. Delia's journey is the essence of the journey of Carcinosin; the way she plays out that journey does not matter in defining the constitutional theme of Carcinosin.

The next story is of Greta, played by actor Parker Posey. The story is reflective and told through a series of flashbacks as she goes through the same process of trying to define self. Greta gave up her privilege of a Harvard education to look after her mother, who is dying of cancer. By giving up herself to support her mother through cancer and death, Greta redefines herself in a "Florence Nightingale" role, as someone with no drive or ambition. After her mother's death, Greta continues the same pattern of abandoning herself by being supportive and loving toward her husband. Greta also gives up on herself when she settles for a job as a cookbook editor instead of pursuing her ambition and drive to be a fiction editor. The decision to look after her own needs and find out what she actually wants for herself is the life-long journey of Carcinosin. First, she decides to leave her husband, who, even though he is sweet, she finds uninspiring; second, she decides to leave her job, which she finds equally unchallenging and uninspiring. Greta finds within herself an emerging ambitious editor. The decision to find her drive and ambition is the theme of Carcinosin. The desire to find her own drive and ambition again and push the boundaries of excellence is Carcinosin. This story is the opposite of the first, in that the relationship is not abusive; Greta's husband is kind and supportive. But Greta's decision to want a more exciting partner and to know what she needs is also consistent with the theme of Carcinosin. The need to push boundaries to explore and find definition of self is the theme that ties the two stories together.

The last story is about Paula, played by actor Fairuza Balk. It is a story of a young woman who is so emotionally traumatized by a near-death experience she sets out on a journey of trying to find herself. Paula is thrown into a crisis of identity and needs to return to her mother and home to find her roots and self. Her mother is not able to provide the help she needs. On the way back to her mother's house she picks up a hitchhiker who has been physically tortured and injured. In the process of reaching out to him and sensing his pain, she starts on the journey of her own discovery of what she wants in life. He pushes her sense of self and compassion to explore who she is. She discovers her need to return to her lover, and she discovers she wants to have the child she is carrying. Each story has the same theme of Carcinosin in the sense that each woman is pushing the limits of herself to find out who she is. Each woman is exploring the boundaries of experience of self and expression of self; each woman is pushing to find a sense of who she is in order to be able to define herself.

The story of the character Rose, daughter of An-Mei in the film *The Joy Luck Club*, is also the journey of Carcinosin. Rose is the subservient wife of the executive husband Ted. The couple is on the verge of divorce. Ted has left because he is no longer able to find a person in the caricature of a wife he has been left with. Rose has given up her career, and as a result of her ambition to be the dutiful wife, she has abandoned so much of herself she is crippled with anxiety, and lacks confidence even to know what to cook for dinner. An-Mei pleads with her daughter to know her worth, to know what she is worth to herself so she can then know her own value and know herself. The struggle for Rose to know her worth is also the struggle for Carcinosin to know worth. The film *The Joy Luck Club*, directed by Wayne Wang and based on the book by Amy Tan, is littered with the skeletons of Carcinosin. The relationship of Lena with Harold, the Arsenicum who is counting every dollar he spends, is also the struggle of a Carcinosin to find worth and enough boundaries to know what she wants and how much she is worth as a person. The high expectations of Chinese society to perform and the high expectations to achieve and succeed as immigrants in America are portrayed in the Carcinosin daughters. A healthy Carcinosin is the person who is at peace, a person no longer being suppressed by one's own expectations or the expectations of others. Healthy Carcinosins do not need to obsessively push themselves to the limit; they will be happy to acquiesce to others' feelings, without losing sight of themselves in the process. They will not be crippled by guilt or by a sense of failure if they do not live up to the expectations of family or their partner. They will still be open but will know where they start and finish as a person and they will know their worth.

Carcinosin and Ignatia

The Theme of Ignatia

Ignatia is derived from a dilution of the seeds of a St. Ignatius bean, which contain the poisons strychnine and brucine. As with *Nux vomica*, strychnine is a poison that produces characteristic extreme hypersensitivity of the senses and a tendency to produce convulsive spasms. *Ignatia* has a higher proportion of the poison strychnine than the remedy *Nux vomica*, and the consequence of this is reflected in the fact that the constitution Ignatia, in contrast to the mentally strong Nux vomica, is weak mentally and uncontrolled emotionally. The destruction of the emotional in Ignatia means that the remedy has traditionally been used by homeopaths for hysterical[40] grief. The homeopathic remedy *Ignatia* is used by homeopaths for suppressed grief, which cripples so much that it always ends up consuming the sufferer simply because it has not been given free expression. The hysterical nature of Ignatia carries over into the presentation of the constitutional picture. Constitutionally, Ignatias are unable to express grief, the expression is cramped within, and they are literally gagging hysterically in a desperate struggle to hold down their grief. The classic keynote symptoms of Ignatia are easily recognized. Ignatias will always attempt not to cry by sighing endlessly instead, and even if they do let out any little sobs they will constantly gulp back tears, bite their checks, twitch and quiver, tighten their mouth, suck it all back inside, and start sighing again. Ignatia mirrors the extreme hypersensitive nature of strychnine in the sense that the physical sensations and mental and emotional feelings are contracted and cramped, and struggle for expression. The more that the expression of emotion is controlled, the more extreme and hysterical it is when finally expressed.

The Challenge for Ignatia in Relationships

The portrayal of the woman Grazia, played by actor Valeria Golina in the Italian film *Respiro,* directed by Emanuele Crialese, is Ignatia. Grazia's *respiro* (which means breath) is her desire for emotional expression. She is a passionate woman whose need for excitement and freedom cannot be fulfilled or expressed in the small, stifling Italian community where she lives. Her need for excitement literally pulsates so strongly through her veins that it drives her to perform acts that are considered outrageous or crazy by the rest of the village. The film opens with her swimming naked in the sea; just this act, and her rage at the violence inflicted on her son, are viewed by the rest of the village as dangerous "mood swings" that require treatment. The first "attack" of her uncontrolled emotions mirrors beautifully the physical, manic, contractive, and hysterical, convulsive nature of Ignatia. Her highly strung temperament is viewed by the community as requiring clinical treatment and her family deals with her hysteria by injecting her with sedative anticonvulsive drugs to get her to calm down. Not every Ignatia will be as explosive and emotive as Grazia. But put Ignatia in such a suffocating community and the expression of the untamed hysterical Grazia is very reflective of the true nature of Ignatia in an unhealthy, suppressed state.

The character of the stepmother Topaz, played by actor Tara Fitzgerald in the film *I Capture the Castle* by Tim Fywell, is also Ignatia. Topaz is a far healthier presentation of Ignatia than Grazia. Topaz is healthy because she has been given free rein to be emotional, and she has been able to make an occupation out of her natural Ignatia skill to be extraordinary and exciting. Topaz has found an occupation and community in which her Ignatia nature is able to be used to her advantage. Topaz thrives in the bohemian art world; she is not controlled by an Italian husband who is fearful of being shown up in his community because he can't control his wife, nor is she trapped in a small, stifling Italian community that is trying to make her conform. The wonderful scene of Topaz standing stark naked on top of the hill in a fierce storm with the rain pelting down on her naked flesh mirrors the hysteria and the passion of the nature of Ignatia. She clearly verbalizes in the film that she needs to do this to be able to calm down and find herself; it is as if her Ignatia nature is only calmed when she is able to find its emotional soul mate in the untamed fury of the storm. The other fantastic scene in the film is when Topaz is overcome with the desire to dye, with the result that every article of clothing the whole family has is dyed green. This is both the hysterical passion, and the hysterical enthusiasm, of Ignatia. The two presentations of Grazia and Topaz intensely highlight for me that emotional health is so dependent on the understanding and compatibility of others around us.

Ignatia has very high ideals and expectations, and a strong desire to see them fulfilled. This strong drive is also seen in the personality of Nux vomica; however, Nux vomicas have the strong mental control to be able to reach their goals. Ignatia does not have strength on the mental plane and, in comparison to Nux vomica, Ignatia is all emotion. With Ignatias it is as if they have overreached or tried too hard, and the expectations are not feasible. The area where this emotionalism manifests the most is in relationships. Ignatias are so romantically idealistic, and their ideals of romantic love so high, that it could be quite easy to accuse them of setting themselves up for inevitable disappointment and grief. Ignatias have a need for the perfect love affair or the perfect job or the perfect family, and if reality does not match their ideals Ignatias become distraught. More important, Ignatias need to have the perfect relationship all the time and any small fight, disagreement, or disapproval will cause Ignatias to become hysterical. Consequently, they will often have very volatile relationships filled with lots of recriminations and jealousy. Nux vomicas have the same issue; however, with Nux vomicas it is expressed on a more competitive mental level and is reflected by how competitive they are in the world.

The theme and nature of the poison strychnine carry the energy or memory of elimination; consequently, both constitutions carry a fear of being dispensed with or discarded. With Ignatias this is expressed emotionally and is manifested in their tendency to suffer terrible jealousy in relationships; with Nux vomicas it is expressed strategically and manifested in hypervigilance to any loss of worldly position or status. The extremely hypersensitive nature of the poison strychnine is manifested in Ignatia as emotional touchiness or hypervigilance to being hurt, offended, or abandoned. Ignatias are often viewed by others as being overly emotional because they always cry at the least provocation. The problem for Ignatias is that the crying will have been preceded by strong anger, but they can't maintain their anger because they lack enough mental strength to hold anger. Nux vomicas will have the same degree of dissatisfaction and hypersensitivity if they are not satisfied, or if they perceive rejection, but the difference is that Nux vomicas have the mental strength to hold their anger and push for what they want. Ignatias cannot cope with disharmony; they need to have perfection all the time, and if they do not achieve their goal of the perfect love affair, they brood. It is as if their expectations are so high that Ignatias have no choice but to emotionally turn the grief back on themselves. The expression of their grief at this point then becomes very suppressed and cramped, and they hold back their tears; the only expression of grief will be their continual sighing. Ignatias will not only hold in their emotions; they also withdraw from people and the world, thus appearing to others to do the complete opposite of what would be expected for a person suffering from hurt or grief.[41] Ignatias are so emotionally erratic they can also sob hysterically over not getting their own way for such a long time[42] that they end up trapping themselves into never being able to let go. Within both states is the theme of spasmodic contraction, which mirrors the poison strychnine. Whether you analyze Ignatia as hopelessly idealist or fatalistic in the area of love and relationships is immaterial; the most important thing is that Ignatia will find a soul mate in the constitution Carcinosin.

Carcinosin is as driven to find perfection as Ignatia. Carcinosins can also be seen to be martyrs to the cause of finding true love. Ignatia and Carcinosin will find a kindred spirit in each other, and their partnership will have the endurance of Nat-mur with Nat-mur but with the romance and idealism of Romeo and Juliet.

Carcinosin and Ignatia Together in the Film *I Capture the Castle*

James Mortmain, played by actor Bill Nighy in the film *I Capture the Castle,* is Carcinosin. James is married to Topaz, who is Ignatia. James is a writer with "writer's block." He is so crippled from the typical Carcinosin overstriving and seeking of perfection that he is no longer able to write; he sits in his room dreaming up endless possibilities for a second book, all of which are predictably fantabulous. James is also crippled by his failure to live up to the expectations of family and society; in particular, he is overwhelmed by feelings he has let down his family financially by not producing a second book. James is so overwhelmed emotionally that it is impossible for him to write. His children, irritated by his lack of progress and worried by their financial ruin, decide to lock him in the old castle on the agreement he is not let out until he has written a book. When he is locked in the castle he is finally able to break through his block to find himself emotionally. James discovers in his entrapment that he has been locked and trapped in grief over the death of his first wife and crippled by his feelings of guilt over his treatment of her. Both Ignatias and Carcinosins have the same emotional Achilles heel; they both tend to disappear and lock themselves up inside of themselves if they are overwhelmed with sadness or grief. The entrapment of the castle is significant in itself. Carcinosins lack a sense of limits or boundaries, so much that they find it impossible to define feelings within themselves. The theme of the origins of Carcinosin is the nature of indiscriminate cancerous growth that knows no boundaries. The confined walls of the castle literally force James to find his own definition or self, and it is not until he is confined that he is able to break the effect of his "writer's block."

Once he is able to find himself, James is also able to know that he needs and loves his second wife, Topaz. Topaz becomes completely distraught with jealousy and grief at one point in the film when she thinks that James does not need her as inspiration. James momentarily thinks he can get support from the mother of his landlord, Mrs. Cotton. Mrs. Cotton is Lachesis; she entices and charms, but on her terms or territory, and even though she is very wealthy she is definitely not about to really give James any money. Lachesis enjoys the game of seduction. Topaz leaves James when she thinks she is no longer needed. The idealism of romantic love and the perfection of idealistic love would never let Ignatias stay in a relationship that does not meet their ideals. Topaz only returns when James is able to convince her that she is the only source of his inspiration. The theme of the origins of Ignatia found within the poison strychnine is elimination and death of the emotional. Ignatias are only truly happy and secure if they are the only source of passion and inspiration for their partner.

James and Topaz have the perfect relationship for both of their natures. Carcinosins and Ignatias struggle in life to find people who are able to embrace and accept the contrasts and emotional extremes in their personalities. Ignatias and Carcinosins will put a lot of effort into pleasing each other because in each other they will find a perfect mirror image of their own high ideals and expectations. This will be a case of the obsessive nature of each of these constitutions having found a positive outlet in each other. Carcinosins will live up to the expectations and idealistic romantic visions that Ignatias have of love, and Carcinosins will probably, for the first time in their life, feel totally accepted for being obsessive. Carcinosins will have much more of a chance to be healthy with Ignatias. Ignatias will have an understanding of the drive of Carcinosins to seek perfection, and Carcinosin will live up to the perfectionist ideals of Ignatia. Ignatias will find a kindred spirit in the sensitivity and empathic nature of Carcinosins; vice versa, Carcinosins will be caring and sympathetic to the idealistic vision of love that Ignatias aspire to and are inspired by. Carcinosins will understand the need Ignatias have to be given free rein with emotional expression, and will never be confronted by or feel the need to control the untamed, wild passion of Ignatia. Rather, the opposite will happen: Carcinosin will be inspired by Ignatia's hysteria. The film *I Capture the Castle* is worth watching just to see the relationship between the Ignatia Topaz and the Carcinosin James.

The person you are in an emotionally compatible relationship with is a mirror reflection of your own emotional state. Two compatible constitutions will always be able to identify with the pathology of each other's emotional grief and hurt, and will be inspired to arrive at the same goal. Their pains will mirror each other's, but each constitution will be motivated by different perceptions of the origins of their pain, even though each constitution will be able to identify with a common goal in their true partner. The defining differentiation of each constitutional homeopathic type is based on identifying the emotional pain in the origins of the homeopathic remedies.

Carcinosin and Mercurius

The Challenge for Carcinosin and Mercurius
Mercurius is so overreactive and debilitated by change it will not be possible to deal with or comprehend the undifferentiated and

ungrounded changeability that is the core psyche of Carcinosin. The constitution Mercurius needs a constitutional partner who is solid and defined. Mercurius with Carcinosin will literally scatter into balls of mercury and fall through the holes of the egoless Carcinosin persona. Carcinosins are permanently, whether healthy or unhealthy, detached from the conscious part of their mind that defines individuality or ego. The thermometer in Mercurius will literally go nuts. The core issue is that Mercurius will find it very hard to trust because Carcinosin is constantly involved in a spectrum of change. Mercurius will not be able to know what Carcinosin wants. Mercurius will feel on insecure ground. With Carcinosin obsessively needing to push limits and controls, to find definition of self, Mercurius will not be able to feel safe. Mercurius will be threatened by the perfectionism and control of Carcinosin. Mercurius will sense the inherent lack of structure and react as if being attacked. Feeling attacked or humiliated can spark Mercurius' paranoia. The difficulties are numerous; there is a healthy ground here, but both Carcinosin and Mercurius will have to work at trusting and understanding, and not reacting — this is especially true for Mercurius.

The Theme of Mercurius

The first example of Mercurius that I want to describe is the character of Rob Gordon, played by actor John Cusack in the film *High Fidelity*. Rob is struggling with the fact that his latest girlfriend Laura has just walked out on him. Laura, played by actor Iben Hjejle, is Carcinosin. She is unsure of what she wants or who she is, and she is particularly unsure of Rob and his commitment. The fact that she walks out on him sets him off on a self-indulgent, paranoid exploration of all the times he has been hurt in love. Rob dissects all the injustices and wrongs done to him by the "Top Five" most painful relationship break-ups in his life. The film is a tirade of Rob's confusions and regrets about old girlfriends who have left him and his fears about future commitment to Laura. Initially, it could be possible to consider that Rob is a hurt Nat-mur who is struggling with fear of future commitment and vulnerability. It could also be possible to consider that Rob could be Lycopodium struggling with relationship loyalty and fidelity. The theme of the "Top Five Break-Ups of All Time" is the key defining theme in the analysis of Rob being Mercurius. Rob is not hurt like a Nat-mur is hurt, nor is he emotionally detached and able to walk away like a Lycopodium. Rob is angry and outraged, and spends the entire film in a verbal, mercurial dissection of the injustice of the situation that he finds himself in. Rob is Mercurius.

Mercurius is exposed when the paranoia thermometer registers humiliation. Rob perceives himself as having just been dumped and subsequently humiliated, shown up, and exposed.[43] Carcinosins will leave any relationship they perceive as not being perfect. Laura is Carcinosin and she is confused about the fact that the relationship with Rob is not perfect. Carcinosins in their indecision and fragility can become very confronting for Mercurius. The thermometer in Rob's brain is literally going nuts. The Mercurius character of Rob in this film is a great example of the prolonged mercurial mental dissection of every aspect of life. Ironically, it is the Carcinosin Laura who is a lot more emotionally fragile than the Mercurius Rob. This partnership combination is an example of the old saying "it takes two to tango." Rob senses her Carcinosin fragility and perfectionism, and interprets this as potential rejection; consequently, he will not commit until he can be sure he won't be humiliated. Laura in turn senses his mercurial fear of being humiliated and interprets his fear wrongly as a fear of commitment to her and their relationship. The dissection and destruction of their relationship also goes deeper in the sense that Carcinosins obsessively control to find definition of self and they obsessively break down structures to find definition of self. Mercurius will not be able to feel safe because Mercurius is threatened by control and threatened by the possibility of no control. Mercurius will always sense a lack of structure within and will react to someone seeking perfectionism as an attacker. Rob's way to attack in return is to undermine the structure of commitment by having an affair. For the Carcinosin Laura this provides the impetus to doubt everything and question existence as only a Carcinosin can do. It is this scenario of girlfriend leaving boyfriend because he has the affair which opens the film and leads Rob into a mercurial dissection of the "Top Five Break-Ups of All Time." Laura is the healthy version of Carcinosin so she is eventually able to move out of continuing to doubt him and reach out emotionally. Rob is a healthy Mercurius and, even though he is struggling to come to terms with commitment, he is eventually able to break through his mercurial fear of humiliation and ask Laura to marry him.

The next example is a more unhealthy presentation in which Carcinosin is totally overwhelmed by an unhealthy Mercurius. Mercurius, if threatened and humiliated, can be very dominating and destructive in the attempt to protect an inherent instability. The inner knowing of Mercurius reflects the reactive nature of the metal mercury. The intuitive Carcinosins who lack boundaries and are unable to psychically protect themselves can easily be overwhelmed by the unstable nature of Mercurius. Both Carcinosin and Mercurius are similar in that they are emotionally dealing with a history of being dominated or suppressed. The difference with Mercurius is that, even when scattered, confused, or reactive, Mercurius will still have an intellectual ego that draws its strength from the changeability and adaptability of the quick, mercurial mind. Mercurius is strong mentally and more aware and present than Carcinosin; thus, Mercurius is able to survive much more intact than Carcinosin, who has no sense of emotional or mental boundary.

Carcinosin and Mercurius Together in the Film
The Way I Killed My Father

The French film Comment J'ai Tué Mon Père (The Way I Killed My Father), directed by Anne Fontaine, contains a beautiful example of an unhealthy Mercurius and an unhealthy Carcinosin in a relationship. Jean Luc, played by actor Charles Berling, is an award-winning gerontologist with a successful clinic specializing in anti-aging treatments for the rich of Versailles. Jean Luc is Mercurius. His perfect social image is undermined by the return of his derelict father Maurice, played by actor Michel Bouquet, who walked out on him when he was a child. His disheveled father reappears at the community ceremony rewarding Jean Luc for his great work. The film is primarily about the rage and humiliation he feels toward his father for abandoning him and his mother. The fact that his father returns at the ceremony to recognize his social standing in the community is significant. Mercurius are very sensitive to any social slight or humiliation. Mercurius need structure and social status to help stabilize the lack of structure inside. Their biggest fear is that they will be found out to be unstable. The grip that Jean Luc has on sanity is shaky, and he does not want anyone else to find this out. The presence of his father starts to undermine his stability. His fear reflects the structural instability of the metal mercury.

His need for social respectability and his mercurial sensitivity to social humiliation is also evident in his choice of wife. Isa, played by actor Natacha Regnier, is a good choice in terms of social standing and personal kudos. Jean Luc even tells her that she is desired by many important people for her perfect beauty and background. When he tells her this, there is no sense that he is in love with her; she is seen by him purely as an object of social status able to boost his respectability and standing, and he knows that she is able to make up for the loss of status he suffered by not having a respectable father. The aspect of the film that interests me is the way he is able to manipulate his wife and the motivation behind this manipulation.

Jean Luc controls Isa's medical treatment. Isa struggles with a sense of herself and with the grief of not being able supposedly to have children. Jean Luc is treating her for her insomnia and depression with sleeping tablets and antidepressants. Aside from being on antidepressants, Isa has the classic stunned, suppressed look of an unhealthy Carcinosin. Isa is unable to emotionally connect or feel any emotion; she is totally disconnected from herself sexually and emotionally. There is a sense that neither are able to connect to each other, as is particularly evident in the bedroom scenes between the two of them. Their lovemaking is totally devoid of connection or feeling. His father Maurice develops a friendship with Isa. Maurice sees the damage and manipulative abuse of Isa by his son and tries to save her. Maurice helps Isa understand that she is actually able to have children, and that Jean Luc has lied about her sterility to protect himself from feelings of rage and vulnerability associated with becoming a father. For Jean Luc, fatherhood reminds him of the humiliation he associates with his own father.

Jean Luc knows that he is being attacked and threatened from two sides: first, in his community by a potential loss of face over his derelict father, and second, at home by being exposed as a liar. The underlying unstable nature of the metal mercury creates a persona in Mercurius that is dictatorial and violent in its need to protect the illusion of structure. Mercurius will literally want to kill or destroy anyone who contradicts or humiliates them, as is particularly evident in the scene where Jean Luc attacks his father and tries to strangle him. It is also evident in the fact that he is prepared to lie, manipulate, and cause immense grief to his wife to avoid getting in touch with his feelings about fatherhood. He is prepared to have his wife addicted to sleeping tablets and antidepressants, rather than be confronted with his feeling of vulnerability.

Mercurius is reactive. Jean Luc is unable to control himself and he starts to lose control with his patients. His façade as the respectable doctor starts to fall apart. Jean Luc seeks out his Nat-mur mistress for grounding and self-definition. He tries to create stability and order by setting his mistress up in an apartment, but she tells him she does not want him to control her. His mercurial reactivity starts to undermine his feeling of sanity. He reacts impulsively. He is unable to control his sexual desire and has to find relief in risqué behavior with prostitutes. The most distinctive element of the psyche of Mercurius is the destructive hypersensitivity and hypervigilance to contradiction. This is the egoism of Mercurius. Eventually, Jean Luc tries to pay his father money to leave because the consequences of having his father stay will only continue to undermine his stability in his community, in his marriage, and in his affair with his secretary.

Isa is the classic example of an unhealthy Carcinosin. She is disassociated and disconnected from herself. At the end of the film there is no sense that she has been able to escape his control and manipulation. The final scene in the film shows Isa in the background, lying on a sun lounge in the garden, looking very fragile. Maurice predicted Isa would forgive Jean Luc for his lies and manipulation, and she would never leave him, and it appears that he was right in his assessment of her. Healthy Carcinosins will no longer allow themselves to be suppressed. They will still be easygoing or happy to acquiesce to others' feelings, but they will not lose sight of themselves in the process, nor will they be crippled by guilt or a sense of failure if they do not live up to the expectations of family or their partner. Isa, if healthy, would no longer oscillate between the extremes of loss of control and the obsessive need for control, nor would she need to suppress both of these feelings with antidepressants and sleeping tablets. She would not allow herself to become the victim of his need to protect himself from feelings of his own inadequacies about fatherhood. Healthy Carcinosin is on the journey of self-discovery, not self-suppression.

Carcinosin and Silicea

The Theme of Silicea

The theme of searching for connective strength is visible in the psyche of Silicea. Siliceas know they lack inner fiber and confidence, and they pride themselves on putting a lot of effort into refining moral codes and ideas, to give them structure and strength within. Siliceas are involved in a rigid self-assessment program; the more perfect their outer image, and the more righteous their inner beliefs, the more secure they become. Siliceas will never step over their line in the sand; it is there to make sure everything is predictable. Nothing is exaggerated or overextended physically or emotionally. The more unsure Siliceas become, the more obsessive they are in tightening the inner and outer parameters. Siliceas have developed these rules to be able to survive the harshness of the world. They will feel secure in a relationship with a constitution who will provide them with inner and outer protection. Carcinosins by their very nature are not able to provide structure or protection.

The Challenge for Carcinosin and Silicea in a Relationship

Carcinosin and Silicea are involved in the same process of trying to develop self-confidence and self-definition, but they go about the process of self-definition in completely opposite ways. Carcinosins quite often have no idea what they are feeling until they have explored an experience by indiscriminately pushing social and emotional boundaries or constraints. Siliceas find out how they feel by defining structure and assimilating ideas into tight, moralistic belief systems. Carcinosins obsessively need to push their boundaries of excellence, and one of the ways they do that is by discarding fixed belief systems. It is possible to imagine that Carcinosin could appear overwhelming or threatening for Silicea.

Siliceas in all relationships with Carcinosins are quite likely to react with increasingly tighter rules because they will always be confronted by Carcinosins' indiscriminate and unbounded approach. Carcinosins have a critical need for unconditional love and acceptance. Siliceas, by the very fact that they have developed such tight rules of behavior in life, will appear judgmental to Carcinosins. Carcinosins do not need to go into another relationship that constrains or limits them in any way; they already carry with them a painful family history. Carcinosins must be able to find inner peace and will only be able to do this in a relationship with someone who does not pressure, suppress, or control. The more Carcinosins feel pressured, the more likely they are to suppress their feelings, to the point that they become depressed.

Carcinosin and Silicea Together in the Film *Intermezzo*

This relationship between a Silicea and a Carcinosin is played out in the film directed by Gregory Ratoff called *Intermezzo* (which means interlude). The Silicea in this film is the male character Holger Brandt, played by actor Leslie Howard. The female Carcinosin is the character Anita Hoffman, played by actor Ingrid Bergman. Holger Brandt is a famous concert violinist. The film opens with his return from a world concert tour. Holger finds the process of touring very disintegrating and exhausting, and his Silicea need for rest and structure is clearly relieved and satisfied by being once again at home with his wife and children.

Holger first notices Anita, his daughter's piano teacher, at her birthday party. Anita plays the musical piece *Intermezzo,* and he is totally overwhelmed by her unbounded passion for the piece. It is not until he meets her again at a concert, and she inspires him with her passion for music, that he realizes he needs her to accompany him on tour. It is obvious when Holger arrives home from touring he is totally exhausted, and struggling with finding the internal strength to go on tour again. Siliceas can internally scrutinize themselves so intensely, they become exhausted, and they then need others around them to lend strength to their purpose. Holger is starting to feel old and stuck in his ways, and Anita is able to move him creatively and inspire him emotionally. Siliceas can also become so fixed and un-changeable in their opinions they lose the ability to be inspirational. Holger is acutely aware of his exactitude and lack of adventure in both his life and music; he knows he is at a static point in his career where he needs her intellectual and artistic inspiration to ignite his own musical passion. Holger is a Silicea constitution aspiring for excellence. Siliceas are aesthetically devoted to their career because they seek appreciation by others and for others. Siliceas aspire to such great heights of refinement, they can also become too exacting in refining details that they lack imagination and inspiration.

Anita is Carcinosin; the passion of her expression for the music transforms her and transports her to another realm. Holger is hap-pily married, but he finds his attraction and fascination with Anita's musical passion totally overwhelming, and he cannot help falling in love with her. It is precisely his Silicea devotion to career and need for artistic refinement and approval that trap him into starting an affair. From the onset of the film it is acutely obvious that it is not sexual passion that inspires him. Holger is sensitive and delicate enough to know he is morally outraged by his own actions. Holger knows it is his Silicea aspiration for excellence and passion for the music that overwhelm his moralistic Silicea questioning. Holger does not have the motivations of a Lycopodium man who finds infidelity a boost to his egoistical potency, nor does he have the motivations of a Nux vomica man who is stimulated by sexual conquest.

His honesty and moral conviction in telling his wife the truth is reflective of the refinement of Silicea. Anita and Holger go on tour together. As soon as the concert is over the relationship starts to show signs of strain. Holger starts to long for the security of his family, and Anita soon realizes that her love and passion for him has not been able to replace his need or longing for family and structure. Holger tries very hard to reassure her that she is enough, but he is not happy, and she realizes that. The relationship is not working for her either; as a result of his becoming emotionally tighter and tighter, she is surrendering more and more, and becoming more insecure and depressed. The strength of their relationship and attraction was based on their inspiration for music, not on a strong desire for each other. Anita leaves because she knows he needs to return to his home and family. Anita also leaves because she knows that it is not healthy for her to give up her own career and aspirations. She leaves to take up a scholarship, and he returns to his wife and family, and his brief "intermezzo" with Anita ends. He returns home and is reunited with his family after his daughter is injured in a car accident.

Carcinosins often skirt very close to the edge of self-martyrdom. This is similar to Nat-mur, but Nat-murs use their inherent lack of identity to overempathize with another's hurt. Carcinosins will also become martyrs as a result of their inherent lack of self-definition; but they do not just overidentify, they lose themselves in the other person's feeling because they do not know what they feel. Carcinosins need structure, but in contrast to Silicea, they find it in an unbounded exploration of themselves by surrendering into a void of passion. This is why Carcinosins need to be constantly pushing the boundaries of achievement. Carcinosins have to have space and expanse to discover what they feel, and if they don't have this freedom they become depressed, and disappear inside of themselves. Carcinosins will feel suppressed and restricted by Siliceas' tight need for structure. Anita wanted to spend her whole life with Holger, traveling to new places and experiencing new creative horizons in their music.

Initially this appealed to him as well, but he was not able to match her unbounded Carcinosin drive for new experiences; he longed for his Silicea sureness and structure of his home and family.

This would be a very hard partnership for Silicea to maintain; Siliceas need to respect the person they are in a relationship with. Carcinosins do not hold a fixed enough position for Siliceas to be able to say that they could ever be sure of Carcinosin as a person. Siliceas have an integral disrespect for the process that Carcinosins need to go through to be able to find out who they are. Siliceas need stability. Carcinosins, because they are so unsure of who they are inside, have a continual need to explore and push outwards. Siliceas will view this process as completely opposite to how they self-assess. Siliceas in this partnership could have a tendency to become more and more fixed to compensate for what they will view in Carcinosin as disintegration. Both constitutions are ironically involved in a process of self-discovery but they will not be able to help each other because they need to discover their inner selves from completely opposite directions.

Lycopodium Partnerships

The Theme of Lycopodium

The following quote comes from the famous homeopath Dr. Rajan Sankaran. It describes so beautifully the underlying dilemma for Lycopodiums that it would be a disservice to the discussion of Lycopodium not to use it. Once we understand this dilemma we will be much more likely to be forgiving of Lycopodium's egotistical, bombastic behavior:

> I have been told that several thousands of years ago, *Lycopodium clavatum* was actually a huge tree and that over the years it reduced to a small fern – the club moss. The main feeling in Lycopodium is that if the person remains small, his survival will be difficult, he will be humiliated, and he will be nowhere. The main theme of Lycopodium therefore, becomes ambition, a desire to grow bigger, a lot of effort which is concentrated fully on becoming bigger, being more powerful, reaching a higher position – the top rung of the ladder.
>
> (Sankaran, p. 117)

Lycopodiums are burdened with the legacy of this fight for survival. They carry deep in their psyche a knowing that they are potentially under threat of annihilation. The main concern and theme for Lycopodium in life is acquiring success and power in order to survive. Their main fear in life is the loss of power – the loss or failure of their business, the failure of their marriage, their loss of position in society. Lycopodium is a constitution that is acutely aware of needing to succeed and perform. Lycopodiums do not outwardly acknowledge feeling vulnerable, and when you meet a Lycopodium this is not the personality picture that is presented. The need to be successful and to win favor in society is so paramount, they over-compensate, and present as bragging and arrogant. The anxiety of failure is so threatening, they literally bust their gut to prove to them-selves and the world that they are not a failure. Their hard work usu-ally pays off; Lycopodiums are good and they know it, and they are also good because they have had to work harder than others to achieve their success. Lycopodiums are under continual stress and strain. Every new situation is a potential threat to their existence, and every new encounter could potentially undermine their author-ity and position. It is not easy for Lycopodiums to continually strug-gle with the feeling that one mistake could undermine their very existence. It is possible, then, to understand why they present with overinflated opinions of themselves. If Lycopodiums convince the world that they are good, they also convince themselves.

The Emotional History behind Lycopodium

Why a Lycopodium constitution comes about is an interesting ques-tion. The parent of a Nat-mur child will be as critical and conditional with love and approval as the parent of a Lycopodium child. Nat-mur has the same fear of failure and the same fear of being rejected as Lycopodium, but the difference is, if Nat-murs perform and are good, they will receive love. Lycopodiums know they are always on their own in life; even if they succeed they will not get approval or reinforcement from their parents. At the end of the day, Lycopodium children know they have no support, regardless of whether they fail or succeed; they have nobody to rely on but themselves. This creates in Lycopodium a very interesting need. Consequently, the hurt of rejection, and the fear of failure is much deeper in Lycopodium, and Lycopodiums will doubly make sure they are never in the same pow-erless situation as they were when they were children. Lycopodiums have to be in control, and they do this by winning power, prestige, and position in society.

Lycopodiums will not be comfortable in a vulnerable position. This fear is projected onto their relationships, and is manifested as a kind of aloofness and seeming lack of enthusiasm in expressing love. Lycopodiums will act as if they are romantically uncommitted because they do not want to be put in a position where they lose power over their own feelings. Ironically, Lycopodiums, on top of fearing loss of power, also fear losing the relationship, because that failure will reflect badly on their social standing in the world. Always anticipating failure can potentially create an enormous amount of anxiety; the compromise Lycopodiums make is to have a partner, but to also protect themselves by holding the partner at a comfortable enough distance so as not to threaten their sense of power and position. This delicate balance of power and control means it is more probable that Lycopodiums will have successful relationships with people who they feel they can control. The most successful relationship for Lycopodiums is with a partner who needs them or who looks up to them for support. Their ideal partner is the person who is in rapture of their skills, and truly in awe of their successes. The other compromise or psychological ploy on the part of Lycopodiums is to have their partner, but to also have lots of affairs. This ploy allows Lycopodiums emotional safety and distance.

Because of their inherent self-reliance, Lycopodiums will always hold something back from making commitments. Other people in a partnership with Lycopodium will never quite have a secure sense they are a permanent fixture. Lycopodiums do not necessarily set out to be unfaithful; it is just that they are constantly looking out for "number one." The theme Sankaran alludes to of once being a "huge tree" and now "reduced" to only a small moss is constantly undermining the security of Lycopodium. If Lycopodiums lose ultimate control, and become dependent on the other person, they will feel like they have lost their power. Lycopodium literally transfer this feeling of loss of power into their physical tendency to suffer impotency. It is at this point that Lycopodiums will often look outside of the relationship and have an affair. The entire exercise is to reinforce their power and control over their feelings, and has nothing to do, in their mind, with not truly being in love with their current partner. The same scenario will also happen if their current partner threatens the status quo. Lycopodiums are always protecting a very sensitive underbelly, and their need to appear strong and potent is paramount. If Lycopodiums are feeling threatened, they will actively create a sense of incompetence in their partner. The partner of Lycopodiums could easily lose confidence; not only do Lycopodiums always need to be right, they also appear on the surface to be good at every single thing. It takes some time of living with a Lycopodium to see they are riddled with fears and anxieties. Lycopodiums succeed because they work twice as hard as anyone else to ensure their success, but they also succeed because they have to. Lycopodiums embrace the meaning of the saying, "Life owes you a living but you have to work hard to receive it." Lycopodiums never forget anyone who has helped them climb up the ladder of success, and they will always repay the debt, but they will never have the same loyalty as Nat-mur because they are essentially concerned with "number one."

Lycopodiums Can Float on the Surface of Water

Moss is supposedly one of the oldest surviving plants. To survive, it has had to adapt its form from being a large tree to a small moss. Moss climbs and grows on most surfaces. This ability is also true of Lycopodiums, and the theme of Lycopodiums is that they are able to adapt to all that life throws in their path. Lycopodiums possess natural sales abilities; they possess a built-in psychological astuteness that helps them make sure they always come out on top and are always liked by everyone in the process. Lycopodiums are natural born charmers; they know how to socialize and work a room to their advantage. Professionally, Lycopodiums will always put in that extra effort and pull out all stops to look after their clients. They need to secure their business, their financial security, and their worldly image.

The C.C. Baxter character played by Jack Lemmon in the film *The Apartment,* directed by Billy Wilder, is Lycopodium. An accountant for a large insurance agency, C.C. Baxter has a small, insignificant desk situated on the seventeenth floor, and he wants to be located up on the managerial twenty-seventh floor instead. He comes up with an ingenious scheme to loan his apartment out to upper-management executives for their extramarital liaisons, or affairs, with their secretaries. In return he wants to be favorably pushed ahead of others for promotion. C.C. Baxter is ambitious; he wants to get somewhere and he has no particular scruples about how he does it. C.C. Baxter wants and needs to be seen to be "someone." His neighbors, who are frequently disturbed by the sound of lovemaking coming from his apartment, wrongly assume that he is a womanizer with a different woman every night. The fact that they think he must be some incredible lover is quite pleasing to him even though they scold him for his lack of morals. C.C. Baxter is not a ruthless, power-hungry Nux vomica; rather, he is an amicable and charming Lycopodium, always nonconfrontational and always ready to smooth over situations with jokes and witty comments. His Lycopodium abilities really come to the fore when he returns home to find one of his bosses' girlfriends who just tried to kill herself because her boss would not leave his wife. His ability to get his neighbor the doctor and the doctor's wife to help save her and get him out of a very tight fix personifies the quick-thinking, quick-talking charm of a Lycopodium. C.C. Baxter unfortunately finds himself falling for the same girl, but C.C. Baxter is only interested in one thing, his own office on the top floor, and this is what he achieves.

The plot of the film is characteristic of films of that era: two men falling for the same woman, with the good guy (him) getting the girl. The interesting Lycopodium twist is that C.C. Baxter gives up his aspirations and his vice president's assistant's job, and his office with the three windows on the twenty-seventh floor that he finally achieves. Why? Because the ultimate insult comes when he finally sees that his boss does not truly recognize his dedication to the job, or acknowledge his brilliant statistical economic rationalizations; he just wants him for his apartment. C.C. Baxter was manipulating his way to the top because he truly believed he was a good accountant. C.C. Baxter also realizes that the girl the boss wants to take back to the apartment is also the girl he is in love with, but at the point in the story where he told the boss to keep his job he did not know she loved him rather than his boss. C.C. Baxter walked away from his job because he knew he did not want to be in a vulnerable position with his boss anymore; he did not throw in his job because he was in love with the same girl. Lycopodiums may want to survive[44] and be important, but they will not give up their ego to achieve success. Morals are something Lycopodiums will blend to any situation and Lycopodiums will float on any surface to get what they need, but Lycopodiums will not be prepared to suffer denigration. Lycopodiums need to be seen as big and important; C.C. Baxter needed to move to the top floor, but he also needed to make sure that he was not going to be upstaged or belittled at any point in the transaction. C.C. Baxter needed to give up all he had achieved to maintain his own ego and potency. This can be interpreted as either the egoistic strength or egotistic weakness that results in Lycopodium "shooting themselves in the foot"; either way, it is the Lycopodium twist that makes for an interesting constitution.

The Emotional Challenge for Lycopodium in Relationships

Lycopodiums take all these sensitivities into their relationships; consequently, they will not tolerate being contradicted or upstaged by their partner. They will always want be the best and be seen to be the best at every task and interaction. It could be hard for a lot of constitutions to be able to live with a Lycopodium, and vice versa, Lycopodiums will not be compatible with a constitutional type who questions their opinions. Lycopodiums are only ever empathic to others' feelings in a work situation or in a social situation because ultimately it will be to their advantage. In a personal relationship Lycopodiums will not necessarily have the same warmth or tireless empathy for their partner's feelings. Lycopodiums will view the relationship as "workable" as long as they do not feel they are stretched too far emotionally. Lycopodiums will become reserved and detached if they feel the relationship is too unstable or taxing. Lycopodiums are experts at avoiding feeling vulnerable or out of control; they never overextend themselves physically or emotionally, and they always make sure they have enough strength left for themselves. They have the ability to temper their emotions and personality so that at all times they will be viewed as socially acceptable and pleasant. Lycopodiums have the reputation of being dictatorial tyrants in relationships because they never want to hear that their opinion could be wrong. They will never even consider arguing about an issue; they are right and there is no doubt about it. Lycopodiums will love and respect their partner but they will also be emotionally comfortable viewing their partner as "the weaker sex." Lycopodiums essentially need to view themselves as the stronger one in the relationship; even when they view their partner favorably, they will always view themselves more favorably. This is why Lycopodiums come across as arrogant and bombastic.

Lycopodiums will be attracted to constitutions they can both dominate and boastfully impress, and who can't outdo them in social charm or worldly success. Most important, the partners of Lycopodiums must not stand out too much; they must be delicate and tasteful. They must also be moderate and temperate, especially in spending tastes so as to not threaten physical security. Lycopodium is a constitution with one face for society and another at home. Lycopodiums will always survive the rockiest of relationships. Even if they decide they have married the wrong person, they will figure out how to work the relationship to their advantage. And if they get divorced, which is one of Lycopodiums' biggest fears, Lycopodiums will continue to thrive in their new role as "single and unattached," at least for a week, and then Lycopodium the eternal charmer will have a new partner. All new relationships will create a level of anxiety for Lycopodium because a new situation represents uncharted waters, but Lycopodium will quickly work out how to float on the surface of the new relationship.

As you would expect, when Lycopodiums fall, they fall harder than anyone else. Any threat to their health – especially, as one male Lycopodium patient put it recently, "to his works" – or to their career will be devastating to their sense of personal power. Loss of potency, loss of social success, and fear of disease can throw Lycopodiums into a very deeply depressed state. Lycopodiums carry the pain of being big and then becoming small as a theme of personal failure. If I only knew the homeopathic persona of a bombastic, healthy Lycopodium, I would not recognize an unhealthy Lycopodium and I would prescribe the wrong remedy in the consultation. Lycopodiums shrivel up and become as small as moss when they perceive they have failed in the world. They withdraw and get depressed and can develop such extreme fears they can't leave the house or even be alone at night. Lycopodiums will believe they are about to die; ironically, even at this point they are still Lycopodium, because they will never call the doctor for help.[45] I have a Lycopodium patient who constantly tells me how sick he *was,* or that he *was* so depressed he couldn't get out of the chair, but he will only tell me this when he is back in command and in a position of power and health.[46] Only the partner of Lycopodiums will see their weakness. A sick Lycopodium will always have a very strong need to be looked after and mothered,[47] because this level of intense anxiety about health and failure will take an exhausting toll. The fear of failure,[48] and the stress of potential illness, ages[49] Lycopodiums and they become very tired. Failure in relationships can cause the same degree of distress. This is why Lycopodiums will often take a long time to commit emotionally, and even if they have been in a relationship or marriage for twenty years, they will still remain separate. The theme of survival by remaining separate mirrors the chemical nature of the substance that Lycopodium is derived from. This emotional distance is evident in the relationship between the man and the woman in the film *Nowhere in Africa.*

Nowhere in Africa is set in Kenya at the time of the Second World War. It is the story of a man and woman from wealthy Jewish families who perceive the impending danger and manage to escape Germany to Kenya. Both portrayals of the woman Jettel and the husband Walter, played by actors Juliane Kohler and Merab Ninidze, are Lycopodium. Jettel is used to being indulged in luxury and comfort. Walter is used to recognition and social importance. The individual struggles that both characters go through are the issues of Lycopodium.

Both struggle to emotionally connect to the other. Their emotional distance is compounded by their individual losses — their lost identity, their lost social position and wealth. On top of that, the isolation of Kenya also conspires to pull them apart. The portrayals of both Lycopodiums are the fractured, unhealthy version where the ego strength of Lycopodium is struggling. Even though they have both lost so much, it is still possible in the film to see the arrogance of the Lycopodium nature and imagine the ego power that each Lycopodium could feel if they were once again in a powerful position in society. This is reflected in the way Jettel hangs onto, and needs, her expensive crockery to show herself to be a person of wealth and importance. When she is fleeing Germany, she spends the survival money on a ball gown. In the luggage she wastes space and packs the family crockery rather than the survival necessities that Walter had told her to pack. She makes these choices based on her need for standards and status. Walter is equally unable to cope or adapt to the requirements of a meager farm manager's position in Kenya. Walter also emotionally needs to have his title of manager, and when he loses that he is totally shattered. Walter's decision to join the English army in Kenya is based on the need to redefine himself as a person with position and status. Neither character is able, even when feeling isolated from Germany and their family, to emotionally give to or rely on each other.

Lycopodiums do not emotionally turn to and rely on another in a crisis. Lycopodiums are used to surviving alone. Jettel and Walter reflect the crisis of Lycopodium when faced with failure and loss. The obsession they both have with societal position nearly causes the destruction of both of them. Both characters have the desire to survive and the drive to calculate what it is going to take to achieve that, and it is only their desire to survive that bonds them together. At one point in the film Jettel sleeps with an army officer to secure release for her and Walter. The only way that Walter deals with his jealousy is to analyze it on the basis of survival even though it eats away at his Lycopodium potency. Their daughter Regina, a Nat-mur, plays the role of an emotional bridge that bonds them together. Both of them relate to each other through her and she becomes the emotional link that eventually heals their crises of loss of status and ego.

Both Jettel and Walter know their marriage was conveniently based on family and position, and societal advancement. The decision to return to Germany at the end of the war also reveals their need for status. The need to be important again in society far outweighs any potential difficulties of returning to be with a race of people who have actively sought their destruction as Jews, and the destruction of their families. Walter returns to Germany to take up the position of a court judge. Jettel knows she needs to return to have position and wealth again. Position is viewed as an integral part of life for Lycopodiums. This is also, of course, important in relationship choices. Lycopodiums will choose partnerships that lead to advancement in society.

The above scenario of a Lycopodium need for advancement is also played out by the character of Mrs. Latour, played by actor Isabelle Huppert in the film *Une Affaire de Femmes (A Story of Women)*. The film is based on the true story of Marie Louise Giraud, an abortionist who was guillotined for her crimes against France at the end of the Second World War. The film is set in German-occupied France. When her friend, a Jewess, is arrested, she is shocked into the stark reality of war. This experience has a profound effect on her and suddenly she realizes that she might not survive. Her husband is in a labor camp; she is the sole provider for herself and her children, and they are hungry. The first abortion she performs is done as a favor for her neighbor, but she quickly sees an economic opportunity and starts to perform more abortions. She is calculative in being able to see and take advantage of all sorts of opportunities, and this is the picture of Lycopodium when forced into survival mode. Mrs. Latour not only wants a way out of her poverty and lack of education; she also dreams of being a famous singer, and it is this dream that fuels her astuteness. She even takes her abortion fee from the sister-in-law of a woman who died as a result of her botched home abortion; she relationalizes that, if she did not take the money, it would be foolish and sentimental, and would possibly equate to admitting guilt. This is the calculative process of Lycopodium survival. C.C. Baxter was in a healthy Lycopodium state; he had much more of his ego intact and was able to walk away from his job. Mrs. Latour does not have his strength to be able to face her poverty, nor has she had his educational opportunities; consequently, she is not able emotionally to cope with any potential threat to her potency. The picture of Lycopodium is also visible in the way she treats her husband when he returns home from the labor camp. Mrs. Latour is charming to everyone else, including her lover, but she is not prepared to allow her husband any control over her. Ironically, it is her husband who has the final control, as he is the person who informs the police of her illegal abortions.

Even at the end, when facing the guillotine, she cannot see the logic behind the outrage[50] for her crimes; for her it was always about what she needed to do to survive. I am not making a judgment on abortion or on her actions. What interests me in this portrayal of Lycopodium is the ability Lycopodiums have to cut off from their feelings to deal with survival. The fear of poverty and loss of position can throw Lycopodium into a very deeply depressed state and it is in this shut-down state that Lycopodiums can then shut off their feelings. Lycopodiums carry the pain of being big and then becoming small as a theme into all of their personal failures, in life and in relationships.

Lycopodium and Calcarea Carbonica

The Theme of Calc-Carb

The homeopathic remedy *Calc-carb* is derived from the inner layer of an oyster shell. The most obvious function of the oyster shell is to provide protection for the soft oyster inside. Calc-carbs struggle with the same issue of how to protect their soft inner being from the world. They look at the world as potentially very threatening, and they feel all alone, unprotected and defenseless, without an outer shell to protect them. Calc-carb is filled with fears and concerns that all revolve around immediate personal security issues such as money, home, security, employment, and health. If their partner is able to provide protection by taking care of all these issues, Calc-carbs will be a lot happier.

Lycopodium and Calc-Carb Are Complementary Remedies

Lycopodiums and Calc-carbs are seen in homeopathy as *complementary remedies*. This means that when Lycopodiums are physically sick they will often need to take a dose of the homeopathic remedy *Calc-carb*. Lycopodiums in a love relationship with Calc-carb will equally feel as emotionally "healed" as they do physically.

Calc-carbs are not complex or complicated; they like the simple routines of living and are natural stay-at-home types. Calc-carbs are warm and sociable, but they will be happiest entertaining friends at home. Their home will be filled with genuine warmth and caring; it will evolve around family, and more than likely will have an embroidered "Home Sweet Home" on the kitchen wall and scones in the oven. Lycopodium the eternal survivor will always seek the refuge of stability and security, and will feel very safe with the routine and protection of living with Calc-carb. Calc-carbs make very devoted partners because they live[51] to make others content and happy. Calc-carbs are natural homemakers, a "balebo'ste"[52] of the constitutional types. The character of Peggotty in the novel *David Copperfield* by Charles Dickens is a wonderfully rounded picture of a Calc-carb woman. Peggotty is a good, simple person who is happy looking after her house and her husband Mr. Peggotty. She gets anxious in a Calc-carb fashion and frets and worries over security and the future. She doesn't like adventure and doesn't like traveling far from home unless she has Mr. Peggotty to accompany her.

The Emotional Challenge for Calc-Carb

Calc-carbs hate the responsibility of responsibility. Calc-carbs will more than likely have a job outside of the home, but they will not cope with a high-powered job that requires a lot of stress. Calc-carbs are hard workers but they will always worry intensely if they are the only one looking after everything by themselves. Calc-carbs in a more unhealthy state will often respond to responsibility at work the same way that an oyster responds to any perceived threat. Calc-carbs will often narrow their focus and become so tight they become totally consumed with the everyday activities of their work place. Calc-carbs will then become overly responsible and overly conscientious, working harder and longer that anyone else. In this state Calc-carbs become very fearful and anxious, and think the entire financial success of the business is on their shoulders. In a family, Calc-carbs also know they cannot take on the responsibility of worrying about the day-to-day finances or the overall running of the household; they know they need a strong partner to take care of all the worry over finances and security. This also is true for their career; Calc-carbs are happy working in large, secure organizations, but definitely not in their own business. In the summaries I mention the character of Ted in the North American production of the television program *Queer As Folk* as an example of Calc-carb. Ted ran his own business and was happy doing this, but his business had the support and protection of his friends and community. In the second series of *Queer As Folk*, Ted loses not only his business, but also his secure footing in the community and within himself. When Ted loses his outer protection in the world, he also loses his ability to feel secure within himself, and his insecurities with the failure of his business are indicative of the fearful persona of Calc-carb. Calc-carbs are happy standing by the side of their partner, knowing their partner is taking the responsibility of the world solely on their shoulders. The problem for Ted was emotionally he did not feel that he could rely on the protection of his Phosphorus partner Emmett. Calc-carb would be much more likely to feel secure and trusting of a boasting, egotistical Lycopodium. Lycopodiums can also feel very good in this relationship with Calc-carb because they will always be relied upon for guidance and assurance.

Lycopodium and Calc-Carb Together in the Film *Persuasion*

This combination of Lycopodium and Calc-carb is played out in the Roger Michell film *Persuasion*, based on the Jane Austen novel of the same name. The film is set in England in 1814, when class position and wealth meant everything if you were to advance in society. Anne

Elliot, played by actor Amanda Root, was, several years before, engaged to a young naval officer, Fredrick Wentworth, played by actor Ciaran Hinds. Anne allowed herself to be talked out of the engagement by the trusted friend of the family, Lady Russell, who assured her that Wentworth was not a good match because he could not "provide for her in the manner to which she has been born." Anne is Calc-carb; she is unsure and anxious, and believes she should trust Lady Russell because she represents the security of family. Anne, however, has inherited none of her family's pretensions to achieve status and wealth. She is very plain and understated, with none of the flowery airs of her father or sister, and although she is happy in her supportive role to her family, her heart is longing to be married with a family of her own. Fredrick Wentworth returns to England with societal position and status as a Captain. He has also managed to amass a considerable fortune from taking risks on the high seas. Fredrick is Lycopodium.

Anne's frivolous, pretentious father is dwindling away the family fortune and he needs to rent out the family homestead to save himself and his family from ruin. Anne meets Fredrick Wentworth again because it is Fredrick's sister and her husband the Admiral who lease the Elliot family home. Fredrick is charming and yet very reserved toward Anne until he finds out it had not been her decision to reject his proposal of marriage. When he finds out that Lady Russell had influenced her, he decides to pursue her heart and hand in marriage. When Fredrick asks Anne's father for her hand in marriage everyone is shocked; her father even declares, "Whatever for!" Fredrick is the archetypal dashing, rich, and charming Captain and no one is expecting that he would be slightly interested in the "plain Jane" Anne. Fredrick is the charming Lycopodium bachelor who is very cynical and untrusting of the motivations and frivolous pretensions of women. In Anne, however, he sees someone who will stand by him on his ship and be totally devoted and pleased to be just with him. Anne is not impressed by high society, and in Anne he knows he is able to find the love and admiration that he as a Lycopodium needs. In Fredrick, Anne is able to find a strong man on whom she can rely. Anne is in love with Fredrick because she can rely on his command and strength. Because Lycopodiums need to have someone look up to them, and because Calc-carbs need to be looked after, this relationship combination has the potential to be very satisfying for both parties. The last scene in the film is of Captain Fredrick Wentworth at the helm of his ship with a very contented Anne at his side.

The Emotional Legacy for Calc-Carb

If Calc-carb is unhealthy and afraid to trust in the bravado of Lycopodium, this relationship combination could be problematic. Both constitutions are potentially anxiety ridden and equally cautious about all change. If Calc-carbs feel threatened, they calcify and literally become brittle and immovable. Calc-carbs could respond very differently to Lycopodiums when they feel anxious, and this is the emotional legacy Calc-carbs carry with them that could potentially get in the way of allowing them to trust Lycopodium. It is precisely this fear and insecurity that allowed Anne to be influenced by the family friend Lady Russell in the first place. Calc-carbs' focus becomes smaller and tighter, reflecting the theme of the oyster shell clamming shut against any perceived threat to their existence. Calc-carbs will mirror the same tightness of an oyster shell, in that they become virtually impossible to budge.[53] The greater their fears, the smaller Calc-carbs make their world.

Lycopodiums also fear the responsibility of new ventures in life, and suffer from anxiety about financial failure, but they respond in an opposite manner to fear. In contrast to Calc-carb, the greater Lycopodiums' fears become, the bigger they inflate their ego and expectations of the world, and the more bombastic and bragging they become, the more likely they are to convince themselves of their own power and greatness. Lycopodiums need to expand; they need to be able to "fly by the seat of their pants." To survive and grow bigger and gain power and prestige in this world means having to take risks. Calc-carbs could potentially be viewed as people who could fill their head with doubt and fear. In contrast to Lycopodium, Calc-carb could be viewed as being comfortable with underachieving in life. Lycopodiums do not like to remind themselves of their fears and anxieties; they need to have their ego boosted and feel omnipotent. Calc-carb will not push Lycopodium to take any risks, and there is a risk in this relationship that Lycopodium will not get a chance to grow and expand. Lycopodiums definitely cannot lead their lives shut tightly inside an oyster shell – they need ego expansion. The dilemma for Lycopodiums is that they also want to come home to a secure, known territory, and Calc-carbs would be comforting to Lycopodiums. If this relationship combination is going to work, the Calc-carb in the relationship has to be able to trust and rely on the Lycopodium. If Calc-carb is crippled by fears and anxieties, then Lycopodium could also run the risk of being crippled by Calc-carb doubts and fears.

Lycopodium Man and a Lachesis Woman[54]

The Theme of Lachesis

The homeopathic remedy *Lachesis* is derived from a dilution of the poison of the Surukuku snake of South America, commonly known as the bushmaster snake. As the name implies, this snake is master of its territory. The personality of the constitution Lachesis has the same stunning and disabling qualities as snake venom. Lachesis has a built-in ability to disarm, charm, entice, and seduce. Lachesis carries an energy and theme that are reflective of the hypervigilance of the bushmaster snake. Lachesis do not relax, even when charming and enticing; they are continually aware of any sort of perceived competition or threat to their autonomy or territory.

The Emotional Legacy for Lycopodium

There is a rather crude expression that is often applied to men and that could be very relevant in this combination of a Lycopodium man and a Lachesis woman. Lycopodium, for all his astuteness in life, can often fall victim to one of his own great weaknesses, his "dick." A Lycopodium man will often "think with his dick" because he has a need to look good. His need to bolster his ego and prowess will equate in his mind with the people he can conquer sexually. A Lachesis woman for a Lycopodium man would be nearly impossible to resist. This is a woman who has made sexual magnetism an art form. Lachesis is a very passionate woman. She is exciting and gorgeous, intense and lustful – and very attractive to Lycopodium. She is a possession and acquisition that a Lycopodium man will want more than anything. All his survival skills will go out the window. For a Lachesis woman a Lycopodium man will risk everything – money, security, the lot. The temptation of a Lachesis woman is too great for the part of his nature that likes to brag and show off. This is a woman who is highly skilled in temptation and he will not be able to resist her charms.

Lycopodium and Lachesis Together in the Film
A Touch of Class

This relationship of a Lachesis woman and a Lycopodium man is played out in the film *A Touch of Class*, directed by Melvin Frank. Vicky Allessio, played by actor Glenda Jackson, is Lachesis and Steve Blackburn, played by actor George Segal, is Lycopodium. Through a series of fluke coincidences, Steve meets Vicky. The attraction between the two is obvious from the start. Vicky instantly turns on the seductive charm of a Lachesis woman and he is immediately stopped in his tracks. Steve is able to assess the situation very quickly and, with true Lycopodium astuteness, he proposes a mutually convenient arrangement. Steve admits to his married status, and proposes an affair that would be advantageous to both parties – especially considering Vicky is recently divorced and, as she herself puts it, only wants occasional sex.

They meet for lunch at a hotel in London. On the first date Vicky makes it very clear that if he wants to have sex with her it will not be in a cheap hotel; he will have to book a nice hotel room in the country for the weekend. The power struggle is immediately off and running. Steve has to outdo her; he books a hotel room in Spain for the whole week. The tension between them until they consummate the affair is very funny; both of them fight and bitch, each vying for power and the best position on top – literally. Vicky is the sharp-tongued Lachesis who can cut to the quick. Steve is the Lycopodium man who wants his power and ego in the world boosted. After the first night he wants confirmation of his sexual prowess; he wants her to tell him how much "the earth moved" for her. Her cutting Lachesis attacks over his questionable sexual power and his Lycopodium need to have his sexual ability applauded make one of the best scenes in the movie. A nice touch in the film is that she goes back to bed to read *The Female Eunuch* by Germaine Greer and he storms off to play golf.

Eventually the tension explodes in a passionate physical fight and they lasciviously fall for each other. They return to London and commence an affair. The affair ends when the Lachesis Vicky realizes she is falling in love and is turning into a jealous wife. Lachesis does not want to feel vulnerable by falling in love. Vicky does not want to need him; needing him equates to losing her power and position within her territory. The affair ends for the Lycopodium man when he realizes he is also starting to fall in love and he can't stop thinking about her. Lycopodiums also do not like to lose control over their position of power and they do not like feeling like they are in a vulnerable position. The substance *Lycopodium* was used originally by chemists as a coating agent for allopathic medicines to prevent the tablets sticking together. Lycopodiums mirror the same natural qualities of the substance: They do not want to be stuck or tied down, but rather to act as a coating agent and smoothly charm themselves through life. This is why they both need and like to have affairs.

Lycopodium needs potency and importance in life. If Steve can conquer a woman like Lachesis, all his underlying fears of failure and lack of confidence will literally fade from his consciousness. Lachesis also needs to be the one to conquer and dominate in this relationship. Vicky will not want Steve to shine or attract more attention than she does. Lachesis presents with charm and enticing sweetness; the viciousness comes when threatened, and Lachesis will only become threatened in a relationship that proposes any threat to autonomy.

Not only will Vicky not want any competition, she will also know[55] that essentially Steve is a man who is looking out for his own needs in life. Lachesis thrives on conflict; it becomes an integral part of well-being. The very nature of holding back their lasciviousness or trying to hold back their vicious cutting tongue is apt to make them physically sick.[56] The characters played by the actor Bette Davis are the archetypal homeopathic picture of Lachesis women. Her characters are always women who are enticing and stunning but bitingly quick to viciously attack anyone stupid enough to get too close and presume ownership. The character of Margo in the film *All About Eve* (which I discuss in the chapter on Sulphur and Lachesis) is a classic example of the sexual charm, enticement, and bitchiness of a Lachesis woman. Lachesis can appear as a very jealous constitution because Lachesis is very sensitive to any perceived competition. Survival in the bush for Lachesis depends on being one up on everyone else.

This relationship will be a venomous fight to the end. Vicky will want to dominate because she is intolerant of any restrictions or controls put on her. Lycopodium, even in the thralls of passion and lascivious desire, will also want to dominate. Steve will find himself in a very dangerous situation; she will kill him after the act of sex. In the affair between Vicky and Steve, Vicky slowly makes him feel uncomfortable about himself. It might have been Steve who sent the final telegram to end the relationship but it was Vicky who ate away at his flesh. By the end of the affair, Steve was not the same cocky, charming Lycopodium man who had walked into it. Vicky might have walked away bitter but she walked away with her strength intact. When Steve walked away I was left with the feeling he will never be able to cope with another affair, and for a Lycopodium man this might not necessarily be a good thing.

When sick or unhealthy, Lachesis can suffer from intense fears of being poisoned and of being pursued. When they suffer from a fever these fears and suspicions can become totally paranoid and overwhelming. Admittedly, this is the extreme unhealthy picture of Lachesis, but even in the healthy picture of Lachesis these fears exist and relationships for Lachesis are a potential trigger for these fears to manifest. Often the underlying motivation behind the lasciviousness of Lachesis is the desire to maintain power. It is this game of seduction[57] and enticement that enables Lachesis to disarm any potential intruders. Lachesis will not willingly choose to marry or commit to a permanent relationship unless there is a way out. The energy that Lachesis put into seduction is amazingly powerful and, even if a Lycopodium man was not "thinking with his dick," the passion of a Lachesis woman would be very hard to resist. Lycopodium and Lachesis will always have problems over power; Lycopodium wants to remain in the top position of power and Lachesis wants to be the one who controls the power. The very first fight Vicky and Steve have in the film *A Touch of Class* is about who is going to be on top when they have sex!

Lycopodium and Natrum Muriaticum

The Challenge for Lycopodium and Nat-Mur in a Relationship

The dynamic between a Lycopodium[58] and a Nat-mur is played out in the film *Full Moon in Paris,* directed by Eric Rohmer. The film is set during the ending stages of their relationship and, even though it is obvious they still love each other, the problem is they love each other in different ways and with vastly different needs. The emotional needs of Lycopodium and Nat-mur prove to be too different; both are unhappy and the relationship is not working. The woman Louise, played by actor Pascale Ogier, is feeling stifled and suffocated by the controlling, possessive nature of her partner Rémi, played by actor Tcheky Karyo. Rémi is Nat-mur and he is miserable because she is not satisfied by only being with him, while his whole life revolves around being committed to her. Louise tells him that she feels like she is being "loved too much," and she needs to create a feeling of independence so she can feel free to truly love him. Initially, she could be Sepia or even Medorrhinum but her deception is the deception of Lycopodium. She does not in fact want to be alone because she needs space or freedom; she wants to be able to play the game of Lycopodium the seducer, and this becomes obvious as the film progresses. The controlling love and loyalty of her Nat-mur partner is too stifling; she is bored with him and needs to restore her power and prowess.

Louise and Rémi live outside of Paris in a modern housing condo complex and Louise works in Paris, commuting daily by train. Louise finds her life with Rémi boring and unfulfilling, and decides she needs to socialize more. Louise has an apartment in Paris that she has rented out; she tells Rémi she wants to renovate the apartment so she can use it to stay overnight after a party and not have to take the long train ride home. In reality she wants to keep her apartment for a Lycopodium *pied-à-terre*. Rémi is totally fulfilled by being with her at home but that is not enough for her. Louise does not define herself as being able to be fulfilled by a life in the suburbs[59] with Rémi; she tells him she is unsatisfied and needs to have more fun without him. Louise needs to socialize and indulge in her fantasies of seduction. But she does not present it to Rémi in those terms.

The Nat-mur Rémi would have initially looked attractive to the Lycopodium Louise. Nat-murs have enough drive and success in the world to appeal to Lycopodiums' need to climb up the rungs of the social or economic ladder and accumulate power and prestige. Nat-murs will also provide financial security to ease Lycopodiums' fears of ruin. The Nat-mur Rémi, very early in this relationship, saw how Louise struggled with financial fear and insecurities.[60] Nat-murs will provide the nurturing and mothering that Lycopodiums need. This could potentially be a dangerous trap because they can easily slip into the "helper" or "therapist" role. No degree of love and nurturing on the part of Nat-mur is going to overcome the insecurities of Lycopodium. It takes Nat-murs a long time to realize that if a situation is not working it is not their fault and it will also not necessarily be fixed by their "martyring themselves to the cause" and putting in more effort. It often takes a lot of suffering for Nat-mur to leave a relationship. Rémi has been miserable and unhappy for some time, but he continues to put up with Louise treating him very badly. There is one scene in the film where he turns up at a party and she virtually ignores him, flirting and dancing with other men. She is demanding and always looking for her own pleasure yet he is continually prepared to compromise what he wants out of the relationship so she can go off and have her so-called "aloneness." Rémi is consistently more understanding of her needs and puts her first and, even though he is angry with her, he forgoes his own rage to hang onto her at any cost to himself. Being alone is interpreted by Nat-mur as proof of failure to succeed in relationships. Nat-murs concentrate so much on blaming themselves and feeling ashamed of failure, they get trapped into hanging in there through loyalty and martyrdom. Each time Louise confirms she does not need him, Rémi gets hurt and rejected and feels inadequate.

The Theme of Control between Lycopodium and Nat-Mur

Lycopodiums cannot love if they feel they could lose potency or power in the relationship. Lycopodiums retain control by having affairs. Louise wants to escape from Rémi because she feels controlled by his need for love. Nat-murs and Lycopodiums both control, and it is a power struggle that will not translate to a successful partnership. Relationships and love are the most important goal in life for Nat-mur. Nat-murs want more than anything in life to find a partner who loves them and they love in return. It is also not enough for Lycopodium to feel financially secure with Nat-mur. Lycopodiums, even though they want security, also need the ego satisfaction they get from seduction. In a different relationship combination they would be able to "have their cake and eat it too," but Nat-mur has control issues and Rémi is too much into control and possession to ever be able to boost her Lycopodium ego. Nat-murs need to be in control by being the most important person in their partner's life. Lycopodiums do not respect the emotional needs of Nat-mur and they also control by not committing emotionally. Both constitutions will eventually attack each other over this difference, again and again, until the hurt that Nat-mur feels is too great and the relationship ends. Nat-mur will need to pull back because the accumulated pain and hurt will be too great. The core of the problem lies with the fact that Nat-murs emotionalize everything and Lycopodiums intellectualize everything.

The other Lycopodium in the film is Louise's married friend Octave, played by actor Fabrice Luchini. Octave is also involved in the game of seduction and would love to sleep with Louise. Octave and Louise play a game of seduction with each other but neither wants to give up their ultimate control over the game, so they never consummate their titillations.

The twist and undoing of the Lycopodium Louise comes about in the process of charming and soothing Rémi's hurt and anger from her treatment of him at the party where she flirts with all the other men. In the process of trying to manipulate and convince him she needs the apartment, she inadvertently plants a seed of doubt in his mind as to whether she is the right one for him. She plants the thought he could find someone who would love him and be satisfied with life in the suburbs. These are ideas she presents to him under the guise of "you can have an affair as well," and at no point in the argument did she ever really believe he will listen to her because she is so sure of his Nat-mur martyrdom. Louise eventually goes to bed with a man she falls for at a party, and then she conveniently realizes she wants to be with Rémi. When she returns home to Rémi she is confronted with the fact that Rémi has listened to her telling him he could fall in love with someone else, and he has gone and done precisely that. Rémi is immensely happy because he has found someone who loves him as much as he loves her. The film ends with Louise crying and, in true Lycopodium style, calling Octave to arrange a dalliance for that evening. Lycopodium Louise would have been very happy to be able to have everything; she wanted to have Rémi at home in the suburbs to provide her with security, Octave in Paris to titillate, and new lovers to regularly seduce in her apartment. The interesting aspect of Lycopodiums is they do not necessarily see or analyze themselves as "having their cake and eating it too," and to judge Lycopodium for being a cad or a womanizer or a seducer does not acknowledge the depth of insecurity Lycopodium struggles with.

Lycopodiums need to see that they are powerful and successful, and seduction is the easiest way to enforce their sense of potency.

Lycopodiums will not need to play the game of seduction if they are in a relationship with a constitutional type that boosts their ego. Silicea, Pulsatilla, and Calc-carb all need Lycopodium and look to Lycopodium to provide strength. Nat-mur has too much of a need to remain in control for this relationship to have any great depth or passion. Nat-murs will not boost a Lycopodium's potency and importance. This relationship will not have the emotional sensitivity of Lycopodium with Pulsatilla, or the depth of intimacy and appreciation Lycopodium will have for Silicea, or the sexual excitement of Lycopodium with Lachesis. Nat-murs do not have the emotional openness and softness to penetrate Lycopodiums. Both constitutions will stay in their own emotional corners in this relationship. Nat-murs are too competent for the delicate Lycopodium ego – they don't need Lycopodium enough. Lycopodiums might hang onto the relationship with Nat-mur because it offers security, but over the years their potency and prowess will suffer and then, consequently, so will their health. Lycopodiums need to feel all-powerful to be healthy. Nat-murs are too realistic to ever let Lycopodiums enjoy their delusions of greatness. It is, of course, in this sort of relationship combination that Lycopodiums will have an affair. The affair will be needed to restore prowess and potency, as shown by the scenario behind the relationship of Louise and Rémi, and this also plays into the expectations of Nat-mur to be hurt and rejected. Nat-murs will not be happy in a relationship with a Lycopodium who will not commit and who will always be unfaithful. Nat-mur craves love with true romance and commitment.

Lycopodium and Pulsatilla

The Theme of Pulsatilla

I have often read in the herbal *Materia medica* of the delicacy of the *Pulsatilla* flower, but seeing it in the flesh is completely enchanting.

I was recently lucky enough to see a *Pulsatilla* plant in the botanical gardens in Padua, Italy. The flower possessed a softness I had not seen in Australia and I am not sure whether it was the romantic Italian surroundings or the fact that the environment was less severe and punishing than the harshness of the Australian sun, but the delicacy of the flowers overwhelmed me. It was fantastic to see the collection of herbs in these gardens because they were planted more than 300 years ago and the gardens are still used by the University of Herbalism next to the gardens. The common herb name for the *Pulsatilla* plant is wind flower. The flower sits precariously at the end of an amazingly thin and delicate stem, and bobs to and fro with the wind, all the time constantly moving and changing position with the wind. The homeopathic constitution Pulsatilla possesses all the qualities of the flower.

The Emotional Fragility and Needs of Pulsatilla

Whether female or male, gay or straight, the persona of Pulsatilla is soft and malleable. It is as if their inner psyche knows they need to be able to flow with the wind if they are going to protect their delicate flower. Pulsatillas are fragile and they feel very comfortable with this inner knowing of weakness. While Lycopodiums and Siliceas struggle with feeling insecure, Pulsatillas know they need to be looked after and the only dilemma for Pulsatillas is whether they are getting the love and affection they need. Pulsatillas will always endeavor to make sure they receive what they need in terms of assurance and security because if they feel alone or abandoned they truly despair. Pulsatillas delicately flirt, with the same quality of the flower allowing the wind to move it. Pulsatillas are extremely attractive and endearing in this process; they do not take without giving in return, but their desire for assurance and consolation is so strong they are constantly seeking attention. The exchange for Pulsatillas comes in their sweetness and nurturing. Pulsatillas are genuinely happy when they are devoted to their loved ones. Pulsatillas will fuss over and concern themselves with the care of their family or partner. This is true for either sex. A Pulsatilla man, gay or straight, will also have the same endearing softness and willingness to placate his partner as a Pulsatilla woman.

Pulsatillas have the same theme as the flower, and they are constantly changing emotional and mental positions. Their changeability is reflected in their continual need for reassurance and acknowledgment; any perceived change to their importance and they become emotional. If they feel deprived at all, they are very likely to be irritable one moment and burst into tears the next. Pulsatillas are not willing to let go of anything they need and if one thing is not right they can be very fussy, petulant, and critical. The negative moods of Pulsatillas are usually very rare; because they have such an endearing nature, they are usually able to get what they need.

If they do not feel they are getting all the attention they need, Pulsatillas will become very insecure. A secure state of mind for Pulsatillas is completely dependent on being noticed and loved by their partner. A literary character that might help in defining Pulsatilla is the portrayal of David Copperfield's first "child-wife" Dora in the novel *David Copperfield* by Charles Dickens. David Copperfield, a Nat-mur, quite often became exasperated with his wife and although he was totally in love with her endearing nature, the Nat-mur qualities he looked for in a wife were practical. Dora lacked any practical skills like being able to cook or run the household. Dora was adoringly in love with him and in awe of his skills as a writer; she would often sit for hours just to watch him write. This sort of adoration would have been highly valued and sought after by Lycopodium but the Nat-mur Copperfield tired of her frivolity and emotionalism. Pulsatilla is susceptible to being overexcited and will be likely to burst into tears,[61] not just from any small slight but also from feeling joy.[62] Dora was forever bursting into tears and being irritatingly frivolous. The character of Copperfield was far more compatible with his second marriage, to Agnes, his lifelong loyal friend and companion and also another Nat-mur. A constitution compatible with Pulsatillas will love their childlike, sweet, adoring nature and their fragility.

Pulsatillas are healthy and happy in a secure relationship; if they do not have this in their life they will always replace it with a religion or group that gives them a strong sense of direction. The character Michael in the North American production of the television program *Queer As Folk* is Pulsatilla. Michael emotionally needs to be the most important person to his partner. When his first partner left to be with his son, Michael knew he would not be able to sustain the devotion he previously had, and although he followed, he returned to be with his family and friends. Pulsatillas live for their partner but they also need their partner to look after them and be devoted solely to them. When they do not have the support of their partner or family, Pulsatillas become very unsure of themselves. Pulsatillas need to be looked after[63] and they suffer from the feeling that they are all alone. Pulsatilla crave to be carried along in this world by a close group of loved ones, just as the pulsatilla flower needs the wind to move it. If Pulsatillas feel their partner's attention waning, they will get upset. Because Pulsatillas are more than likely to cry for attention it cannot be assumed that Pulsatillas are weak. Pulsatillas are very strong and determined to always secure a relationship in their lives and this is what they crave. Pulsatillas will always feel more secure in a partnership.[64]

The Challenge for Pulsatilla in Relationships

The character Judy Roth, played by actor Mia Farrow, in the Woody Allen film *Husbands and Wives* is Pulsatilla. The film *Husbands and Wives* is very similar to the French film *Une Liaison Pornographique*, which I use in the Nat-mur and Sepia discussion, in that the documentary-like style of the film allows the viewer into the private thoughts and motivations behind each character's actions. Judy Roth is married to Gabe Roth, played by actor Woody Allen. Judy, who has a child from a previous marriage, would like to have a child with Gabe, who is her second husband, but Gabe is resistant to the idea. (The reasons for his resistance I discuss in the chapter on Nat-mur and Arsenicum.) The important dynamic to discuss is the resistance is interpreted by Judy as a rejection of her importance to him because Judy is Pulsatilla. Judy immediately sinks into typical Pulsatilla insecurities over whether he really loves her and whether he is still attracted to her or whether he concentrates on his writing and his students more than on her. The documentary-style interviews allow us to see the motivations behind each character's hurts and pains. The most important aspect of determining your constitution is to identify the theme behind your core emotional traumas and motivations. No one individual constitution is more together or less insecure that the other; each constitution will simply be affected by different fears, different insecurities, and different hurts.

The crisis for Judy is precipitated by their close friends separating. Judy takes the disintegration of the close group of the two couples very badly. She consequently projects her insecurities onto her relationship with her husband Gabe. The loss of support makes her more vulnerable to her husband's rejection; she then questions the integrity of her husband's cynicism about children. The new man at work, Michael, played by actor Liam Neeson, immediately becomes a real possibility as a source of support and attention she is not getting from her husband. Michael reveals in one interview that when he first met Judy, he was sure she was flirting with him even though she was married. This is the nature of the flower that moves and gently flirts with the wind. Pulsatillas will change the direction of their affection as much as they change their mind, especially if they are feeling like they have not been noticed enough. Pulsatillas will not devote themselves to their partner unless they have a guarantee their partner is totally devoted to them. Judy knows she is able to show her poems to Michael but cannot show them to her husband. Emotionally she sees this as the first sign she has started to withdraw from the marriage. Judy concludes that, if Gabe is so cynical and critical, he will eventually criticize her, as well as her poems. Judy decides their marriage is over and she transfers her love and need to Michael. Pulsatillas crave support from a strong person equally as much as they need to be supported and surrounded by a strong network of loving and supportive family and friends. The documentary style of the film is great in that we are also privy to Judy's previous husbands' opinions about how needy they have found her. The last interview of Judy and Michael is very revealing; he immediately jumps in to support her and make her feel totally secure at all times, and this is exactly what she needs. Not all constitutions are going to be able to be malleable to the tears and needs of Pulsatillas, and an Arsenicum Gabe was definitely one constitution who was not able to be manipulated by Pulsatilla.

The Needs of Lycopodium in Relationships

Lycopodiums will revel in the demands of Pulsatillas. As with Siliceas, Lycopodiums will see this as the perfect description of a suitable partner. Lycopodiums like to take control and make all the decisions, and this will be a partner who will make them feel all-powerful. Lycopodiums will feel very potent with this degree of dependence. Pulsatillas are "feminine" and tenderhearted, and Lycopodiums will feel their prowess and performance boosted with Pulsatilla. Pulsatillas will not argue with Lycopodiums; they will be happy to be dependent and in awe of their partner. Pulsatillas are easily upset and Lycopodiums will be emotionally comfortable with this because they also do not like to be confronted or challenged. For Judy, the Arsenicum Gabe was always bringing doom and fatalistic gloom into their relationship and she needed emotionally to see her relationship through rose-colored lenses. The more cynical and pessimistic Gabe was, the more Judy doubted his devotion to her. This is a dilemma for Pulsatillas that will not present itself in a relationship with Lycopodium, because Lycopodiums will not challenge Pulsatillas. Pulsatillas need to receive approval and constant reassurance of love, and this will appeal to Lycopodiums' need to see themselves as wonderful and needed. The returns for Lycopodiums will be numerous. Lycopodiums love to be indulged and fussed over, and their ego will be in heaven with Pulsatilla because they know Pulsatilla will genuinely be happy to love and adore them. Lycopodiums will be able to feel very important and potent in a relationship with Pulsatillas.

Lycopodium and Pulsatilla Together in the Film
Hannah and Her Sisters

The relationship between Hannah and Elliot in Woody Allen's film *Hannah and Her Sisters* is a typical picture of an unfaithful Lycopodium with a loving and endearing Pulsatilla wife. Hannah, played by actor Mia Farrow, is a sweet Pulsatilla who is always trying to please her husband and family. The Michael Caine character of Elliot falls in love with Lee, Hannah's sister. Lee is vulnerable and Elliot the Lycopodium egoist cannot resist the temptation to be needed. Lee is seen as fresh and new, and young and beautiful, and subconsciously a boost to his ego and self-importance. Elliot is at a mid-life crossroad and his marriage with Hannah has been "so stable for four years" he is facing "boredom." Lycopodiums' infidelities have always to do on some level with the need to be seen as important and Elliot even explains it to Lee in those terms. He doesn't think that Hannah really needs him; even more telling, he also says Hannah spends too much time devoted to the children and he barely gets a look from her. For any constitution in a relationship with Pulsatillas this can be a real danger as Pulsatillas can often fall totally in love with their children and totally ignore their partner. Hannah does not find out about the affair before it ends, so she is spared any hurt or possible jealousy, which for Pulsatilla can be very painful. Elliot will never make the decision to tell her he was unfaithful[65] because he sees Hannah as being too good and wonderful to ever hurt. The reality is Elliot does not want his Lycopodium security with Hannah shaken or threatened. Lee eventually realizes Elliot will never leave Hannah and she allows herself to fall in love with someone else. Elliot of course falls back in love with the wonderful Hannah.

If Lycopodiums do not pay due attention to their Pulsatilla partner, it will not go quite so smoothly for Lycopodium, and even the smoothest of Lycopodiums will be exasperated with the neediness of Pulsatilla. Even though they love and live to acquiesce to their partner, Pulsatillas will not tolerate being ignored. For Pulsatillas, security in life is based on the knowledge they are loved and adored. The fatal mistake made by Gabe Roth in *Husbands and Wives* was to reveal he was still in love with the woman from his last relationship, even though she turned out to be crazy. The relationship for Judy ended when Gabe revealed the reason he was attracted to Judy was that she physically reminded him of his previous true love in life and he only chose her because she was a saner version. It was at this point she acted upon her attraction to Michael. If their love and attention is not returned, Pulsatillas are apt to make themselves sick to get the sympathy they feel they deserve. Sickness is how Pulsatillas will express all emotional tension through their body. The most important aspect to remember about Pulsatillas is at times in their life when they feel unsure you will always see the effects of stress very quickly, and if Pulsatillas are not given permission to express their tension emotionally they will suffer physically. A person in a relationship with Pulsatilla who thinks that Pulsatilla is being "a little girl," or, in the case of a man, "too sensitive," or, in the case of a child, "a little baby," will cause Pulsatillas to suppress their fears and worries. Pulsatillas need to cry to release, and they need to release their emotions to be healthy. The logical, analytical Arsenicum nature of the Woody Allen character Gabe Roth in *Husbands and Wives* was eventually going to be incompatible with the emotional sensitivities of Judy; from the onset of the film it was obvious he found her emotionalism tiresome and irritating.

Ironically, for all their petulant behavior and perceived jealousy, Pulsatillas will ultimately forgo themselves to their partner if it looks like they risk losing the partnership. Jealousy will upset and hurt Pulsatillas, but abandonment will destroy them far more than their partner's unfaithfulness. Lycopodiums will also acquiesce; however, Lycopodiums acquiesce out of not wanting to lose any financial and emotional security they have established.

If Pulsatillas are not in a relationship with a strong and dominant partner, they can become fixed in a very similar way to Silicea. The unique understanding constitutional homeopathy is able to offer in terms of understanding each individual person is very poignant in the acceptance of the health and motivations of Pulsatilla. Pulsatillas are genuinely happy when devoted to their partner or children or parents. Pulsatillas are healthy when they hand over responsibility to someone else. If they feel the decision-making processes are up to them they often get very fixed, rigid ideas, or rely on religious beliefs to give them the sense of security they need. They also at these times are more likely to get sick and hang onto illness as a form of eliciting sympathy from others. Pulsatillas need strong direction and they will be more likely to be happy and healthy in a relationship with a constitution like Lycopodium.

Although Pulsatillas are devoted to their partner, Pulsatillas are not "down to earth" and practical in the same way Calc-carbs are. Lycopodiums will have to allow for a housekeeper when budgeting the household finances because Pulsatillas generally will not stoop to the mundane cleaning of the bathroom. Pulsatillas are "princesses" or "princes," and Lycopodiums will love them even more for this quality.

Lycopodium and Silicea

The Theme of Silicea

The homeopathic remedy *Silicea* is derived from a dilution of pure flint silica. Flint supplies the strength or grit of sand on the beach. Siliceas can seemingly appear to lack grit or strength in their delicate personalities, while at the same time they possess moral grit and strength of personality. Silicea is concerned in life with finding true connective structure and strength and this creates an emotional conflict that is very similar to the one experienced by Lycopodium. Both constitutions have a pressing fear of failure and inner lack of confidence. Silicea does not have the ability of Lycopodium to cover it up with bravado and show. Siliceas will have similar anxiety and apprehension, but because they lack connective structure they move into a small, fixed state that then becomes their inner force against the world. The more Lycopodiums feel threatened with anxiety and apprehension, the larger they inflate their egos to compensate. The more Siliceas are threatened, the tighter and smaller their focus becomes. It is as if their thinking process is, "If I doggedly hold onto my opinions, the very power of my conviction will reinforce the weakness I feel inside." Siliceas reinforce their inner force by developing fixed, unchanging, completely inflexible[66] ideas and belief systems. Because Siliceas know they struggle with inner strength, they also spend a lot of time creating a perfect outer image to try to rein-force their internal shakiness. Both responses of Silicea and Lycopodium are coping mechanisms; with Lycopodium it is inflated and big, and with Silicea it is refined and precious. The underlying anxiety about survival is the same.

The Emotional Legacy for Silicea

Practically, this translates for Silicea into a personality picture of someone who is struggling to have inner confidence and, because there is such a deep inner lack of faith, Silicea will often give way to stronger personalities. The second Mrs. De Winter in Alfred Hitch-cock's film *Rebecca*, based on the book by Daphne Du Maurier, is the perfect presentation of Silicea. The story is about a man who accidentally kills his first wife. After covering up his crime, he goes on vacation to recover. On holiday, when he is supposedly recover-ing from the death, he falls in love with the woman who is to become his second wife. She is a companion to a wealthy woman at the expen-sive holiday resort where he is staying. Her emotional nature is to give way and please, and he falls in love with her because she pos-sesses all the personality qualities that are opposite to the harshness of his first wife. Her previous role in life as a companion or personal assistant is also how she defines herself, and when she marries she takes this identity into her marriage. The dilemma is that she moves from being seen in life not as a companion but rather a wife and mis-tress of a vast household and estate. She is totally overwhelmed by the pressures and expected demands of her new position as the second Mrs. De Winter. Played by actor Joan Fontaine, the second Mrs. De Winter defers to her husband Maxime all the time. She is an unhealthy Silicea. She is understated as a person and it is not until she becomes the second Mrs. De Winter she even has a name. In the film *Rebecca*, she becomes so terrified of the housekeeper, who was devoted to the first Mrs. De Winter, that she starts to feel very shaky and threat-ened inside, as if she is about to splinter into tiny pieces of glass. The shakier she becomes on the inside, the tighter her appearance on the outside becomes. As the film progresses, her choice of clothes reflects her inner need for perfection and structure. Siliceas' outward appearance will always be very refined and delicate, and they will always put a lot of effort into personal appearance and presentation. Nothing is overstated or exaggerated; first, they do not want to attract too much attention, and second, their inner tightness is simply reflected in the outer image. The second Mrs. De Winter's inner crisis comes to a crescendo when she accidentally breaks a delicate sculpture on the desk in the study and it symbolically shatters into small pieces.

Siliceas are a seemingly contradictory personality type. They can appear timid and unsure, and then conversely, they can hold strong, determined moral beliefs and ideas. In contrast to Lycopodium, their determination is exceedingly understated and it is important to understand that although Siliceas are fixed in their opinions, it does not translate into inner strength. The weakness of Siliceas is consistently present in both states. The more unsure Siliceas become, the more obsessive they can become on the outside, to protect themselves. Siliceas will also tighten and refine their beliefs and morals to such a degree they can appear to be inflexible. Siliceas can also become completely obsessive about one thought or aspect of how they look. The issue here to remember is at this time Siliceas are more worried and unsure about themselves than usual.

The character of Mrs. Cathy Whitaker, played by actor Julianne Moore, in the film by Todd Haynes, *Far from Heaven* is another presentation of Silicea. The film is set in Connecticut in 1957, when racial integration was frowned upon by both the black and white communities. From the very start of the film, Cathy is caring toward her black gardener, who has just lost his father. Cathy Whitaker has strong principles and morals and needs to have her outer perfection match her inner moral perfection, and even though she is shy, she is prepared to follow her principles. As the film progresses it also becomes obvious Cathy does not have the social bravado and arrogance of her friends; she is a lot more sensitive. This is the nature of Silicea. The film is tackling the tightness of American society in the fifties and the effects it had on the choices people were able to make in terms of personal freedom and individuality. Cathy is confronted with her need for a perfect world and perfect husband, when she discovers her husband's homosexuality. Needing emotional support from the trauma of discovering her husband's sexual activities, Cathy reaches out to Raymond, her gardener. The community and times conspire to make this an impossible relationship and she knows she does not have the strength or opportunity to make choices. Given a different time in history, Cathy could quite possibly have had the opportunity to fulfill her emotional connection with her black gardener, but the prejudices of the time made it impossible for both of them to find a community, white or black, that would accept them as a couple. For a Silicea, it would have been impossible to make a stand without support. Raymond is also faced with the improbability of his feelings for her ever being realized. Cathy has to return to her husband and the status quo of her position in society.

The Theme of Lycopodium and Silicea in Relationships

Silicea will not threaten Lycopodium; Silicea is very unlikely to argue or challenge Lycopodium, who needs to always be right. Siliceas are so unsure of themselves they will be perfect for the confidence of Lycopodiums because Siliceas will always need them. If Lycopodium were to write a job description for a partner, Silicea would come very close to perfect. This is not such an outrageous concept; it would be quite within a Lycopodium's thinking process to do such a thing. The fact Silicea is not loud or bombastic will also allow Lycopodium to shine in all social situations. The refinement of Siliceas will appease the senses of Lycopodiums because Siliceas will not show up Lycopodiums or confront them or embarrass them in social situations. Lycopodiums are always looking for anything that enhances social appearance. For Silicea, Lycopodium will provide a welcome relief from the stress of having to perform socially. Lycopodiums are able to bluff through most situations regardless of how anxious they feel underneath. Siliceas are not able to be so thick-skinned, and are more likely to become so consumed with self-doubt that they talk themselves into giving up altogether. The one strength Lycopodiums have is that, through the process of deluding the world about their own greatness, they often convince themselves and everyone around them that everything is going to turn out just right. Lycopodium's bravado will consequently be able to give Silicea a lot of confidence.

Silicea has a tendency to become very fixed and tight as a consequence of feeling tremendous anxiety. The positive side of this process is a discerning, principled, and moralistic nature; the negative side is a brittle, unbending, exacting pickiness, which can have a stifling effect on everyone else. It is at these times that Silicea will be the hardest for Lycopodiums to get on with. Lycopodium will need to show respect for the opinions of Silicea. Siliceas are exacting in maintaining their moral image and Lycopodiums will have to give in. The most wonderful thing, for Silicea, is that Lycopodium will give in and fall in love.

Lycopodium and Silicea Together in the Film
Adam and Evelyne

The most romantic film of Lycopodium and Silicea is *Adam and Evelyne,* directed by Harold French. Adam, played by actor Stewart Granger, is Lycopodium, and Evelyne, played by actor Jean Simmons, is Silicea. As with films of that era, there is a hard-to-believe set of circumstances that brings the two lovers together. Evelyne has been brought up in a strict God-fearing orphanage, all of her life believing her father to be dead. She is rescued after her father's death by his best friend, who promises to look after her. He is, of course, wonderfully charming and rich, and this is the story of an "orphan Annie" sent away to finishing school to come back as "glamorous Eve." Upon her return, they start to fall in love, but things are complicated by his secret life of gambling, which he cannot reveal to her because she has clearly expressed her distaste for it.

Adam is a charming Lycopodium who has for years had lots of women, but has avoided making any commitment. His latest girlfriend, who has waited for years for him to pop the question, sees very clearly how in love he is with the exquisite Evelyne. She stabs him in the back by informing on his illegal gambling to the police;

she knows if Evelyne finds out about the gambling she will leave. She is too late in taking revenge because the Lycopodium Adam has already decided to give up his life of gambling for the delicately principled Silicea Evelyne. The ending of the film is true to character to the last detail: When asked by the policeman at the raid whether gambling had been going on, Evelyne tells the truth and Adam is arrested. Siliceas will doggedly stick to their principles, as does Evelyne. This dichotomy of appearing delicate yet strongly holding onto principles is the theme of the silicate nature of breaking glass, and the silicate strength in the stems of plants. Evelyne then tells Adam she is in love with him, and for a brief moment he has the typical Lycopodium fear of commitment, but then he turns and asks her to marry him. Adam will be very happy with Evelyne for all the reasons I have outlined above. She will not threaten or confront his importance, and she will live up to his concept of the refined, delicate woman he will want the world to see him with. For her, Adam will continue to provide guidance and security from the harshness of the world. Siliceas, even though they appear to be very strongly principled, do not have anywhere near the sort of worldly coping skills of Lycopodiums.

The Emotional Challenge for Silicea

The issue to remember is that Silicea does not have a great store of strength and endurance. Survival for Silicea is often dependent on pulling back emotionally, as well as mentally and physically, to conserve energy. Siliceas lack internal grit and need to rely on making tighter and tighter rules to reinforce their personality. Siliceas can become almost completely paralyzed by their inability to decide which direction to take, and they will often pass up career opportunities rather than make difficult decisions. When you consider this degree to which they become crippled, it is easy to understand why they also create such tight rules. Lycopodium will seem like a great relief for Silicea. Lycopodium loves the power of making decisions for someone else. This is a partnership where both constitutional types are able to truly complement the other without the relationship being a co-dependent one. Because Siliceas will never allow Lycopodium to control their principles and beliefs, Silicea will always be able to remain inter-dependent and not co-dependent.

If Lycopodium does not respect Silicea, Silicea will not cope with conflict. Because of their sensitivity and vulnerability, Siliceas avoid all arguments and disagreements, and will choose to end the relationship rather than have conflict. Even though they seemingly lack confidence, Siliceas will walk away from a relationship that does not live up to their ideals. Lycopodiums are also adverse to arguments. Both constitutions are unable to deal with too much reflection or internal critical assessment. Lycopodiums are truly cowards when it comes to hearing anything critical and Siliceas depend so fully on their high ideals to give them strength that anything which shakes this structure is terrifying. Siliceas' need for continual praise and acknowledgment also makes them unlikely to enter into arguments. Lycopodiums know their haughtiness is a façade to cover up insecurity. Ironically, although Siliceas suffer greatly from a lack of self-esteem, they will possess more backbone and integrity than Lycopodiums and will be the strength behind a Lycopodium partner. Siliceas will also be happy with this position in life; they do not need an important position in society, nor do they approve of social boasting and self-promotion. Lycopodiums will be viewed by Siliceas as a pillar of strength because of how well they deal with the world, but if Lycopodiums momentarily lose position or power in society, Silicea will ironically give them the strength to pick themselves up and try again.

The Rationale behind Lycopodium's Commitment to Silicea

Siliceas will not tolerate unfaithfulness in any form. Lycopodiums will quickly figure out that Silicea has a heightened sense of morality, and Lycopodium will not even be able to flirt if this relationship is to last. Lycopodium will amazingly concede to Silicea. Silicea will also consider the boasting self-congratulation of Lycopodium in society to be distasteful and will, of course, tell Lycopodiums so, when they get home. Ultimately, because Lycopodiums pride themselves on psychological astuteness and taste in all matters, they will concede to the opinions of a Silicea partner and then congratulate themselves on having chosen such a tasteful, refined, intelligent, and sensible partner.

Lycopodiums love being chameleons. Lycopodiums like to be able to read each situation and trust in their astuteness to adapt to each new circumstance; consequently, they fear holding fixed opinions in case this goes against them. Lycopodiums will, however, respect Siliceas' fixed opinions because of their integrity. Lycopodiums will then get a lot of strength from knowing that Silicea has chosen them. The convoluted rationalization involved in this process is a beautiful example of the inflated ego that is integral to the constitutional picture of Lycopodium.

Natrum Muriaticum
Partnerships

The Theme of Nat-Mur

The essence of Nat-mur is the theme of control. The homeopathic remedy *Nat-mur* is derived from a dilution of sodium chloride, or common salt. The physical side effect of too much dietary salt is fluid retention. The emotional side effect of salt is that Nat-murs do not allow their feelings to flow. The mental side effect of salt is Nat-murs' overcontrolling everything by being perfectionists. Nat-murs are so controlled as children that they grow up to be adults without ever having explored their emotional nature or identity. Nat-murs have never had the chance to allow feelings to develop or envelop them, so they are emotionally immature and inexperienced in being able to deal with feelings of love and hurt. This does not mean they are cold or emotionless. In fact, the complete opposite is true: They feel things very deeply, but the emotional side is so restrained by their strong mental methodology that it is has not developed.

All the following expressions, which wonderfully describe the emotive nature of salt and the emotive nature of Nat-mur, I found in the book *Brewer's™ Concise Phrase & Fable*. Shakespeare uses salt as a metaphor to convey the flavor and depth of youthful passion in the reference, "Though we are justices and doctors, and churchmen, Master Page, we have some salt of our youth in us" (*The Merry Wives of Windsor*, 11, iii). Shakespeare also uses salt to convey love in *Othello* when Iago refers to amorous passion as "hot as monkeys, salt as wolves in pride" (*Othello*, 111, iii). Both of these expressions convey the intensity and depth of Nat-mur's feeling about love. Love is the most important thing to Nat-mur. Nat-murs are wonderful to have a relationship with because they put a lot of effort into trying to please and they are always sensitive and emotively attentive to their partner's needs. Love comes with all the trappings of romance for Nat-mur: meaningful presents, candlelight dinners, and intense sunsets shared together. Nat-murs are very conscientious and take their role as the "giver" very seriously. Nat-murs try to "do" relationships and will be the best possible lover, wife, or husband. Nat-murs are very responsible and will also be the one in a partnership who will look after the finances and cook all the meals.

The expression "a covenant of salt" refers to salt as a symbol of incorruptibility, a state that cannot be broken or undone. Nat-murs are the best of people. In the book of Matthew the disciples were told they were "the salt of the earth" (Matt. 5:13). Nat-murs put a lot of energy and importance into making sure they have achieved their best. Relationships are approached with the same seriousness they apply to everything else. Nat-murs are perfectionists. They excel at whatever they take on and they tackle life methodically and systematically; everything will have a place, and everything is in its place. Nat-murs will always be the one to achieve and accomplish all tasks. They are "true to his salt" – that is, true to their word. Nat-murs are dependable, loyal friends and lovers, the "salt of the earth," but behind this quality there is an ulterior motive, which is their need to control in order to protect themselves.

The expression "like adding salt to the wound" gives insight into the reasons behind the need to control and emphasizes the intensity of the hurt or slight, and the depth to which Nat-murs will feel wounded. Nat-murs try to control and hold onto their outer world as an insurance policy to protect themselves from experiencing further pain or rejection. The need to hold back from life and restrain everything gives an indication of the degree of sensitivity that Nat-murs experience. If *Nat-mur*, the homeopathic remedy, needs to be prescribed in a consultation, it indicates the person has been very painfully hurt in life. The expression "the pillar of salt" refers to

God's punishment of Lot's wife, who disobeyed God's command and was turned into salt when she looked back on the cities of Sodom and Gomorrah: "She became a pillar of salt" (Gen. 19:26). If Nat-murs fall from grace they feel like they will never be repaired: "If the salt have lost its savour, wherewith shall it be salted?" (Matt. 5:13). Given the degree of serious consequences for Nat-murs, relationships and love are very serious. The intensity with which they care is matched by how sensitive they are to being criticized or hurt in love. Nat-murs interpret the dynamics of giving in terms of what is fair. If they have gone to a lot of trouble to care for you and look after you, and then you criticize them, it does not seem fair and the process becomes very confusing. Nat-murs spend a lot of time alternating between it being the other person's fault, and it being their fault, because they should have given more. Every hurt or insult or perceived criticism will be mulled over and over, and the outcome can go either of two ways. They could overcompensate, martyr themselves, and give even more, or they can withdraw and get defensive. The most important theme of both choices is that Nat-murs do not let go easily. The expression "to salt away" reflects their emotional need to hide away their supplies for future use or reference. They "salt away" and hang onto the hurts, or they hang onto the relationship and martyr themselves. Nat-murs also hold onto partners and this is reflected in the tendency to hang onto a relationship way past its "use-by date."

Nat-murs care so much for true love and romance it can potentially be very anxiety producing. They have a lot at stake here and they do not want to be rejected or hurt. Ironically, they respond to most interactions with the expectation of that very scenario happening. For Nat-murs it all gets too serious and the level of anxiety over not being in control is critically high. Therefore, they decide to pull back. They present with a veneer of reservation and an "I don't need you" attitude. The expression "an old salt" refers to a weathered sailor who has been well-salted by his experiences at sea. This attitude has many faces in Nat-murs but the essence is the same: Nat-murs will not reveal their vulnerability. Ironically, one of the most problematic aspects of relationships for Nat-murs is that they struggle with making a commitment. They overprotect and guard themselves so much that in the end they are unable to commit and open up to the relationship. They not only "salt away" relationships, they also project this excessive control onto every area of their lives. The most important thing for Nat-murs is not to fail at anything. Consequently, when you put together all of the above conditions and anxieties, it is possible to see that Nat-murs have set themselves up for difficulty on many levels.

The Emotional Legacy for Nat-Mur in Relationships

The character of Justin in the North American production of the television program *Queer As Folk* is an example of Nat-mur. He is the loyal partner of Brian, the Medorrhinum who is always off seeking sexual experiences with someone else. Justin plays out the dynamic of being hurt and denying hurt, and the line is blurred between love and devotion, and martyrdom. Justin takes his devotion to the relationship very seriously, and his perfectionism and need to be successful in love lock him into staying. Nat-murs will have no need to have any relationship of any sort outside of the commitment they make to their partner; Justin has no need for other partners. In the story line, Justin agrees to have other sexual partners because Brian does not want to be confronted with the fact that Justin is totally in love with him. Justin agrees because he also has alternative motivations: first, to try to control Brian by making him jealous, and second, to prove to Brian he is not too dependent. Justin knows that Brian will not want to stay in the relationship if he thinks that Justin is too dependent or needy. Medorrhinums have a strong need for freedom, and they will not allow themselves to be trapped and imprisoned by jealousy, so Justin's manipulative tactics fail. Justin locks himself into the only possible outcome of alternating between hurt and martyrdom. Justin needs someone who will love only him, because he gets too hurt and because this is what Nat-murs crave and need. In subsequent episodes, Justin eventually leaves Brian for what he thinks is true love with someone else. Unfortunately, he is also hurt in this relationship, and he returns to Brian because he realizes that Brian does truly love him. Brian does love him although his Medorrhinum nature always needs the excitement of new partners. Consequently, he will never really be able to meet the emotional needs of a Nat-mur for perfection in love.

Another expression can also aptly be applied to Nat-murs: "Too much salt makes a man dry." This is particularly relevant for Nat-murs at the end of an unsuccessful relationship. Nat-murs hang onto a relationship way past its "use-by date," and they often feel dried up and embittered. A Nat-mur who has been disappointed and hurt in love will be more guarded and more driven to remain in control, and will subsequently struggle with making a commitment. In their next relationship, they will have a pre-nuptial agreement ready to sign, or they will build lots of emotional barriers to break down. It is the fact they care so deeply that leads them to develop more ways to protect themselves. The ways in which their control manifests are varied and Nat-murs can possess all the archetypal "Type A" personality traits of compulsive competitiveness. Nat-murs can play the "therapist" who is very happy to remain in control while their partner plays the "patient." They can present as a sensitive "New-Age" person who meditates every day and has perfect control over all of their feelings. Nat-murs can be someone who is cynical and critical all the time, or they can be someone who is always telling jokes and laughing. Nat-murs may present as "exercise freaks" who are highly competitive, or they may practice yoga and be very serene. They can also be very nice and giving people who never really allow you to see their inner hurt or pain. All of these are ways for Nat-murs to cover up their sensitivity and hurt, and remain in control. Nat-murs, more than any other constitution, need to think about their future partner. Nat-murs have intense loyalty and need to look after others, so they will not easily leave even the most negative of relationships. This can be disastrous because, as they get more hurt, they barricade themselves in more and dwell on their hurt. It is then hard for them to break down their barriers to feel love and closeness again. The problem for Nat-murs behind all the barriers is they also are removed from how they feel. Over several years of containment, Nat-murs manage to arrest their emotional development and maturity; consequently, they can often appear emotionally immature and inexperienced in love.

Nat-murs also subconsciously play out their immaturity by setting up emotionally impossible relationships. Nat-murs can remain protected from having to feel vulnerable in life by involving themselves in a relationship with someone who needs constant help and looking after. Nat-murs can also set up their non-commitment in relationships by falling in love with people they know will eventually leave them (like a married lover), or by falling in love with someone from a different religion where the family differences are so insurmountable they know the relationship will never work. This is just another form of control that protects Nat-murs from ever having to feel vulnerable about needing someone in their life.

The other trap for Nat-mur, once hurt or rejected, is to endlessly seek revenge. Nat-murs will hold onto past slights and hurts and will not let go of their anger until they have rubbed "salt into the wound" of the person who has offended them. This all sounds so negative, but sadly it is played out in divorce courts and bitter separation battles. The 1979 film *Kramer vs. Kramer*, directed by Robert Benton, is a classic character portrayal of a Nat-mur Ted Kramer, played by actor Dustin Hoffman. The struggle for Ted to let go of the pain and hurt of being abandoned, and not to continue with his need to seek revenge, reflects how hard it is for Nat-murs when they get hurt. The emotional need of Ted's wife Joanna, played by actor Meryl Streep, to leave her son and husband so she can find herself, is reflective of the needs of a Sepia woman. Sepias panic, feel encroached upon, and desperately need to flee to find their grounding. The impossible struggle for Ted to understand the feelings of his wife became a seventies icon for feminist literature. The aspect of the struggle that interests me is that Ted portrays the struggle of Nat-murs to deal with hurt and revenge. Ted's subsequent abandonment of himself into the obsessive care of his son Billy is also a classic portrayal of the fine line that Nat-murs have between duty and martyrdom.

Nat-murs also have the ability, after years of marriage or commitment to a relationship, to cut the person off and walk away. They realize one day they have hung in there out of an overly responsible, "salt of the earth" sense of duty. Their ability to walk away at this point reflects the degree to which Nat-murs ultimately like to remain in control. They will not let their emotions be placed in a vulnerable position even if they have been in that relationship for twenty years. They literally will cut all ties and never see the person again. Nat-murs who have spent some time "healing"[67] after a painful relationship will not be afraid of feeling their emotions. They might still be Nat-murs, but the Nat-mur need for control is not squashing down their emotions, or controlling their partner. Healthy Nat-murs are warm, generous, and comfortable with showing the intensity of the love they feel. Healthy Nat-murs are also able to maturely ask for their needs to be met. The overgiving that Nat-murs often resort to when they are actually needing to be looked after themselves is just another of the defense mechanisms that I referred to earlier. Healthy Nat-murs are a lot more in balance and know how much to give and how to receive.

The Emotional Depth of Nat-Mur

This chapter on Nat-murs may sound very intense and potentially negative. It is important to repeat that Nat-murs are a wonderful constitution to have a relationship with, because the one goal Nat-murs take the most seriously in life is to find a partner and devote themselves to their partner. They are caring and devoted to providing the best for their family and humanity. Because of Nat-murs' intense capacity to feel hurt, they are a lot more sensitive and aware of others' hurts, and this enables them to care about the rest of the human race. The best portrayal of Nat-mur I have seen in a film is the character of Daniel, played by actor Philippe Torreton, in the 1999 French film *It All Starts Today (Ça Commence Aujourd'Hui)*, directed by Bertrand Tavernier. The story is set in a poverty-stricken, small town in France. Daniel is the pre-school teacher who doubles as a social worker fighting the poverty and lack of financial help from the local government. Daniel is Nat-mur in all its faces: He cares, he gets angry, he cries, he struggles with his feelings of rage and revenge, and he dedicates his life to helping others. The line admittedly is very blurred between Daniel being portrayed as a patriarchal martyr or an upholder of humanist values amidst the twentieth century's ever-widening gap between rich and poor. But the world would be a very self-centered world without the caring and effort that Nat-murs put into humanitarian goals. When you look at the depth of feeling in the hearts of Nat-murs, it is possible to understand how intense their reaction will be if you reject or hurt them, and this is why relationships are so serious for Nat-murs.

Natrum Muriaticum and Arsenicum Album

The Theme of Arsenicum

The homeopathic remedy *Arsenicum* is derived from a dilution of the poison arsenic. Arsenic as a poison has an infamous history because death from arsenic poisoning was always horribly painful and violent. The well-known crime writer Agatha Christie often preferred her characters to use arsenic to poison their victims because death by arsenic poisoning was always dramatic. The distinctive acrid taste of arsenic always alerted the victims in her stories to the fact that either they were being poisoned slowly, or that it was too late and they had already drunk or eaten the fatal dose. Arsenicums carry a theme of the possibility of a potential poisoning and the threat of destruction deep within their psyche. They perceive the world as threatening and potentially dangerous. Arsenicums are much more wary and cynical in approaching the world than, for example, Nux vomica, which is also a constitutional picture derived from a poison. Nux vomicas interpret the psyche of potential poisoning with a much more aggressive attitude and they fight to the bitter end. Arsenicums, in contrast to Nux vomicas, absorb the possibility of destruction and become crippled with survival anxiety. Arsenicums are always hyper-vigilant and guarded about all potential diseases that could attack them. Arsenicums are exacting in their attempts to protect themselves from destruction. They suffer from extreme fear of being weak or sick because it makes them defenseless to a potential poisoning. The fear that they will not notice the poison is dynamically and somatically played out in the exacting perfectionism that is unique to the Arsenicum nature. This is the underlying psychodynamic trauma and theme of Arsenicums. The theme of potential destruction means that Arsenicums will always be fearful about taking any sort of risks in their lives.

The author Chris Bohjalian wrote a fantastic personality portrayal of an Arsenicum man in his novel *The Law of Similars*. It is an archetypal example of the survival anxieties and exacting, perfectionist traits of the constitution Arsenicum. It is the story of a man who is plagued by a chronic sore throat and emotional anxiety after the sudden death of his wife in a car accident. All of the conventional doctors he tries have been unable to find a cure and he considers homeopathy as a last resort. The intense worry over his sore throat and the need to find a cure is reflective of the need for perfect health. The character Leland Fowler agonizes over whether to trust the local homeopath Carissa Lake and, most important, whether to trust her prescription, which is the homeopathic remedy *Arsenicum*. He realizes that the homeopathic remedy is derived from a dilution of the poison arsenic. The degree to which he intellectualizes and questions is a fantastic description of the Arsenicum persona. He is the local district state prosecutor and is obviously quite conservative in his views. He is so anxious about his health and her prescription that he convinces himself she could poison him with the homeopathic remedy *Arsenicum*. Although confronted by his own cynicism and his firm belief that Carissa is into some form of "esoteric" healing, he decides to take the remedy.

Carissa gives him a book on homeopathy and the constitutional picture of Arsenicum to read to help him understand she is not trying to poison him. The more he reads about the "fear" and "anxiety" and "restlessness," the worse his "burning" throat becomes. It is an interesting portrayal of Arsenicum because it is very true to character. Arsenicums will always doubt and agonize over whether to trust, and whether to trust the process of homeopathy. It would really have made no difference if Carissa gave him a hundred books on the dilution process in homeopathy; Leland would still have worried and lacked trust. Arsenicums will always be hypervigilant to any perceived threat to existence and the character of Leland is no exception. He eventually decides to take the prescribed homeopathic remedy *Arsenicum* because, after analyzing the dilution process of "one part arsenic to ninety-nine parts water to one part arsenic and a million parts water" (Bohjalian, p. 45), he decides it is all "quackery" and can do no harm. Needless to say, after taking the homeopathic remedy *Arsenicum,* he starts to improve. The homeopathic cure that Carissa gives cures not only his burning sore throat and anxiety but also, of course, the underlying problem of grief and loss over the death of his wife. In true Arsenicum character, Leland takes over his own prescribing because he knows best, and overprescribes the remedy. This is, of course, classic Arsenicum arrogance and perfectionist need to control their destiny!

Arsenicums are so fearful of disease that the most extreme unhealthy Arsenicums will not venture outside in case they become susceptible to illness. Even in the healthier presentation of Arsenicum, there is an obsessive need to be on guard that is reflective of the potentially destructive nature of the poison arsenic.

The Emotional Legacy of Arsenicum

The best archetypal picture of an unhealthy Arsenicum is the character of Mickey, played by Woody Allen in his film *Hannah and Her Sisters.* Woody Allen adds a humorous twist to the character that could be interpreted as a Jewish caricature, but the character is still Arsenicum regardless of any exaggeration. Mickey is obsessed with the fact that he has cancer. His compulsive, obsessive hypochondria is characteristic of Arsenicums' hypervigilance. Even when he eventually finds out his health is intact and he is not going to die of cancer, he is obsessed with the fact that he will eventually die and that death is the eventual destructiveness of his life. He is worried that he has no control over his death and he decides the solution is to have control over God. He becomes obsessed with finding the ultimate answer and the right God to follow so he can eliminate any chance that he might not be covered in Heaven. The film is particularly funny as he abandons his Jewish allegiance and moves from following Hari Krishna to Jesus. His control and cynicism are Arsenicum, and his perfectionist need to have the ultimate issue of death covered with the right God is also Arsenicum.

Arsenicums are difficult to have a relationship with because they use arrogance and cynicism to protect themselves when they are particularly threatened. Without their exacting fastidiousness Arsenicums are potentially vulnerable to attack. Arsenicums have their survival to protect with these guards, and lowering of their standards is interpreted as a threat to survival. This fear of destruction is reflected in the use of *Arsenicum* in homeopathy. The homeopathic remedy *Arsenicum* is always needed when the disease matches the destructive nature of the poison arsenic. Arsenicums project this fear of destruction onto their relationships. Arsenicums feel emotionally and physically exhausted if they are emotionally threatened or emotionally confronted by their partner.

The character of Gabe Roth played by actor Woody Allen in his film *Husbands and Wives* is another perfect example of Arsenicum. Gabe's wife Judy Roth is a Pulsatilla,[68] and from the onset of the film it is obvious that he finds her tiresome and has no patience for her insecurities and emotionalism. The disintegration of their relationship comes about initially over the fact that he is filled with cynical, pessimistic views about bringing a child into the world and she is desperate to have a baby. Her insecurities and need for a child are treated very arrogantly by him and she can never bypass his mental dissection and cynicism to be able to justify why they should bring a child into this world. What is interesting from an Arsenicum point of view is that, as she becomes more emotional, he also becomes more insecure and unsure of himself. Judy is directly confronting and undermining his sense of security in himself by the very fact that she is criticizing him. Woody Allen tends to always play a character[69] who presents as the caricature of a hassled Jewish husband having to deal with the emotionalism of either his wife or mother. However, aside from the caricature aspect of his character, the interesting play that occurs between Gabe and Judy in this film is revealing of the Arsenicum fear of attack. As soon as she becomes emotional, he becomes more vulnerable to disintegration and perceived destruction. The fears and hurts and motivations behind each individual constitutional picture are completely unique and individual. Arsenicums feel threatened about their continued existence if they are emotionally challenged.

The aspect of the film that also interests me in relation to Arsenicum is that the character of Gabe resists his attraction to one of his aspiring students. Gabe is a rather arrogant college lecturer. Gabe becomes infatuated with one of his students, Rain, played by actor Juliette Lewis. The film *Husbands and Wives* is a mock documentary-style film so the viewer is privy to the thoughts and emotional motivations behind each character. Gabe kisses Rain at her twenty-first-birthday party, but he doesn't follow it up by having an affair – he walks away. He reveals later to his therapist that he walked away knowing he had made what could possibly be the biggest mistake of his life. Gabe also very clearly states that to face "change" and the relationship with Rain would be equivalent to "death." Arsenicums will not risk change because it is synonymous with destruction and death, and it makes them feel defenseless. Rain is the constitution Carcinosin. Gabe the Arsenicum has the ability to know that her unbounded expansiveness could very possibly be threatening to his need for structure. Arsenicums know they need a constitution that is solid and stable.

The Emotional Legacy of Arsenicum and Nat-Mur Together

Arsenicums would consider that Nat-mur was going to be safe enough for them to fall in love with. Arsenicums are meticulous in their desire to achieve absolute and total perfection. Arsenicums need to cover up their emotional vulnerability and they need the self-containment that perfectionism gives as a guard against feeling weak and insecure about their existence. Their unrelenting drive for perfection and their domineering authoritarianism over themselves to achieve perfection protect an intense anxiety. Nat-murs have the ability to meet the standards of Arsenicums. An emotional and changeable Pulsatilla would always have made Gabe feel very insecure. For Judy, a cynical and critical Arsenicum is equally difficult. Arsenicums will not prove too harrowing for Nat-mur. Nat-murs will rarely be the target of Arsenicums' sarcastic, critical observations[70] of incompetence or inefficiency. Nat-murs also fastidiously need to control the environment but for different reasons. Nat-murs need to protect their pain and it is this understanding that gives Nat-murs the empathetic sensitivity to see beyond Arsenicums' dictatorial arrogance. Between Nat-murs and Arsenicums, there could be a few arguments over the best way to tackle a problem, because both are "control freaks," but ultimately the arguments will be resolved because they basically respect each other's perfectionist streaks.

Arsenicums are a domineering personality that always likes to take control in a situation. The fact that Nat-murs are able to tolerate this characteristic in Arsenicums and not, for example, in Lycopodiums is because Arsenicums are always loyal and faithful. Healthier Arsenicums are supportive and generous to their family because the family is viewed by Arsenicums as a haven. The security of family allows Arsenicums to relax and be much more open and intimate than they are in the world. Arsenicums are not likely to threaten the security of family by having an affair. Both the Woody Allen characters of Mickey and Gabe Roth in the two films *Hannah and Her Sisters* and *Husbands and Wives* are not the ones to walk away and pose any threat to the continuation of the marriage. In both films they remain loyal to the ideal of stability within marriage and are motivated by the desire to find security with a partner.

If Arsenicums get physically sick or if they are feeling emotionally threatened, they can become paranoid about financial security. It is at this point that the perfect relationship between Nat-murs and Arsenicums will start to show signs of fracturing. Arsenicums are morbidly fearful of the destructiveness of illness or financial ruin and this is why they fight so hard to maintain control. Unhealthier Arsenicums can become so obsessive that they can become downright mean. Ebenezer Scrooge in Charles Dickens' *A Christmas Carol* is a classic version of this picture. Nat-murs will interpret this shift in Arsenicum as a rejection. Nat-murs are easily offended and hypersensitive to rejection and they will interpret the frugality of Arsenicums as withdrawal of love. Nat-murs have a very overromanticized version of love and relationships; indulgence in presents is seen as positive reinforcement of love for Nat-murs, and when Arsenicums withdraw this, Nat-murs will feel hurt. Arsenicums view money as security. Nat-murs view money and presents as proof of being needed and loved. Nat-murs have the underlying fear they are ugly and bad and they are always ready to consider it their fault or that they should have tried harder when a relationship breaks down. It is this tendency that traps them into being "martyrs to the cause." It is also this underlying fear that makes them so sensitive to any rejections or any perceived slights.

Arsenicums do not set out to deliberately hurt. Arsenicums' anxieties and obsessive nature are intricately tied up with themselves and their own survival. It is important for Nat-murs to remember that to have a positive outcome in their relationship with Arsenicums, they should not concentrate on their perceived hurts. Arsenicums will need time to get well and return to their healthy former self, and it is important that Nat-murs do not "add salt to their wounds" and seek revenge.

The novel by Amy Tan, *The Joy Luck Club*, has a wonderful example of an unhealthier Arsenicum whose frugality has not been held in check. The character Harold is Arsenicum. His partner Lena is Carcinosin. Lena does not know her own value and worth and has not been able to stand up to Harold. Harold is petty and ruthless in the handling of the finances. There is finally a ridiculous fight over the division of the grocery bill that provides the impetus for ending their marriage. Lena does not eat ice cream but he bills her for half of his ice cream. This is a picture of Arsenicums in the extreme, but it is good to view because Arsenicums, if not controlled by an equally strong partner, can be out of control with their tightness. Nat-murs have the strength not to be manipulated by the meanness of Arsenicums but Nat-murs have to remember not to "add salt to their wounds."

Natrum Muriaticum and Causticum
....

The Theme of Causticum

The homeopathic remedy *Causticum* is derived from a diluted tincture of potassium hydrate. Potassium is used by the body to stimulate nerve impulses for muscle contractions, and severe potassium deficiency results in physical paralysis and emotional anxiety. The personas of Causticums are an interesting mixture of emotional sensitivity, empathic reactivity, and mental stagnation. In Causticums it is possible to see the physical results of a nervous system that has been so totally overstimulated and exhausted that it has frozen and become stuck and paralyzed. Causticums are constitutionally excitable and overstimulated, and restlessly driven by their reactive intensity. They are so highly tuned to everyone's feelings around them that they are constantly in a state of high alert.

At first Causticums can appear very shy, even to the point of being introverted or emotionally paralyzed; then, in stark contrast, they can be passionately angry. Nothing will have changed from one moment to the next – they will still be Causticum. The change will simply be caused by the one point in the conversation that has sparked off their intensity about a particular issue, and the reactivity of Causticums will immediately come to the fore. Causticums are often confused with Phosphorus on the basis of their sensitivity and reactivity. Phosphorus is sensitive because the nature of light lacks a solid persona. Phosphorus blend in to other people and this helps to form what Phosphorus is feeling. Causticums are just as sensitive, but they are reactive to the feelings of the people around them. Causticums take on board the other person's feelings, issues, or causes, and try to "fix" them. It is important to emphasize the role of potassium in the body; note that potassium is needed to stimulate nerve responses, but a deficiency or an overdose of potassium brings about a contracted, paralytic state. This is why Causticums can be shy and introverted or angry and extroverted. Causticums can also be fixed and rigid in their ideologies. Causticums are prepared to throw themselves into the responsibilities of living in this world. Causticums are anxious for the plight of others and these anxieties are not just concentrated on family and friends; they can take up the cause of any threatened race, animal, underprivileged group, or political group. Phosphorus is very unlikely to take on the misfortunes of a group and fight for their cause; Phosphorus is much more interested in floating on the surface of life and enjoying the world. Causticums can become so overexcited and manic they can obsess about checking every little detail in whatever they are organizing. Causticums will be worried and overcome by all sorts of fears about what could happen to the world, and to the people they care about.

Examples of Causticum in Films

It is not possible to be sure of a very famous person's constitution unless you know that person personally. The portrayal of a personality in a film is also often the interpretation that belongs to the director or writer. The portrayal of the Indian leader Gandhi by actor Ben Kingsley in David Attenborough's film *Gandhi* is an interpretation of a Causticum that is the closest I can find to the above picture of Causticum. Gandhi is presented as an intensely sensitive person who is compelled through his depth of empathy about human suffering to act on behalf of humanity. Even though a pacifist,[71] he is Causticum in the intensity of his outrage and anger toward the injustice that he sees around him. Causticums have the obsessive nature and compulsion to push to whatever extreme they analyze is needed to achieve their goal. The portrayal of Gandhi, exhausted in his struggle to free India from imperialism, is the picture of Causticums when they are physically sick from the intensity of how deeply they feel for their cause.

The film *The Blues Brothers*, directed by John Landis, has Ray

Charles[72] the actor and musician in the role of a music shop owner. The scene where he shows The Blues Brothers Band how to play the electric piano is reflective of the stimulated, passionate nature of a Causticum. The passion and enthusiasm he has is transferred into a classic Causticum spasmodic energy pulsating throughout his whole body. This is also the physical, emotional, and mental intensity of Causticum, which is reflective of the theme of potassium being needed by the body to stimulate nerve impulses for muscular contractions.

The Theme of Nat-Mur and Causticum in a Relationship
For such serious and sincere people to fall in love, they will need to be able to respect the other person. In Nat-murs, Causticums will be able to find someone who they respect because Nat-murs also care about others. Nat-murs possess a social, moral, and ecological conscience and integrity that will be in tune with Causticums. Nat-murs take responsibility for themselves and their involvement in the world as seriously as do Causticums. Nat-murs are as likely to passionately take up a cause or fight. Because both constitutions are concerned with the welfare of their family and with looking after others, this combination would have the hallmarks of being one of the most enduring of relationships. Problems for Nat-murs always come in relationships when they feel hurt or unappreciated, but Causticums would be extremely unlikely to ever be unsympathetic to Nat-mur. Causticums will be so sensitive and empathically attuned to Nat-mur that the Nat-murs' need to build walls around themselves will not be present.

Nat-murs, in contrast to Causticums, can appear very controlled. Nat-murs will not display the same degree of enthusiastic passion for a cause and, when faced with ideological dilemmas, Nat-murs are more likely to try to control the issues at hand. Causticums are a lot more likely to appear out of control and manic because they are so worried or upset. Nat-murs will feel as intensely as Causticums but will not be the ones madly rushing around. Because they do take things so seriously, Causticums can easily flip into the more contracted unhealthy side of their nature and lose a sense of balance. Causticums will overwork and overorganize, obsessing to the point they become completely exhausted. Causticums will feel so deeply they will not able to rest until they have solved whatever problem they are tackling. It is this depth of empathy for others' suffering that can cause Causticums to go into deep depression. Because they feel so deeply they start to imagine all sorts of terrible things happening, and it is at this stage the nervous exhaustion manifests in the physical. It is important to point out that Causticums will react this way to all situations; it does not have to involve a deadline or a crisis like meeting a deadline of sending off food parcels to thousands of starving children to produce such an overreaction. Causticums take all tasks very seriously and are overly conscientious. The owner of a failing business will definitely be able to sleep better than his Causticum employee.

Both Causticum and Nat-mur will have a deep understanding and sympathy for each other. It is often hard to live with Nat-murs because they are so guarded and emotionally immature – with Nat-murs "you can be damned if you try to help and damned if you don't." Nat-murs do not deal well with vulnerability, so they might take offense at offers of help or, alternatively, resent you for not helping. Many people will be exasperated with the oversensitivity of Nat-murs; Causticums will by their very nature be able to soften the barriers that Nat-murs put up.

Nat-murs take on causes based on their personal experience or pain, and this is an essential difference between Nat-mur and Causticum. Causticum might fight for more funding for breast cancer research because it is a worthy cause, while Nat-murs will fight for the same issue because their mother died of breast cancer. For Nat-murs it is always personal, and if Nat-murs fail at a particular task they will hang onto pain and their thoughts about revenge for a long time. If Causticums feel they have failed, they don't just contemplate revenge like Nat-mur – they actively enact it. The driving force of Causticums is their emotional sensitivity and they will have no choice but to take their cause further because they are so moved by the suffering or predicament of others in the world. The degree of anxiety that Causticums experience at this point of a conflict will have a physically, emotionally, and mentally crippling effect on their health. The immovable mental stance that Causticums take throws them into the classic Causticum paralysis. Causticums become intolerant and highly idealistic; they can become terrorists to defend their views. This combination of Causticum and Nat-mur would make a formidable social-activist team because both constitutions become incensed about the suffering of others. Both will work tirelessly for a cause and in each other they will find someone who takes things as seriously as they do. Causticums are a lot more emotively reactive than Nat-murs; they will cry when they see starving children on the television news. Nat-murs, because they have arrested emotional development, are more likely to remain in control. The mental control of Nat-murs will come to the fore in their ability to map out and organize a program of food parcels. It will be Causticums who will emotively take their anger and outrage that one step further into violent resistance or rebellion and terrorism.

Nat-Mur and Causticum Together in *The African Queen*

The romance and adventure of Causticum and Nat-mur is enacted on screen in the famous movie *The African Queen,* directed by John Huston. Rosie, played by actor Katherine Hepburn, is Causticum and Charlie, played by actor Humphrey Bogart, is Nat-mur. The film is set in the Congo at the start of the First World War. Rosie, a fervent Causticum Christian missionary, is rescued from advancing German soldiers by Charlie, a rebellious, "rough and ready," gin-loving Nat-mur. Their escape turns into a struggle not only of survival but also against each other as they realize they are not only in the middle of a tumultuous war and river, they are also in the middle of a tumultuous love affair. The Nat-mur Charlie struggles with opening up and trusting, while the purist Causticum Rosie struggles with whether she can respect the rough-hewn river trader. She realizes that Charlie might have an external toughness but she also sees he has an internal softness that makes him not only likable but also able to be respected and trusted. This tough, closed exterior of Nat-mur with a soft interior is a very typical picture of how a Nat-mur presents. Rosie has the drive and determination and idealistic passion of a fervent Causticum, while she is also the "uptight," judgmental Christian fundamentalist who disapproves of his taste for gin. Rosie has to work very hard to let go of her contracted, purist Causticum views. Rosie is also the Causticum idealist and she is able to see that he has the "good heart" of a Nat-mur.

Rosie is the classic picture of the Causticum who is excited and passionate about a cause and will not let go or give in for anything. Charlie is the typical picture of the Nat-mur who is soft and caring and romantic underneath but hard-edged and rebellious on the exterior. Causticums and Nat-murs together will have the romance, adventure, and purpose of Rosie and Charlie. Together, Rosie and Charlie are able to join together to defeat the shipping might of the German Navy. This film is a must to watch as both constitutional presentations are classically archetypal of Causticum and Nat-mur. Nat-murs often feel they are totally alone in the world and no-one understands them. They are constantly struggling with the issue of whether to open up their heart and let people in: especially in relationships, they can be very cautious in case they get hurt or disappointed. Causticums are such strong idealists and believers in love and justice they will have the strength and tenacity to be able to wear down the reserved Nat-murs, and in Nat-murs Causticums will find a kindred spirit.

Natrum Muriaticum and Natrum Muriaticum

The Nat-Mur Challenge to Fall in Love

This is probably the most enduring of all combinations because both Nat-murs will have chosen carefully in this partnership. Life and relationships are a serious business involving long-term commitment and hard work for Nat-murs. Both will be attracted to each other because in each other they will perceive the qualities they need for a long-term partnership. Even though Nat-murs take time to get over their initial reticence to fall in love, this union of Nat-mur with Nat-mur will blossom into a loyal companionship for life.

The film *Go Fish*, directed by Rose Troche, is a romantic love story of girl-meets-girl. In this film each woman takes an inordinately long time to let down her Nat-mur guard and fall in love. Both women are Nat-mur and the entire film is about the emotional reticence of each to trust and let go enough to fall in love. Max is played by actor V.S. Brodie, and Ely is played by actor Guinevere Turner. Max has not had a relationship for ten months and Ely is in a somewhat suspicious commitment to a two-year-old relationship with a girlfriend who lives in another city. Both Max and Ely are struggling with making an emotional commitment to falling in love and take the whole film to even get to the starter blocks; Max oscillates over whether Ely is suitable and Ely hangs onto her committed, convenient two-year-old relationship. Nat-murs take a long time to let down their guard because they feel everything very intensely. The film unfortunately ends just after they have finally consummated the relationship, but based on their personalities, and the length of time they both took to assess each other's suitability, I am confident in saying their partnership will be very long-term.

This relationship combination contains love, but it is not a feverish, tumultuous love affair filled with passionate longing and agony. Ely is ecstatic after her first night with Max but when her housemate Daria (definitely a Lycopodium) asks why she did not stay for the entire day in bed with Max, she answers she is "playing hard to get!" Her reply to the question is revealing of the time Nat-murs take to fall in love, and even after all that time and the whole film, and the entire community trying to bring them together, her answer is still reflective of the retentive nature of Nat-mur.

The Emotional Legacy for the Unhealthier Nat-Mur

The film *Bedrooms and Hallways*, also directed by Rose Troche, has another example of two Nat-murs who end up together. In *Go Fish* the two Nat-murs, Max and Ely, come together out of carefully considered issues of compatibility, but in *Bedrooms and Hallways* the two Nat-murs come together because they identify with the hurt and pain they see in each other.

Leo, played by actor Kevin McKidd, is a gay man who is persuaded to join a men's group made up of supposedly straight men. Initially Leo is reserved, but, because of his attraction to another man in the group, Brendan, played by actor James Purefoy, Leo eventually brings up in the group his gay status and attraction to Brendan. The film is a very funny, quirky exploration of identity and sexual preference. Brendan decides to have a relationship with Leo because he has never had a gay relationship before and he wants to experience what it is like. Brendan is not in love with Leo and he is not likely to fall in love with him. The character Leo is Nat-mur, desperate for love and commitment. Brendan is on the rebound from Sally, and his sexual dalliance with Leo is an adventure and experiment that he views as a fill-in until he can return to Sally. Brendan (definitely a Lycopodium) struggles with fidelity, commitment, and loyalty, and it is blatantly obvious he is not the true love Leo is looking for. Leo wants to fall in love with someone special and he is tired of not being the special person in someone's life and of being hurt and rejected. By a strange twist of fate, it turns out that Sally was an old school-yard flame of Leo's. Sally, played by actor Jennifer Ehle, is also a Nat-mur. Eventually the love triangle is revealed and Leo is left hurt and abandoned by Brendan. Once she sees Brendan's true colors, Sally also feels hurt and rejected, and ends the relationship with Brendan because she feels disgusted by his infidelity.

Sally and Leo eventually sleep together. Their emotional connection is based on identifying rejection in each other, and the consummation is based on their desire to protect themselves from falling in love in the future. Whether the relationship will last and how they will in the future resolve the question of Leo's sexuality — being gay, straight, or bi-sexual — are not addressed by either of them because they are both immature in acknowledging their emotional needs. It is also this same desire to not be hurt again that can trap Nat-murs in relationships that do not meet their needs. Given the issue of Leo's sexual preference, Sally's relationship with Leo would definitely fit that scenario. Also taking into consideration their sexual preference, both Leo and Sally would also appear to be setting themselves up to be ultimately hurt and rejected in the future. The film also portrays that an unhealthier Nat-mur will also fall in love with an unsuitable person to avoid possible issues of opening up to commitment and love in the future.

The Challenge for Nat-Mur in Relationships

Over the years, small hurts and disappointments could accumulate between Nat-murs in a relationship with each other. Because they are Nat-mur, they will both choose to emotionally withdraw rather than engage. Because they carry emotional scars from a history of disappointment in love, Nat-murs will mistakenly sacrifice emotional intensity in a relationship for the sake of stability. Nat-murs tends not to respond immediately or appropriately to their feelings or to their need for emotional fulfillment. They can love conditionally and make safe choices in choosing a partner because they are not experienced enough with feeling emotionally open. Nat-murs received conditional love from parents and if love has always come with conditions and agreements attached to it as a child, it is hard not to continue this patterning into adulthood and into future relationships. Nat-murs have had such a long time of containing their feelings so that when it comes to picking the appropriate partner they are often emotionally immature and out of touch with their own feelings. Both Sally and Leo are mentally sensible and mature beyond their years, but emotional teenagers when it comes to falling in love.

Nat-murs keep a mental and emotional ledger of all past hurts and wrongs committed over the length of the relationship, and constantly refer to them. Sally had remembered and held onto the very words that Leo had used as an excuse to not sleep with her all those years ago when they were teenagers. Nat-murs also keep a record of the wrongs they have done to others and their accumulated guilt from these wrongdoings hooks them and holds them in a relationship that might have lost its passion long ago. Nat-murs feel so intensely that it is impossible for them to sustain any level of intense openness in their relationships unless they are very sure of the other person's loyalty and commitment. Nat-murs in other combinations will continually question their partner's commitment and motivations. In choosing another Nat-mur, however, they know the relationship is a safe, calculated, interdependent choice. Even if the relationship loses some of the emotional depth and intensity because of accumulated hurts, and becomes more of a friendship than a love affair, Nat-murs will always choose love and affection and predictability, and they will be more satisfied by loyalty and friendship and communication in a relationship than tumultuous passion.

Nat-mur, more than any other constitutional type, will gain insight and knowledge from this book on compatibility. Nat-murs are hopeless romantics because they have an integral need to know that somewhere in life is someone who needs them. Nat-murs have a need to feel that they connect on a deep emotional level with their partner and it is only when they feel this connection that they will allow themselves to truly fall in love.

Nat-murs are not the type of constitution that is going to be sexually excited after a passionate fight or screaming match. Passionate love is too unpredictable for a Nat-mur, and with every twist and turn in a tumultuous love affair Nat-murs are thrown into emotional turmoil. Nat-murs will also not respect themselves if they feel they have lost control over their emotions. Fights are taken very seriously by Nat-murs and they will be more likely to want to sit down with their partner and discuss feelings, going over every detail of any disagreement in a very controlled, calm manner. Nat-murs are so sensitive to any possible rejection they will often overreact to disagreements in a relationship and blow perceived hurts completely out of proportion. Nat-murs in partnership with another Nat-mur will find they can take each other seriously and treat each other with love and respect; they could choose to stay in their emotional corners in a fight but the respect and trust they have for each other will help them leave their emotional corners and come together again.

Nat-murs always seek to support others emotionally and be there in times of need and stress. This relationship, regardless of any protective walls between them, is a long-lasting, deep, loving, and loyal companionship. Nat-murs over time can also decide to let go of old hurts and grievances because in this relationship both Nat-murs know their partner is committed for life. In this combination of Nat-mur and Nat-mur, both see in each other a reflection of their own principles of loyalty and commitment.

Natrum Muriaticum and Phosphorus

The Theme of Phosphorus

Phosphorus as a mineral plays a conductive role in every chemical reaction in the body and is used within cells for the production of energy. The element phosphorus is a nonmetallic conductor that produces its own light and appears luminous in the dark. In Phosphorus constitution is the luminescent essence of phosphoric light, as well as the conductive nature of the mineral. Their luminescence is reflected in their ability to bubble and sparkle along in their lives, often enthusiastically jumping from one thing to another. The conductive nature of the mineral is reflected in their enthusiastic involvement in life and people, and their need to stimulate others. Phosphorus will love being noticed, being excited, and giving to others.

An Example of Phosphorus in the Film *Life Is Beautiful*

My favorite Phosphorus is the character of Guido, played by Roberto Benigni in his film *Life Is Beautiful (La Vita é Bella)*. The film is set in Italy at the time of the Second World War. Guido is Jewish and the majority of the story takes place in the concentration camp where Guido and Dora and their son Joshua have been sent. Guido is desperate to protect and save his son from the reality of death in the camp by pretending it is some sort of convoluted game that must be won. On the truck to the transport trains, he invents a game and adventure that is worth 1,000 points with the reward being a real tank. Guido is able to use his enthusiasm and infectious nature to transform his son's experience from a trauma to a game. His humor, quick-thinking inventiveness, and never-failing ability to look at the positive are the infectious nature of Phosphorus. *Life Is Beautiful* is a Holocaust film and I do not want to show any lack of respect by referring to the film as a love story. But, for me, it is the most wonderful romantic love story of devotion and unfaltering enthusiasm that I have ever seen. The fantasy of the film is the wonderful phosphoric nature of Guido that enables him to transform death in the camps. Whether it was possible for a phosphoric Guido to ever in reality survive in a real death camp is not relevant; the power of the film is the fantasy of a story about hopefulness and dreams. The first part of the film is Guido's infatuation and courtship of Dora, played by actor Nicoletta Braschi. Dora is a gentile[73] and she gives up her family to marry the romantically infectious and enchanting Guido. With the use of a series of chance flukes and well-manipulated coincidences, Guido makes Dora believe it is her fate to fall in love with him. The most romantic scene in the film is when she climbs under the table and kisses him, then asks him to "Take me away." He scoops her up on a white[74] horse and carries her away.

The Theme of Nat-Mur and Phosphorus in a Relationship

Phosphorus has expansive warmth and sympathy that Nat-mur will find attractive. Phosphorus is sensitive and loving and will not threaten or criticize Nat-mur. They like to be noticed and loved continuously and they crave unequivocal adulation. Nat-murs are good at romantic love and Phosphorus will love being swept off their feet. Phosphorus possesses a volatile nature because within the nature of Phosphorus is a theme of conductivity. Because their nature is naturally responsive to the world, they often feel they are empathically pulled all over the place.

The character Emmett in the North American production of the television program *Queer As Folk* is an example of Phosphorus. Before settling down with Ted, Emmett was constantly falling in love with someone new, or starting a new job, or getting excited about a new project. Addicted to the enthusiasm of being "in love," they can also fall out of love as quickly as they fall in love. It is not that their heart is not true; it is simply a case of needing to search out new gratifications to be emotionally healthy. Phosphorus can be childishly[75] aware only of Phosphorus. They are easily carried away by their own enthusiasm or by the enamored state of another, and they will always love the intensity of new infatuations. With such openness, Phosphorus can experience a roller coaster of emotion and feelings, and it would be hard for Nat-murs to provide the excitement and attention that Phosphorus continually craves. Nat-murs, even when in love, cannot remain in an open state for too long; they need to go back into themselves and guard their emotions. The stable nature of Nat-mur might initially appeal to Phosphorus but Phosphorus will eventually need to seek out the emotional excitement of new, passionate love affairs. The natural expansiveness of Phosphorus will eventually make Nat-mur appear very boring.[76] They are aware they lack a solid form and they know they possess within their nature the expansiveness of being able to produce light. Phosphorus will see this as a six-month relationship.

Phosphorus will always eventually lack the emotional steadfastness that Nat-mur will need. Nat-mur will feel let down and betrayed. Nat-murs will initially feel they did not love Phosphorus enough, and blame themselves, and then Nat-murs will feel hurt, and finally will need to seek revenge. This scenario will also definitely occur if Nat-mur finds out that Phosphorus is having an affair, which is more than likely given the phosphoric need for new stimuli.

Nat-Mur and Phosphorus Together in the Film
I Capture the Castle

This exact scenario between Phosphorus and Nat-mur is played out in the film *I Capture the Castle*, directed by Tim Fywell. Rose, played by actor Rose Byrne, is an exquisite example of Phosphorus. The two Cotton brothers Simon, played by actor Henry Thomas, and Neil, played by actor Marc Blucas, both fall in love with the exciting and beautiful Rose. Simon, the older brother, is Nat-mur and Neil is Carcinosin. Neil comments in one scene that there is no one like her. Rose is emotive and alive but she is also stifled and bored by being trapped in her family's poverty. The brothers are rich, and Rose sees her only way out of her situation is to trap the older brother, Simon, into marrying her. The only problem is she becomes very bored with him very quickly because he is Nat-mur. All his money and all her new clothes are not enough to stimulate her. The euphoric, phosphoric Rose quickly fades and she loses her bubbly warm nature because the Nat-mur Simon is essentially just too controlling and predictable for her phosphoric nature.

Rose knows the marriage will be disastrous and she knows she has since fallen in love with the younger brother, Neil. Her emotional dilemma comes about because she finds it hard to contemplate leaving Simon, not because she loves him, but more for the reason she cannot take the risk of being left to the boring state of poverty. She also cannot risk being left alone. Phosphorus constitutional types do not want to be alone in life and this is why they are continually falling in love with a new partner a very short time after the last relationship has finished. Behind the bubble of Phosphorus is a constant desire to be noticed; they are affectionate because affection is what they need in return. This insecurity drives them to seek out new lovers. Phosphorus will always need excitement to be healthy in life and this is also why poverty for Rose was so horrendous; it is very hard to be stimulated by new clothes and new adventures if you are poor. Not every Phosphorus will have the same material drive as Rose, but they will have the same drive for new experiences. New experiences are not dependent on material wealth; it is just that the Phosphorus Rose reflected her frustration in this way because she had felt stifled by her family's life in the castle.

The Emotional Challenge for Phosphorus with Nat-Mur

What is the cost for Phosphorus to stay in a long-term relationship with Nat-mur? The light side of their phosphoric nature is affectionate and childlike in their innocent trust of others and the world, while the dark or unhealthy side is anxiousness and indifference to everything in life. The unhealthy side to their nature is expressed when they become disassociated from their own euphoric body. Their restlessness is their own defense mechanism to the stagnant indolence in their nature. Life with a Nat-mur will not have the spontaneity that is needed by the nature of Phosphorus. On one hand Nat-mur will offer stability and ease their anxiousness but over the long term it will throw them into an unhealthy side. If they deny their own phosphoric, adventurous nature because they think they "need to settle down," they then become the unhealthy, indifferent Phosphorous. They are only happy when they are truly luminescent and conductive. To be healthy, Phosphorus will eventually need to move out of this relationship with Nat-mur. Rose might have been motivated by the belief that material wealth would provide her salvation, but she was also motivated by a need to be liberated from the boredom of her family. Phosphorus has an overwhelming need to be continually stimulated and excited, and Rose hated being bored. Simon was essentially too boring for her and she craved the stimulation that Neil was able to offer. The film has a happy ending for the Phosphorus Rose: She is able to be with the exciting Carcinosin Neil, who will keep her interested and stimulated. She also gets to live in America, which will also be much more stimulating and harmonious for her phosphoric nature than stuffy England. The hurt of the Nat-mur Simon will, however, take a long time to heal. Simon will also need a long time before he can fall in love with someone else, which is the tragedy of the film for Rose's sister Cassandra, who is in love with Simon. Simon is still in love with Rose and Nat-murs hang onto all feelings for a long time – equally to hurt as well as love.

Phosphorus must sparkle and shine all the time. They have to always captivate their audience and continually dance on from one relationship to another or from one occupation to another. This is Phosphorus when healthy. They have an innocent hopefulness and only become anxious when they go against their own nature. We are continually being told by numerous "how-to" books on relationships and commitment that if you are not able to stay in a long-term relationship there is something wrong with you. The most important aspect of this book is that everyone is in harmony with their true constitutional nature. It is not unusual for Phosphorus to have several relationships or several marriages. This is what they need to be healthy; they have to continually move on in relationships until they find someone who is able to excite their responsive nature. They also do not like unpleasantness and will go to great length to make sure everyone loves them; they will also try to make others aware they are truly a victim of their need to be loved and it is not something they can or should be held responsible for. Phosphorus will always be able attract others because Phosphorus has an optimistic, enthusiastic view of the world. I have particularly formed this picture in relation to Phosphorus with a Nat-mur. In a relationship with someone who is lighter and more positive and bubbly like themselves, Phosphorus constitutional types will not be tempted to leave or have an affair to find new stimulation. It is very obvious in the film that Rose will be very happy and stimulated with the Carcinosin Neil. Nat-murs by their very nature will not be able to provide this stimulation. The control of Nat-mur will stunt the growth of Phosphorus.

The Emotional Challenge for Phosphorus if Abandoned in Love

All of the above analysis is based on the assumption that it is Phosphorus who falls out of love and wants to end the relationship. Admittedly, this is the most likely scenario with Nat-mur, but if it is Phosphorus who has been rejected in love then things are completely different. Rejection can produce the emergence of the unhealthy Phosphorus. The intensity of the lightness of Phosphorus will only be matched by the intensity of the darkness. The homeopathic remedy *Phosphorus* is often one I consider using when the patient in front of me is suffering from the most extreme broken heart – literally dying from grief. The phosphoric theme of destruction is mirrored in the nature of a phosphorus deficiency. A deficiency of the mineral in the body can cause a lack of appetite, irregular breathing, mental and emotional fatigue, and nervous disorders. The grief of Phosphorus can be a picture that borders on insanity: a person totally consumed with loss and having no sense of control. The theme of the disintegration of light resonates. They often describe their grief as feeling they are in several pieces and cannot assemble themselves or know how to put themselves back into one piece. They are inconsolable and they feel they will never be able to recover. The homeopathic remedy *Nat-mur* is also a good grief remedy, but constitutional Nat-murs, even in the throngs of the most wrenching grief, will be able to stop and reflect logically on how to seek revenge.

Sense and Sensibility, directed by Ang Lee, is a film adapted from a Jane Austen[77] novel. The story line is constructed after Mr. Dashwood falls fatally ill and is forced by current inheritance laws to leave his estate to his son from his first marriage. The son, encouraged by his greedy wife, throws the family out on the street. The Dashwood family finds their financial circumstances considerably altered – they lose the family home and their rights to the considerable family inheritance. The family's loss of fortune dramatically affects the marriage prospects of the daughters. The despair of Marianne Dashwood, played by actor Kate Winslet, is reflective of the disintegration of Phosphorus when struck down by grief. Marianne's new financial circumstances make it crucial for her to consider a marriage proposal. Marianne is a healthier version of Phosphorus than Rose in *I Capture the Castle*. Marianne rejects the rich Brandon because she knows she does not love him and her aspirations are to fall in love. Marianne falls in love with the dashing Willoughby, played by actor Greg Wise, who is the classic Lycopodium. Marianne is jilted in love by the dashing Willoughby because Willoughby is disinherited by his rich relative at Allenham Court and, for the sake of his own survival, drops Marianne and marries someone else who has considerably more money. It is not that Willoughby does not love Marianne, it is just that he has to make a decision based on his financial survival. Marianne "in love" reflects the open and enchanting light, phosphorescent nature of Phosphorus. When struck down with grief and jilted in love, she quickly disintegrates into the dark, brooding, consuming destruction of Phosphorus. Marianne, when grieving for Willoughby, catches a cold and chill from being out in the rain; she immediately develops pneumonia and looks as if she could die at any moment. Phosphorus has the physical characteristic of mirroring the unstable nature of light in the sense that all illness has the tendency to develop very quickly into something serious. The homeopathic remedy is often my first choice in a case of pneumonia that has come on very quickly.

To be true to a particular constitutional picture you have to be able to see in a grieving or unhealthy stage the same theme presenting as in the healthy or joyful stage. The personality picture of the eldest daughter Elinor, played by Emma Thompson, is the classic picture of the controlled Nat-mur. Elinor is Nat-mur in grief and in joy; both pictures reflect the control that Nat-murs have over their feelings. Although the sisters love each other and are tied together by sisterly love and family loyalties, the stark differences of the light, open nature of Phosphorus and the controlled nature of Nat-mur continually pull them apart. This will always be the nature of Nat-mur and Phosphorus in a partnership. Phosphorus has an interesting physical symptom: Any emotive reaction is followed by a physical heat reaction. It is this sensitivity and excitability that makes Phosphorus so emotive. The warmth of the emotive Phosphorus makes this partnership of Phosphorus with Nat-mur very unlikely to be able to sustain itself. Nat-mur is recognized as an emotional constitution, but Nat-mur in comparison to Phosphorus is nonreactive and concerned with maintaining control over feelings. Phosphorus constitutional types will only stay in any relationship if they are continually excited.

Natrum Muriaticum and Sepia

I recently watched an example of this relationship combination being played out in the French film *Une Liaison Pornographique (A Pornographic Affair)*, directed by Frederic Fonteyne. I sat there absolutely transfixed because there on the screen were a couple enacting the same patterning I had that very day thought about between Sepia and Nat-mur. The actress Baye portrays a beautiful example of a Sepia woman and the actor Lopez a Nat-mur man. "She" (I will call the actor this, because in the film neither character has a name) places an advertisement in a porn magazine looking for an ideal partner with whom to carry out her sexual fantasy. "He" responds to the advertisement and they start an affair. The sexual encounter is from the onset based on her fantasy and her expression of herself; she is the one who is the inspiration behind this adventure.

The film is shot in a mock-documentary style, featuring interviews with both characters. The shooting shifts from the present day to past flashbacks of their affair. From the documentary-style interviews we get to hear the accounts of the development of the love affair, and we are able to hear each character's story and see the discrepancies in the two versions. The viewer is privy to only a small amount of the sexual affair but we watch the gradual development of the tension between the characters. This film is a fantastic piece of writing to use for a book on homeopathic relationship analysis because the differing versions perceived by each character show so beautifully the differing emotional motivations behind the two constitutions of Sepia and Nat-mur.

She is the healthy Sepia – unhindered physically or emotionally, and able to express herself passionately and sensually. At one point in the film he describes her face when she has an orgasm as the true expression of a woman who is a woman. She is dominant and emancipated not only in her sexuality but also in her ability to express her passion and love for him. There is a scene in the restaurant where she tells him how much she loves him. She asks if he has ever declared his love to another woman. He answers he didn't think anyone would want him. This is the tragedy of Nat-mur – he cares so intensely for her that it terrifies him. He has tears in his eyes, genuinely touched and overwhelmed by her passion, but he is also panicking – not because he doesn't love her but because he loves her so deeply he cannot allow himself to feel love or have love. In comparison to her, emotionally he is hiding out in her passion. It is at this point we see the reserves and barriers that Nat-murs put up to protect themselves. The risk of being open is huge. He eventually decides he will declare his love, but at the point he wants to tell her he is overcome with the typical

Nat-mur fear of hurt and rejection, and he projects this rejection onto her and does not go ahead with declaring his love. The irony is, we find out from the flashbacks, that she wasn't going to reject him, but was going to accept his love. All the barriers of Nat-murs are there in his vulnerability and he projects rejection and hurt that isn't there. This is the delusion of Nat-mur. At this point you can visibly see in his face the control of Nat-mur, his self-criticism, his need for emotional protection, and his subsequent rationalization that the relationship would never have worked. She sees this and interprets it as a lack of love for her, and she is not willing to go ahead. She walks away knowing he would never have been able to match her passion. Sepias are proud of their independence. If they lose their freedom and individuality and get trapped by the constraints of another's retentive feelings, they themselves will lose their own independence and sense of well-being.

The only sex scene in the film explains for me why this Nat-mur man is so enthralled with this Sepia woman. Her Sepia passion is far more powerful than his Nat-mur control, and momentarily he is able to let go of those controls and feel. His emotionally powerful experience of her unrestrained passion, and his desire to remain in control, leave him in a predictable Nat-mur quandary. At the end of the film it is easier for this Nat-mur to remember her by mementos of their encounter than to have continued with the relationship.

It is interesting to consider if this Sepia woman did not know herself so well and had settled for a compromise of her needs, what would have happened? I am certain the scenario we would then see would be of an unhealthy Sepia woman. Nat-murs would by their very nature try to control. The Sepia woman in this film knows she can only be passionate in the uncontrolled, unconventional relationship she has set up. There is a sense that if the relationship had continued it would have been difficult for it to find a successful structure and redefine itself outside of the encounter of an affair. He is also aware when he talks of the past that he would have eventually wanted to have control over her and the structure of their relationship. He expresses that it would never have worked, but he is left with and hangs onto sweet memories of having experienced a truly wonderful woman.

Hanging onto, and romanticizing, past relationships is also often a convenient way for Nat-murs to get out of falling in love with a new partner. Nat-murs romanticize past loves even though they know the relationship did not work then and will never work in the future.

Why Nat-Mur and Sepia Are Locked in an Emotional Struggle

Nat-murs initially appeal to Sepia because they are not dependent lovers. Nat-murs are not overly burdening or demanding and this allows Sepias the space and freedom they need. Nat-murs are, of course, also initially uncomfortable with getting too close emotionally. This initial reticence of Nat-murs allows Sepias to feel unthreatened and comfortable.

Sepias are emotional and passionate, and Nat-murs, with their romantic idealism, will seemingly fall madly in love with this sensuality. Sepias soon realize that their depth of emotion is not being matched by the Nat-mur partner. Nat-murs, even when in love, do not have the emotional openness or strength to match Sepias' passion or depth. This seeming lack of depth is not because Nat-murs do not feel deeply; it is because they are afraid of how deeply they feel. Nat-murs are happy hiding behind Sepias' emotionalism and passion. Sepias have an accurate and cutting insight and will see they have become another of Nat-murs' defense mechanisms for not feeling emotion. Nat-murs will hide behind Sepias' passion because they are always trying to protect their vulnerability to getting hurt. The initial space and freedom given by Nat-murs can now be seen for what it is. Sepias do not have a lot of confidence in their ability to be successful in relationships; they can easily doubt themselves and lose their grounding, and sink into old patterns of depression and negativity. Sepias will interpret Nat-murs' lack of emotion as an "I don't need you" attitude. Sepia, if feeling overwhelmed and ungrounded, will quickly react by criticizing and attacking. This relationship is fraught with pain; each constitution sets off the other's negative patterning. Sepias reacts the same way cuttlefish react if threatened;

they immediately squirt out a thick black ink to allow time to escape. Sepias will then descend into depression and hopelessness. Nat-murs can be perfectionist and judgmental, and they will view Sepias' depression as pathetic. Sepias will view Nat-murs as retentive, emotional cripples, while Nat-murs will view Sepias as negative and unworthy of their love.

Nat-murs will lose their romantic vision of the ideal sensuality they fell in love with. Nat-murs will then throw themselves into work, sport, or anything that can reinforce their emotional control. Nat-murs, even when angry or depressed, never let themselves go and always pride themselves on remaining in control. The retentive salt in their nature does not let their tears or rage flow very easily. Nat-murs consequently will build more and more barriers of control. Nat-murs[78] need to protect their vulnerability by trying to control Sepias. This will be the end for Sepias; they do not like to be controlled, especially because they will have insight into the drama being played out between the two of them. Nat-murs are no longer open; they are in their siege mentality. Every time Nat-murs come close to Sepias in this state they will be disgusted with Sepias' blatant display of decline. Sepias have no choice but to leave and restore grounding and creativity because they need their independence for emotional strength. The emotional struggle for Sepia always comes back to the nature of the cuttlefish being comfortable to swim alone.

Sepia Partnerships – The Sepia Woman

The Emotional Need for Freedom within Sepia

Sepia is the only constitution that I discuss exclusively from a female bias. Sepia women need independence and freedom in relationships if they are to remain healthy. The difference between the healthy and unhealthy Sepia woman is so marked it is crucial for Sepia women to understand their emotional need for freedom. In my clinical practice I see far more unhealthy Sepia women than unhealthy Sepia men simply because it is far easier for a man in this society to walk away from family commitment than it is for a woman. Sepia needs to be unhindered physically and emotionally to be able to be healthy. Successful relationships for Sepias have to be with a partner who can allow them independence; otherwise, they sink into depression. If they are controlled or dominated they become ungrounded and out of touch with themselves. The homeopathic remedy *Sepia* is derived from the ink cuttlefish squirt out when they sense that danger is present. If cuttlefish feel hemmed in or threatened they need to quickly create a subterfuge so they can escape. Cuttlefish like to swim alone; they do not collect in groups. Sepias also need to be able to go off and swim alone. Their need for independence and space is essential.

The Emotional Legacy of the Sepia Woman

Sepia women feel they do not have many successful relationships. In relationships they struggle to try to balance their need for a career with their husband's and children's needs. Even if Sepia is not married the expectations and demands of a partner are seen as a struggle. Sepias will feel they are trying to be all things to all people. This, of course, means they will feel absolutely exhausted and worn down. Sepia is striving for her own self-realization and, in her mind, children and a partner can be seen as a hindrance in that process. It is not that she does not love; it is she does not love with the same dependency so many women project onto their children and husband. Sepias do not identify themselves first and foremost as mother and wife, and feeling forced to love and give makes Sepia women feel the need to escape. The Sepia woman is grounded in herself, but only if she is emancipated from the passive role of wife and mother.

Sepias become distraught in relationships when they feel controlled or trapped. An unhealthy Sepia woman will turn into a complaining, nagging harridan. Sepias suffer from terrible fatigue and exhaustion when they feel threatened. The Sepia depression is particularly visible before her menses, and this is when Sepia is most likely to express feelings of being threatened or hemmed in. Their restlessness is so extreme they can become completely disconnected from themselves and their family. There is such confusion in their depression it gets translated as complete apathy, and they cannot find their grounding. Premenstrual Sepia has such strong emotional extremes she can literally be laughing one moment, crying the next, or imploding or exploding with rage the next.

Examples of Sepia in Films

The character of the housewife and mother of Richard in the film *The Hours,* directed by Stephen Daldry and played by actor Julianne Moore, is a classic version of unhealthy Sepia. This is the unhealthy Sepia who is confused and unsure of herself. She is screaming inside with a need to escape and find her identity. She leaves her two children and husband to go off and find herself because she knows if she stays she will eventually succeed in killing herself or go insane. The portrayal of Joanna by actor Meryl Streep in *Kramer vs. Kramer,* directed by Robert Benton, is also a classic example of a Sepia woman struggling to find her grounding. Her need to leave her husband and child to find herself became a symbol of feminist struggle in the late 1970s. However, the struggle of Joanna has always been the struggle of a Sepia woman who has lost her grounding, and it will always be.

The healthy Sepia woman presents as the complete opposite. Healthy Sepia is a vibrant, alive woman[79] who is passionately in touch with her own power and her own body. The woman character in the French film *Une Liaison Pornographique (A Pornographic Affair)*, which I discuss in the section on Nat-mur and Sepia, is the classic version of healthy Sepia. This woman is so grounded in her knowledge of herself she is able to set up a relationship on her terms. She is able to be passionate and present without needing to run away. Her relationship does not threaten her individuality or her need for space and freedom.

It is not unusual in my clinical experience to see Sepia women suffering from depression and confusion. The presentation of Sarah Woodruff, played by actor Meryl Streep, in the film *The French Lieutenant's Woman*, directed by Karel Reisz, is a portrayal of a Sepia woman when she has lost grounding and a sense of herself. Sarah knows she is not able to love Charles; she knows she needs to go away and find her grounding within herself. Charles Smithson, played by actor Jeremy Irons, does not pose any threat or impose any controls; the melancholy and disassociation is entirely in her own head. Sepias can believe it is impossible for them to have a relationship because they cannot possibly meet the demands of their partner. Often the presenting picture is of a woman who has no sexual desire because she has been cut off so much from her passion she can't feel passionate. Sarah was struggling with the grief of being abandoned and deceived, but the melancholy and depression she felt was that of a Sepia woman struggling to find an avenue of expression for her passionate, creative nature. There is a need in Sepia women to find their true sense of self in their occupation or creative pursuit. With freedom and creative input into herself, Sarah is able to free herself from her melancholy and depression. If the demands or perceived threats are taken away, there is an immediate lifting of the feeling of oppression, and Sepias will be able to move into their passionate, healthy selves. Sepia is a sexually passionate woman when there are no constraints on her sense of her own being. Unconstrained, healthy Sepia no longer feels she is likely to scream against restraints and she no longer thinks she is so insane she must run away.

The Emotional Challenge for Sepia in Relationships

Sepia needs her independence and freedom in all aspects of life. This is acutely felt by Sepia if she is forced to give up her occupation or job. Sepias in a relationship with a partner who has to always be right, or one who needs a woman at home in the kitchen looking after children and attending to their every need, will eventually become depressed and feel trapped. It is not always possible to predict life; for example, imagine a married Sepia career woman who has a child and the child falls ill. She feels it is her duty as the mother to stay at home and look after her child; quite possibly her husband might be unwilling to give up his job, or he may also be quite logically justified in this decision based on the fact he can earn more money than she can. He might also see his career as more important than hers. Either way, it doesn't matter – the issue is it will not be a good choice for Sepia to stay at home because she will eventually feel trapped and sink into chronic depression. Other constitutions, as well, would also not necessarily enjoy staying at home, but they are not going to be rendered completely devoid of a sense of self.

A lot of women reading this description of Sepia will, of course, be able to relate to this need for freedom. Many will also be able to say to themselves that this is something they worked out a long time ago, which is why they have not entered into relationships with dominating people. It is the woman who feels trapped in a relationship with overly demanding commitments and feels herself sinking into hopelessness, negativity, and depression who needs to think about who she is and, consequently, what she needs to be happy. Sepias also need to believe it is possible to have successful relationships. Sepias need to know they can have a successful relationship without literally having to rely on antidepressants. The theme of needing space and freedom is seen in both healthy and unhealthy Sepia. Sepias have a constant paranoia they will be forced into situations against their own will. With Sepia's strong need for freedom and space, it is easy to imagine that the relationship between a Sepia woman and a partner who needs to dominate would be disastrous. Sepias have to find the right partner who will not dominate them and Sepias also need to "think outside the box," to create unconventional relationships that match their needs, like the woman did in the film *Une Liaison Pornographique (A Pornographic Affair)*.

Sepia Woman and a Lycopodium Man

I have made the choice to be gender-specific in this discussion. In the case of Sepia it will make the discussion a lot more relevant because the Lycopodium male is the archetypal example of the worst type of male for Sepia to be in a relationship with.

Lycopodiums have strong emotional issues to do with loss of power or potential loss of position. The acquisition of prestige and worldly notoriety give Lycopodiums a secure sense of themselves. To gain power and position in the world you have to be able to take on new ventures. Lycopodiums are like "school-yard bullies" because they use the people around them to boost their ego and sense of importance so they can allay their fears. Ironically, it is often the bully who has an insecure sense of self, not the person who is the bully's victim, and this is particularly applicable for Lycopodium. No one is ever going to see the underbelly of Lycopodiums because the outer picture they present to the world is someone with a lot of confidence. Lycopodiums use the world around them to ease their sense of insecurity. They need to be good at what they do and they have to feel superior to everyone else. The ego they need to develop in order to hold their fears at bay is huge. With so much energy going into the presentation of themselves to the world, it is possible to imagine that when Lycopodiums get home they will need a rest. It is how this rest manifests that is most interesting in this context.

The most successful way to have your ego reinforced is to be needed. The drive of Lycopodiums to achieve and be successful in the world is so intense they are usually dictatorial at home. This will become an issue if the partner of Lycopodiums has her own issues with control, as is the case with Sepias. What is potentially even more shattering for the ego of Lycopodiums is a partner who doesn't need them. A Lycopodium in a relationship with Pulsatilla presents as a completely different person from how Lycopodium presents when feeling threatened in a relationship with Sepia. Lycopodiums need to feel they are "the king of the castle." There are many constitutions who feel secure and happy if their partner is the one who is looking after them; Sepias are not one. Sepias do not like to be looked after or controlled in the way that Lycopodiums like to look after and control. The one insecurity Sepias can have in this world is financial insecurity. If a Sepia woman compromises her freedom and control for the sake of financial security with a Lycopodium man, she will quickly sink into the depressed picture of the unhealthy Sepia.

The Lycopodium man would feel very insecure and threatened by the independence of a Sepia woman. This is not a good partnership combination; there will be endless arguments. The Lycopodium man would have to be right and the Sepia woman will not be told what to do. Even if the Lycopodium man was not too bombastic, the Sepia woman would tire; he will not have her passion or the depth of her emotional feelings. Sepias' passionate emotionalism would also terrify a Lycopodium. Lycopodiums, if threatened, will not commit emotionally. A Lycopodium man would quickly declare she was a "ball-breaker" and wonder why he was ever attracted to her in the first place. The fear of an empowered Sepia woman could threaten a Lycopodium man to such an extent he could be rendered impotent. A Sepia woman would also be far too unconventional for a Lycopodium man.

The Empowered Sepia Woman

This scenario between Sepia and Lycopodium is played out in the film *Venus Talking* by German director Rudolf Thome. Venus, played by actor Sabine Bach, is a healthy Sepia woman. She is a vibrant woman who appears to have put a lot more of herself into her writing and career than her family life. This is confirmed by her husband's expressed grievances that she has continually put herself and her career first. The film is about an unusual writing contract she is given. Her publisher has set her up in a fantastic, modern apartment to write a book that is supposedly going to be a best seller. The twist to the contract is she is linked to an online webcam that allows people to log on and watch while she writes.

She is the healthy Sepia woman who has an awareness and passionate response to her own sexual needs. She starts an affair with a young artist she meets in a bar on the very first night of the writing contract. The other twist is she has been duped and the computer operator has also set up a webcam over her bed. The director Rudolf Thome is, of course, interested in exploring in this modern relationship exposé the dynamics that result from her children and husband seeing her in bed with other men when they log on to the webcam. The relationship that interests me is the dynamic that develops between the Lycopodium entrepreneur Bernhard, who is backing the project, and the Sepia Venus.

The opening scenes of the film are set at her family home in the country, where the people involved in the project are meeting for dinner to finalize details before she takes the contract. Bernhard, played by actor André Meyer, is the Lycopodium backer of the project. Bernhard is shown having a very competitive table tennis game with Venus's publisher. Bernhard is a man who is desperate to win. There is a fantastic scene in which Venus gets up to dance and Bernhard dances against her not with her. She is in her full Sepia state of passion and excitement and expresses it through her body, while he is totally unable to dance with her — he constantly advances and intrudes, and competes, all the time trying to entice and win her over sexually. Initially, he could be mistaken for a Nux vomica; however, the deciding moment comes when he thinks what she has written so far on the project is "New-Age" crap and he immediately wants out of the deal and will settle for a financial ending of the contract with the publisher. Lycopodiums do not take financial risks and will not like to fail in business. The difference with Nux vomica is Nux vomica would push and conquer and fight to the end; Lycopodiums, in contrast, will pull out very quickly. They do not care how it is viewed by anyone; they are only interested in survival. The publisher will not back out of the contract, so Bermhard's decision to charm and entice Venus is seen as the only solution to the possible failure of the project and his loss of money. Bernhard goes to try to seduce her so he can get her to change what she is writing. The interesting dilemma is the Lycopodium Bernhard is emasculated by her in bed and is unable to perform sexually. A Nux vomica would not have that problem. Bernhard pretends he is too drunk to cover up his inability to perform sexually. He fails at manipulating her or controlling her emotionally; she is Sepia and he is Lycopodium.

A Lycopodium man in a relationship with a woman who needs him presents as a completely different man. Lycopodiums treasure all the support and love that is given to them. Lycopodiums in a relationship with a woman who looks up to them are empowered and potent. Sepias need their own empowerment in life; they are not going to want to boost someone else's ego. Sepias are involved with their own journey of finding out how to express themselves. Lycopodiums, if they stay with Sepia, will need to seek emotional gratification elsewhere, and this is when they will have the affairs that Lycopodium is noted for. The relationship between Sepias and Lycopodiums is a typical example of the saying "it takes two to tango." Lycopodium will feel the need to boost his prowess by having an affair, because Sepia will undermine his confidence. But Sepia would not have been so threatening or critical in the first place if Lycopodium had not needed so desperately to bully her. It is always possible to view the cause of a conflict from both sides, especially with Sepia and Lycopodium.

The Challenge for Sepia in Relationships

If Sepia stays in this relationship she will quickly move into the unhealthy presentation of her constitution. She will become defensive and her desire to be alone will increase. Her negative, critical nature will come to the fore so she can ward off perceived attacks, and the more threatened she feels the more overwhelmed she will become. Sepia will move into depression and shut down her feelings. The more she shuts down, the more she loses touch with her own body and her sexuality. This will be particularly threatening to a Lycopodium man, as he needs to feel he is needed as a man. His sexual prowess is an outlet for his feelings of insecurity in the world.[80] He will take this rejection very hard, and it is at this point the unhealthy side of Lycopodium can be seen. He will become more of the "schoolyard bully" to try to overcome his feelings of rejection. Sepias cannot be molded by anyone other than themselves and their power comes from their independence. Sepias are happy when they are independent, and they will only become "ball-breakers" if they are provoked. The degree of anger Sepias have when they are encapsulated and contained is formidable. Lycopodiums could not only be rendered impotent; they will also find themselves with a very large, deflated ego. Sepias have an incredible ability to cut to the quick. This relationship combination will not be successful.

Sepia Woman and Medorrhinum

The Theme of Medorrhinum

The homeopathic remedy *Medorrhinum* is derived from the microorganism *Neisseria gonorrhoaea,* which causes the disease gonorrhea. Medorrhinums contain in their nature qualities of the presentation of the disease state of gonorrhea. Gonorrhea is intense, eruptive, and spontaneous, and this same intensity is a theme in the constitution Medorrhinum. There is also a reflective introversion and need to move inward that mirrors the progression of the disease if left untreated.[81] The extreme polarities of eruption and introversion match the intensity and theme of the disease. If you identify yourself as Medorrhinum, the most important theme is the alternating polarity of behavior accompanied by an intense desire to push the boundaries of experience. Medorrhinums know their exploration of the self will only be found in their excessive thirst for expanse and experience.

Medorrhinum is an extremely interesting constitution and it is fascinating to understand why Medorrhinum will have a successful relationship with Sepia. I have already stated that Sepias struggle in relationships, but Sepia will find a kindred spirit in Medorrhinum. Sepias have the same issue that Medorrhinums have over being forced to do things against their will. For Sepias the situation comes about from feeling like they are being dominated and they resolve the feeling by seeking independence. With Medorrhinums the dynamic is much more complex. Medorrhinums alternate between extreme forms of behavior and they only feel at peace by finding themselves within extreme polarities of existence.

The Emotional Legacy of Medorrhinum

The persona of Medorrhinum is difficult to discuss in concrete terms because Medorrhinums do not have fixed boundaries. There is no sense with Medorrhinums that they possess inner orientation points like a North or South Pole on a compass. They do not necessarily want to know where they are, but they are always looking for themselves; this is the dichotomy of Medorrhinum. They head out in life and push limits – this is how they develop a sense of themselves. There is a push to expand outwards and inwards at the same time. Each point of expanse is the same because in the experience of exploration they are escaping. Therefore, Medorrhinum presents with contrasting extremes.

An overwhelming sense of inner emptiness often disturbs Medorrhinums, so much so that they think they are going insane. At the same time they have an overwhelming need to explore the world and experience the energy of experience. The character Brian in the North American production of the television program *Queer As Folk* is a wonderful example of Medorrhinum. Even though the character of Brian has a successful relationship with his partner Justin, the drive of Medorrhinum is an urgent need to explore and experience more. Behavior is not the issue in the analysis of a constitution. The drive and underlying theme and reasons that motivate the person make up the persona of a constitution. Brian manifests the drive of

Medorrhinum in his need to experience several new sexual partners. Loyalty and fidelity are completely irrelevant, in the context of the need that Medorrhinums have to expand their horizons. Brian has an urgent need to push his boundaries and horizons. To remain[82] with his inner self is disturbing and disconcerting. Medorrhinums are driven by a need to experience intensity.

The drive to cover up inner weakness and conflict brings about anxiety that is unique to Medorrhinums. If you do not have a point of reference, there are always unlimited horizons you can travel to. Medorrhinums can appear to others to lack self-control. If someone else tries to enforce controls or their concepts of conventions in the form of taking responsibility, Medorrhinums are likely to want to escape.

If inside of themselves, Medorrhinums know they do not have a solid grip on reality, they will push in the opposite direction to make sure all possible weaknesses are covered up. At the time Medorrhinums are feeling most unsure and vulnerable, they will often act as if nothing scares or affects them. Medorrhinums are extreme in everything. It is possible to either catch them on the flight out of themselves when they present as the extrovert or on the flight into themselves when they present as the introvert. The essence is the same; they have to always be exceeding all limits. If you do not have an orientation point or boundary that contains you, then you will always alternate between extremes.

The character Smilla in the novel *Miss Smilla's Feeling for Snow*, by Peter Høeg, is a Medorrhinum. At one point in the book she is faced with the possibility of imprisonment. Medorrhinums cannot deal with being restrained or imprisoned, and her inner knowledge that this would send her over the precipice of sanity into insanity is the core of Medorrhinums' struggle with their grip on sanity. It is an interesting book to read because it describes Medorrhinums beautifully. The story line is based on her revenge on the killers of a small boy she has befriended. The friend who loaned me the book commented that she felt Smilla was unrealistic in her pursuit of the perpetrators, and that one minute Smilla presents as an introvert in the story and then turns into "Super Woman." If you see Smilla as Medorrhinum, it makes perfect sense why she did not give up. Smilla's strength lies in the depth of her anger and her need for revenge.[83] Medorrhinums will push to the absolute limits of endurance to inflict punishment and seek their revenge; they do not have in their nature the same restrictions other people have. Medorrhinums will not be constrained by convention or societal expectations. Smilla does not hold back from expressing how she feels. She does not need people; in fact, she hates being manipulated into being nice and she is not even very friendly. Her only friend seems to be the little boy for whom she goes to extraordinary lengths. We also know from her father she can be exasperating in her determination to do what she wants to do – he has never been able to control her. Her father surmises that Smilla's inability to deal with restriction, her desperate need for space, and her inability to work in society all stem from her Greenlander heritage. He sees this as the reason he has never been able to control or restrict her in any way. I on the other hand analyze Smilla as Medorrhinum, and this is not a constitution that anyone can control.

When analyzing your constitution or your partner's constitution, look for the motivating theme behind personality. Don't look at the surface presentation of the character; the emotional motivating theme reveals the constitutional picture. Smilla stays at home reading mathematics books and Brian rages all night in gay bars; the theme or thread that ties these two expressions of Medorrhinum together is the need to defy finiteness and discover infinity. Smilla's passion is mathematics because she is stimulated and expanded by the infinity of numbers, while Brian needs to defy his finiteness through pushing his sexual boundaries.

The Theme of Medorrhinum in Relationships
Medorrhinums only know life through experiencing every bit for themselves. They play for high stakes and party hard – "sex, drugs, rock and roll" is their usual scenario. The film *Loulou*, directed by Maurice Pialat, has a wonderful example of a Medorrhinum who

needs to push all boundaries. Nelly, played by actor Isabelle Huppert, is a middle-class woman who is tired and bored with the man she is living with. She is totally sick of her current partner's possessiveness, and when she meets Loulou at a disco she decides to go off with him. Loulou, played by Gérard Depardieu, is a criminal and layabout and from a completely different social class, but she decides to move in with him. Nelly wants to experience everything with a manic urgency – even Loulou can't work out what she sees in him. He knows she wants his "dick" but he is confused when she does not seem to notice his roughness or criminal history. Her previous partner André is equally confused and distraught over her decisions and can't believe the affair will last. Nelly gets pregnant and has an abortion because she realizes Loulou will not support her and she will lose her freedom. Loulou cannot fathom what drives her to get rid of her child. For him having a child is a romantic ideal. The film ends with Loulou asking Nelly's old partner about whether she ever wanted a child when she was with him. Nelly would never have decided to go ahead with any situation that meant she was dependent or trapped. Medorrhinums need to be stimulated and free and Nelly is Medorrhinum. Everything is tackled with a spontaneous urgency to experience everything. Nelly indulged in everything to excess, always trying to understand her own essence of feeling. Nelly can appear destructive. She is not destructive; the urgency she feels is a desire to be free and unrestrained.

Another character who is Medorrhinum is Carrington, played by the actor Emma Thompson in the film *Carrington,* which is directed by Christopher Hampton. The character Carrington is very similar to the character Smilla. The film, based on Michael Holroyd's biography of the writer Lytton Strachey, is set at the time of the First World War and features the lives of the famed London Bloomsbury artistic set. The film portrays the true story of unconsummated love between the artist Dora Carrington and the homosexual writer Lytton Strachey. Carrington is an unconventional woman struggling with her relationships with men. On first impression the character of Carrington could be mistaken for a Sepia woman struggling with

independence and individuality, but the difference is the love relationship she forms with Lytton. A Medorrhinum woman not only
wants freedom, she needs unrestrained passion. Lytton is the only
man she is able to feel safe enough to love and he is the only man
who she can truly be passionate with. Carrington struggles with being
owned and constrained. The dilemma is more intense than it is for
Sepia. Medorrhinums can only feel their passion when there is no
threat to their autonomy, and they can only feel their own passion
when they are met by an equally powerful expanse of desire. Sepias
can, in contrast, be grounded and healthy in relationships. Carrington had to have the protection of an asexual relationship and this is
why she found herself in love with a man who could not satisfy her
physically. For the times, and particularly for her complex personality, it was the best solution. After Lytton dies she also knows she
cannot bear to live without knowing he is there to stimulate her. She
needs to shoot herself because she knows she will never be able to
be matched energetically by anyone else. Every horizon beckons
Medorrhinums and they usually follow it with great drive and passion.
Sepia is happy swimming alone, and this is what distinguishes Carrington as Medorrhinum and not Sepia.

Sepias equally need to see horizons. Medorrhinums are not going
to be threatened by Sepias' passionate nature or feel the need to control. Medorrhinums will be excited and stimulated by Sepias. Sepia
just *is;* her intuition and insights into life are natural and Medorrhinums who need to intellectualize and rationalize, to understand
everything, or "party" to the extreme to experience passion will be
in awe of Sepias' natural strength. Medorrhinums do not have an
inner sense of knowing or any sense of a continuous spectrum of
reality, so they spend a lot of time trying to analyze everything to
find their own North or South Poles. This combination of Sepia and
Medorrhinum makes a potentially exciting and passionate relationship,
but it will be tumultuous.

Both constitutions are able to love passionately, in the moment,
without ever wanting to surrender their freedom or individuality.
The character of Brian will never surrender himself in love to his

partner Justin. Sepias won't surrender in love either, because if too much is demanded of them they will lose their connection to themselves. Medorrhinums will never surrender because they are essentially too self-centered and absorbed in their own processes of experiencing life. Both constitutions belong only to themselves. Medorrhinums are as unconventional as Sepias in their ability to exist as individuals, never needing to be attached to their partner. Medorrhinums can appear cold and detached and Sepias can appear equally as detached. Each constitution has the ability to exist independent of others. Carrington needs Lytton because he is the only person she has found who can match her passion. Brian equally needs Justin because he is able to match him emotionally. But both Carrington and Brian also express themselves sexually with other partners.

Both Sepia and Medorrhinum can be attacking and critical if they are overwhelmed or pressured. Medorrhinums can be equally as nasty and aggressive as Sepias, but this usually happens when they are contradicted, or forced to expose their emotional or physical weaknesses. Medorrhinums oscillate between extremes, not only of emotions but even in their work performance and life, and are acutely conscious of how the pendulum swings for them. Medorrhinums can oscillate between love and hate, and be very nasty and cruel, if they are confronted with their irrational behavior. Their extremes haunt them and they can be extremely paranoid about any threats or perceived attacks. Sepias react to domination or perceived attacks with defensiveness or critical nagging. With Medorrhinums they react as if they are being rejected. Medorrhinums suffer from an overdeveloped paranoiac fear and anxiety that someone is watching them; consequently, any rejection or criticism is taken much more seriously. Unsure of where their horizons are inside, Medorrhinums imagine everyone else is looking over their shoulder and able to see their instability.

The Emotional History behind Sepia and Medorrhinum
This once again is a relationship that depends on Sepia being healthy. Medorrhinums in a relationship with an unhealthy Sepia will react

to the attacks with all the above negativity and defensiveness. Sepias have a built-in intuition and ability to find their partner's Achilles heel, so this relationship could be very tumultuous and heated. Both constitutions are great at plate-smashing tantrums and need these sessions to release their emotions. Sepias and Medorrhinums both share an emotional history of overbearing fathers and the pain of this makes both constitutions so hypervigilant to all controls, demands, or criticisms. This hypervigilance can make them appear selfish to others. The emotional need of Medorrhinums to find space inside themselves is so acute there is no time for them to think about how this might affect anyone else. This could also explain why Medorrhinums are obsessive adventurers, never staying too long in one place. It could be a short and stormy partnership between Sepia and Medorrhinum, but it will be very passionate.

Sepia and Medorrhinum Together in the Film
Sunday Bloody Sunday

The character Alex Greville, played by actor Glenda Jackson, in the film *Sunday Bloody Sunday* is a Sepia woman in a relationship with a Medorrhinum, Bob Elkin, played by actor Murray Head. Bob is a young designer and creator who is consumed with the Medorrhinum exploration of form and space, and expansive movement, within his sculptures. *Sunday Bloody Sunday,* directed by John Schlesinger, was quite a shocking film for its time because it explored homosexuality and bisexuality. Bob Elkin is having a relationship with Daniel, a man, and with Alex, a woman. Bob is Medorrhinum. He literally leaves her bed to go to his bed. Both Alex and Daniel know about the existence of the other, and they both struggle with feelings of hurt, abandonment, and jealousy. Bob is selfish in the true sense that Medorrhinum is selfish; he is only concerned with finding satisfaction and stimulation. He is aware of how each lover feels but it does not concern him in the least. Bob does not feel committed to either lover and leaves both of them to take an opportunity to pursue his art work in New York.

Dr. Daniel Hirsh, played by actor Peter Finch, is a Nat-mur. At the end of the film Daniel pretends he is one of his patients in a consultation and he relays to the camera what the relationship with Bob has meant for him. Daniel says all of his life he has been waiting for someone courageous to come along so he could fall in love. His speech is a Nat-mur speech of wanting to fall in love with someone, and it is a Nat-mur talking from a place of hurt and pain and martyrdom. Because Bob is not that person, Daniel will hang onto what little he has, because it is better than nothing, and he decides to accept that it was not "nothing" he had with Bob – "it was not nothing, but something." Alex equally wants Bob to stay, but the difference is Bob leaves his toucan for her to look after. With Daniel, Bob returned his key and left with no promise to return. Bob knows Alex is an independent woman who will be able to survive without him; she might wait for him to return but she will not wait alone. Daniel, on the other hand, is in love with Bob; he would not consider it possible to go to bed with anyone else. Alex might want to be with Bob, and she might feel jealous, but she is not dependent. When Bob is not around, Alex could quite happily go to bed with someone else, and Bob knew he could come back to her.

Sepias are often accused of lacking attachment to loved ones or of being indifferent. In this relationship combination with Medorrhinum, there is more of a chance for Sepia to be happy and healthy. If Sepias are not threatened they will not need to hide and withdraw affection and love. Medorrhinums will go off to different parts of the world or to different partners but will feel very comfortable coming back to Sepias because they know Sepias are self-sufficient and will survive while they are away. Sepias will wait for Medorrhinums to return because Sepias also need to be loved without possession, and Medorrhinums can do this.

Sepias are very self-sufficient and will love the space and freedom to do exactly what they want. Bob actually asks Alex if she wants to come to New York with him, and she declines. Sepias sink into their unhealthy side when they allow themselves to be dependent. Sepia, once they are trapped and constrained again, will then want to escape. Alex is a healthy Sepia; she knows she does not want to go back to living with her husband or tag along with Bob to New York. She knows she needs to be free.

Only by putting themselves in high-risk situations can Medorrhinums truly feel what it is to be alive; this theme is continued in their quest for love. Sepias' unbridled need for freedom will meet Medorrhinums in their expansiveness.

Sepia Woman and Nux Vomica

The Theme of Nux Vomica

The homeopathic remedy *Nux vomica* is derived from a dilution of tincture taken from the seeds of a poison nut *Strychnos Nux Vomica*. It was commonly referred to as strychnine because the nut itself contains a high percentage of the poison. Nux vomicas carry the energy, or threat, of this poison deep in their psyche, and it is manifested in their need to win at all costs. Nux vomicas express their position in the world as "you are only as good as your last victory," and they will assess every interaction in life as loss or win. Nux vomicas have a highly developed vigilance to potential threats because they know the potential threat of annihilation is real enough to threaten their survival. Nux vomicas have an unusual fear or delusion that someone has literally taken their bed. This sort of fear reflects a great deal of anxiety about losing their place or position in the world.

The Emotional Challenge for Sepia and Nux Vomica

Nux vomica's fear of restriction is similar to Sepia's, but for different reasons. Both constitutions have a fundamental need for power and position because with power comes freedom. Nux vomicas use power so they can fight off any potential threats, while Sepias use power to achieve independence and individuality. Ironically, they could initially be attracted to each other because in each other they will see a like-minded love of power, but their partnership will be such a continuous bloody battle that it has no possibility of success. Nux vomicas will have to be in charge, and Sepias do not like to be controlled. Nux vomicas view any compromise of position as failure, or having "lost the battle." Security for Nux vomicas equates to knowing they are the only one in a "top dog" position; therefore, Sepias' independence will be seen as a threat to Nux vomicas' need to be victorious. Nux vomicas need to know their partner is loyal and dependent, and the very nature of Sepias' individuality and independence is paramount to saying they are not needed. Nux vomicas do not like to be shown up or humiliated, and they will interpret Sepias' independence as a direct humiliation and attack on their authority. If their partner in life is not dependent on them, Nux vomicas feel like they have "lost face" because someone has literally taken their bed and eliminated them. Sepias' need for independence is equivalent to a "call to arms," and Nux vomicas will need to destroy Sepias. Nux vomicas are the typical "Type A" personality — always competitive, ambitious, and driven to achieve, with a pathological need to win at all costs. Nux vomicas and Sepias would be so incompatible it would be surprising if either of them were attracted to each other in the first place.

I suspect that the most likely scenario would be that Nux vomica spotted a successful, independent Sepia "career woman" at work, and Nux vomica decided to "break her balls" and "show her who's boss." The thinking process would be "how dare she think she could compete with me or tell me what to do"; more than likely she is actually the boss, and this is a situation that would be unbearable. Nux vomicas are such obsessively driven people it would be extremely difficult for them to ever respect anyone as their boss. If the relationship started I can imagine it would be on this basis, and would be a carefully conceived plan on the part of Nux vomica to discredit her professionalism and take over her position. Nux vomica is common among men; however, in my clinical practice I see a lot of Nux vomica women so I am not going to be gender-specific. The combative attitude can be expressed equally by any Nux vomica regardless of gender. Nux vomicas, male or female, are ambitious and driven to achieve and win at all costs.

Nux Vomica's Emotional Need for Power and Devotion

Napoleon is the closest image I have of a Nux vomica. It is always hard to be sure of the constitution of famous figures from history because so much of what is written is influenced by current perceptions of the political history of the time. Napoleon is fairly likely to be Nux vomica, because only Nux vomica would equal his confidence in battle strategies and match his drive to conquer the whole world. Nux vomicas have one significant Achilles heel, however: their delusion or fear of being moved out of their bed and subsequently eliminated. It is the knowing of this vulnerability that makes Nux vomicas so reluctant to make a commitment to marriage in the first place. Nux vomicas know they need to be in a favorable position in the world, and they also need to know they are in a favorable position at home. Their partner must be totally devoted, loyal, and obedient. They will never be happy with a partner who is in the same area of expertise because they do not tolerate being challenged or contradicted in business, and especially not at home. If Nux vomicas do not feel secure in love they will start to doubt themselves, and this is when they will strategically lose confidence in their decisions.

Josephine was infertile and unable to provide Napoleon with an heir. As a Nux vomica Napoleon had no choice but to end the marriage, even though he still loved her. Napoleon desperately needed an heir; offspring for Nux vomicas are a projection and visible proof of their conquering potency in the world. Napoleon was enough of a strategist to realize his downfall in life came when he ended his marriage to Josephine, and when he looked back over his life he saw from the moment he got rid of Josephine he lost confidence in his ability to make shrewd decisions. His second wife did not have the same devotion or loyalty as Josephine, and he realized when he gave up her devotion, he also lost his confidence. Napoleon moved out of the security of his bed and away from the security of Josephine's devotion. Nux vomicas need the security of home to provide them with much-needed repose from the world, and Napoleon had always needed to go home to Josephine to replenish his energy[84] after battle.

His second wife was apparently emotionally demanding and Napoleon was not able to feel he could replenish his energy and rest when he came home. Josephine was apparently very good at spending a fortune on clothes and in indulging herself, which exasperated him, and pressured him into feeling like he had to amass a fortune to keep her happy. However, she was apparently totally devoted to Napoleon, and this is what he needed to emotionally replenish. It is probable she was a Pulsatilla because she remained devoted to Napoleon even though he abandoned her. It is not just a coincidence that at the same time his second marriage started, he also started to feel threatened and paranoid and began to make mistakes in battles. When Napoleon looked like he was failing in battle, his second wife immediately abandoned him for the security of her family.

The Power Struggle between Sepia and Nux Vomica in the Film *Howards End*

The portrayal of Henry Wilcox in the novel *Howards End* by E.M. Forster is Nux vomica. The book has been made into a film, directed by James Ivory, with actor Anthony Hopkins as Henry Wilcox and actor Helena Bonham Carter playing the character Helen Schlegel. The story revolves around the relationship of Henry and the two Schlegel sisters. Henry is a ruthless business man and his desire to own and conquer everyone around him is obvious from the outset. The relationship struggle over the power of Sepia and the power of Nux vomica is played out between Helen and Henry. Helen is Sepia; she is a passionate woman with strong spiritual beliefs that she is unwilling to compromise for societal conventionality. Both sisters appear at the start of the film to be extraordinarily high-spirited and independent. The older sister, Margaret Schlegel, played by actor Emma Thompson, succumbs to the power of Henry and marries him, even though she knows he has no respect for her values. Margaret's love and loyalty are not based on romantic love but rather on societal respect for the role and definition of a good wife as someone who defers to her husband's authority. Margaret is Nat-mur. Helen, on the other hand, has no desire to give her power away and she has the ability and strength to not submit to Henry's lack of care for humanity. She resents her sister's defection and weakness. Helen's passion and power, and unconventional strength, come from her healthy Sepia desire for freedom of expression.

Margaret is the classic picture of the Nat-mur who has so much empathy and understanding for the other person's conflicts it can be viewed as bordering on the unhealthy picture of the martyred Nat-mur. Nat-murs can be easily trapped by their need for loyalty or by their empathy for the other person's pain. Margaret forgives his unfaithfulness to his first wife and she continually forgives his disdain and destruction of her family ties to her sister, but Henry does not give anything in return. His desperate need for power is Nux vomica and Nux vomicas never compromise because to give is to lose power, and to lose power is to be humiliated, and this thinking is the picture of Nux vomica when they are threatened. In his relationship with the Nat-mur Margaret, Henry is quite secure in his control and power, but in his relationship with the independent Sepia Helen, he always feels threatened. Nux vomicas are acutely jealous of anyone else's sense of security, and Sepia, when she is healthy, is grounded and sure of her individuality and will be seen as a threat. Nux vomicas have a strong ego and pride in how they want the rest of the world to see them, and they are ruthless when they are threatened. Nux vomicas also need to respect the partner they have chosen, especially because this can reflect back on their own image of themselves in the world. Nux vomica will not respect Sepia. This combination of similars[85] would rarely even work in a friendship. In a relationship with a different constitution Nux vomica will not be as threatened and uncompromising.

An ironic twist to the story is that Henry's first wife Ruth dies and bequeaths the family home, which she owns, to Margaret Schlegel. The loss of control and power over what he sees as his property is intolerable to Henry. The desire of Nux vomicas to have ultimate control and power over everything is considerable. The history of the bequest haunts Henry throughout the film. Henry refuses to give up the home he sees as belonging to him through his marriage rights.

The power of fate and spirituality overcome his Nux vomica possessiveness and Howards End is finally taken by Margaret. The ultimate insult is that Margaret in turn bequeaths the property to her nephew, the child born out of wedlock to the unconventional Sepia Helen. To lose face in society is to be humiliated for Nux vomica. At the end of the film Henry is portrayed as an elderly man who has been shamed and has lost a considerable amount of his power as a result of being humiliated by the Sepia Helen, but he still has his loyal Nat-mur wife Margaret on his arm supporting him.

The Emotional Legacy for Nux Vomica

The cut-throat Diana Christensen character, played by Faye Dunaway, in the 1976 film *Network,* directed by Sidney Lumet, is another Nux vomica. Diana is a ruthless executive working on a top-rated news show; she is only concerned with winning and getting the ratings she needs to be the most successful executive at the network. The film is about how they acquire an increase in their ratings and how they then deal with the threat to their continued success. Howard Beale, played by actor Peter Finch, is a psychotic, alcoholic newscaster who, for some time, has been able to turn around the ratings of the near-bankrupt TV network by putting on a nightly show that verges on the psychotic ravings of a madman. Howard increasingly starts to lose control and the ratings are plummeting. Diana's boss, Frank Hackett, played by actor Robert Duvall, is also Nux vomica. Nux vomicas will eliminate all opposition and any potential threats to their success. Frank and Diana would rather choose to kill Howard Beale than to face the slow decline of their ratings on his news show. Nux vomicas do not deal and do not want to contemplate failure. Frank and Diana arrange for Howard to be shot.

Diana also will not negotiate in her relationship. Max, played by actor William Holden, wants an emotional commitment from her to their relationship. Diana would rather lose the relationship than lose face and admit she needs him, or feel like she has to commit to anything that could threaten her autonomy. Diana knows she is too "masculinized," as she herself puts it, to be able to be a normal woman in

a normal relationship. She does not want to stop winning and achieving in her job to give love to Max. She would also much rather he
return to his wife so she does not have to witness his slow, aging
decline. Nux vomicas do not like to watch failure and decline; any
fall from grace is reflective of what they fear most.

The persona of the character Rick, played by actor Humphrey
Bogart, in the film *Casablanca* is also Nux vomica. Rick is the hard-
edged owner of the famous night club in Casablanca, Rick's Café
American. The night club is a gambling club, but Rick has the reputation of never drinking or gambling with the clients; he is always
in control. Casablanca is a holding port for desperate people needing a way out of Nazi-controlled Europe in the Second World War.
Everyone is stuck in Casablanca struggling to get a visa or buy a
forged visa on the black market so they can secure a way out of
Europe into another country. One night the only woman Rick has
ever loved turns up in Casablanca desperate to secure a visa for herself and her husband. Ilsa, played by Ingrid Bergman, had been Rick's
lover at a time when she did not know her husband was still alive.
When she found out he was alive, she had left Rick stranded without telling him the reason she left. Rick is a Nux vomica and the
humiliation of being dumped has been acutely eating away at his
soul, turning him into a bitter, cynical Nux vomica. When she arrives
in Casablanca, Rick is forced to confront his humiliation. Nux vomicas will only want to win if it is totally on their terms. Nux vomicas do not negotiate and will not gamble. Rick knows Ilsa will not
choose him. Nux vomicas have a need to be in a "top dog" position;
they need to know they are the only one in their lover's eyes. Rick
has access to a supply of visas and he gives visas to the woman he
loves even though she chooses to leave with her husband. Ilsa is torn
between the man she is in love with, Rick, and her freedom-fighter
husband she loves and admires. Rick does not force Ilsa to choose
between him and her husband Victor Laszlo because Nux vomicas
will never settle for second best; they know they need total devotion
from their partner.

Nux vomicas are similar to Lycopodium in the sense they are

hypervigilant to potential threats to their continued existence and position. On first impression it is easy to confuse Lycopodiums with Nux vomicas because both constitutions have a lot of bravado and arrogance. Both constitutions also have the reputation of being a bully. Lycopodiums need to bully and brag, to cover up their underlying fear of failure. Nux vomicas fight because they need to secure their position, while Lycopodiums fight because they need to survive. The difference lies in their motivations; if Lycopodiums have their back against the wall they will give in and opt for survival, and not give a damn about whether they are viewed as cowardly. Nux vomicas, on the other hand, will battle to save face. Preserving dignity is more important than survival for Nux vomica – if they save face, they will win. Rick from the film *Casablanca* was prepared to give up the girl to save face. Unless Ilsa chose him upfront, he was not prepared to deal. It is their inability to deal that makes Nux vomicas often very hard to live with.

Sepias, by the very fact that they need independence, will threaten Nux vomicas; consequently, the ruthless side of Nux vomica will come to the fore. Nux vomicas in partnership with Calc-carb, Pulsatilla, Nat-mur, or Carcinosin will present very differently. Sepias have their own urgent issues over finding individuality, and therefore they cannot afford to acquiesce to a Nux vomica. Sepias and Nux vomicas share the same fear of emotional commitment. Sepias fear the loss of individuality and space, while Nux vomicas fear the potential loss of position they interpret comes with commitment in relationships.

Staphisagria Partnerships

The Theme of Staphisagria

The theme of suppression and repression has to be able to be seen for the constitution to be Staphisagria. If there is no history of emotional or physical abuse, it would be very unlikely that Staphisagria would be the right constitution. Other constitutions have been abused by family, but Staphisagrias are unique in the sense they turn the oppression around onto themselves in the form of suppression of their own feelings. The main cause of illness for Staphisagria is from suppression of feelings. Staphisagrias are protecting a very painful emotional history of some sort of abuse and the main issues or theme Staphisagrias have to deal with are the negative effects from suppression of their emotions.

Staphisagrias who consult me in my clinic are almost apologetic they have had to seek help. They sit hunched over with their arms neatly by their side, as if they do not want to even take up any space. One thing that is immediately noticeable is they have to literally stop talking to swallow saliva.[86] Every time they swallow I immediately have the feeling that along with the saliva they are also swallowing their ability to stand up for themselves. They seem to get smaller and smaller as they continue to talk. This is a very important constitution to discuss in a book about relationships because a lot of the self-esteem issues Staphisagrias are dealing with come from, and lead them into, abusive relationships.

The Emotional Legacy of Staphisagria

Staphisagrias have the feeling that they need to hold onto all their negative thoughts and reactions, and not share them. *Staphisagria* is listed in the homeopathic repertory in the group of remedies for "egotism," along with *Sulphur, Lycopodium,* and *Nux vomica.* But Staphisagria could not be a more different constitution. The undoing of Staphisagrias is that they do in fact have a very strong egotistical streak. Staphisagrias have an enormous amount of egoistic pride in the sense they feel it is beyond their dignity to ever express any of the "bad feelings" they have. This self-imposed exile from expressing negative feelings causes an enormous amount of subsequent problems. What it means for Staphisagrias is that, if they express anger or outrage, they feel like they have belittled or disgraced themselves, so Staphisagrias then decide to hold onto their negative thoughts and suppress them. This is an absolutely crazy situation to put themselves in because it means they are trying to go through life without ever getting angry, or without ever losing their control or dignity. Sitting under their dignity is egoistic pride that they have not responded the same as other people in this world. Staphisagria can be very righteous and dogmatic in this belief. It is not unusual to find that a lot of very righteous religious people are Staphisagria. What is also common is to find a lot of Staphisagrias involved in religions like Buddhism. A Buddhist Staphisagria misuses the spiritual practice of abandoning negative feelings and reinterprets it to mean control and suppression of "bad feelings." This process is self-defeating. If you try to hold onto and suppress anger, it builds until it explodes with such power and force it ends up being expressed out of proportion to the original feeling. After such outbursts Staphisagrias are mortified by their behavior and sink into guilt and self-abusive shame. Their self-abuse can be expressed in various ways and in varying severity, from religious abandonment of the world, to physical abuse like cutting themselves, to forced bulimia or anorexia, to sexual self-abuse or abuse of others, or it can commonly be expressed as a general suppression of emotional feeling. The other problem, which is even more terrifying, is that Staphisagria will not be able to fight off any future abuse because they are not able to tap into their feelings of anger and outrage. Staphisagrias have suppressed and repressed their feelings so much they don't know how to get angry. If someone can't get angry, they can't fight off future abusers.

The Emotional Challenge for Staphisagria

The third story *Our Friend Judith* in the film *A Man & Two Women*, directed by Valerie Stroh, is a good portrayal of a Staphisagria woman. The stories in this film are based on stories by the feminist writer Doris Lessing. The issues explored by Doris Lessing have to do with women's individuality, self-expression, and independence. From a homeopathic analysis of Staphisagria, the story is about a woman who creates so much independence she ends up abusing herself through the neglect of her emotional needs. The character of Judith is a rather uptight intellectual poet who has an enormous amount of pride and arrogance about her emotional independence. Judith is in a relationship with a married man and she is very content with the arrangement because she can retain her emotional independence. She does not want to deal with facing her feelings in a monogamous relationship. Judith is happy being who she is until she suffers an emotional crisis when she becomes attached to the cat she gets for herself. Her cat is a rather active tomcat that proves very problematic to the nightly peace of the neighborhood. The sleep-deprived neighbors want the cat castrated. The crisis comes because she will not castrate the cat nor will she give it away to anyone in another neighborhood who could get it castrated. She will also not compromise on letting it live, so she decides to have it put to sleep. The problem with her decision is that she has not acknowledged how attached she is to the cat emotionally. She is grief stricken with his death and is not able to deal with the fact that she misses him. The fact she hasn't previously considered or respected her feelings is an acknowledgment of her Staphisagria suppression.

The stress proves too much and she leaves for a working holiday in Italy. One of her friends visits and relays how wonderfully radiant she is. She has fallen in love with the local barber. However, once again she is faced with a crisis over acknowledging her feelings and once again she is faced with a crisis over her feelings for a cat. Her lover convinces her to leave the cat when the cat is about to give birth, to go swimming with him. The cat is too young to deal with the kittens and she kills her babies. The emotional crisis comes for Judith because she realizes she has fallen in love to such a degree she allowed herself to be influenced and manipulated by someone else to the extent she went against her own instincts regarding the cat. The character of the woman Judith ends up trapping herself because she cannot continue in the relationship with the barber. For any constitution other than Staphisagria, the crisis over the death of the kittens would be sad and tragic but the Staphisagria Judith interprets the crisis as a personal insult to her own lack of dignity and character. Judith is horrified that she allowed herself to be emotionally needy enough to listen to her lover. She personally feels guilty over the death of the kittens and she is totally mortified by how she loses her temper by hitting the sadistic boy who causes the cat to lose her litter. Judith is Staphisagria because she is proud of her dignity and emotional independence. Staphisagrias can be very righteous and religious in isolating themselves from their feelings and needs. Judith is a passionate woman who has very strong sexual needs that finally come to fruition with the barber, but she is not prepared to become dependent or acknowledge her own needs. She remains a spinster and does not acknowledge her own passion. Staphisagrias trap themselves through their own inability to allow themselves to be in touch with their own feelings. Within Staphisagrias there is always, on some level, suppression and abuse; with the character of Judith the suppression and abuse were toward herself and the suppression was of her own feelings. In unhealthier Staphisagrias, this suppression of feelings can lead them into abusive relationships where they suppress someone else.

The Emotional History behind Staphisagria

Because of their strong, judgmental pride about the expression of anger, it is feasible that Staphisagrias could trap themselves into relationships that are abusive. Staphisagrias will not let the other person know what they feel, and they will trap themselves into staying through their own pride and inability to get angry enough to admit the abuse and leave. *Staphisagria* is also the constitutional remedy for people who are trapped in an abusive relationship and do not have enough self-esteem to get out because they have never stood up enough to find their own anger. It is also possible they are holding feelings of guilt from the past to justify their staying in an abusive relationship. *Staphisagria* is also the constitutional remedy for the abuser in such a relationship. When people try to suppress feelings, one of two things ends up happening. First, these people become so shut down they do not even know they are being abused; second, they are a virtual powder keg waiting to be lit. In Staphisagrias both possibilities exist — they can be either self-abusive or the abuser, or both.

Along with the suppression of anger in their lives, Staphisagrias also suppress their sexual feelings. As with all sorts of suppression, the more people try to hold down the feelings the larger and more obsessive the thoughts become. This is true for sexual feelings as much as it is true for feelings of anger and rage. Feelings of guilt and shame are often the reasons behind the strict moral codes that Staphisagrias impose on themselves. It is not unusual to find in the history of Staphisagrias that they have been the victim of sexual abuse. The homeopathic remedy *Staphisagria* is often the first remedy I consider using for rape or sexual abuse cases. More than likely the victims will have moved into the constitutional psyche or theme of being Staphisagria and they have been in Staphisagria ever since the abuse. Tragically, they will have struggled with the suppression of their feelings ever since they were raped or abused, and the most common feeling they carry with them is guilt and self-loathing and self-blame. The actual event is carried as deep guilt and humiliation, as if they committed the crime and not the abuser. This humiliation is also the feeling they are confronted with if ever they think they express any future "bad feelings." If there is no sexual abuse in their history, then often they were abused psychologically or they were shamed by society into feeling they were not worthwhile people. A lot of children from poor backgrounds have feelings of shame inflicted on them by society, usually starting at an early age in school.

It is also not unusual to find in their background that they were the children of alcoholics or drug addicts and they feel very ashamed about their parents. An alcoholic parent can be their abuser. Alcoholics often overreact to situations with violence and abuse and then the next day are so overcome with feelings of remorse and shame that they then often abuse themselves by drinking more.

Just as Staphisagrias suffer from neurological sensitivity on a physical level, the same is true on the emotional. The same pride and dignity they have in themselves means that Staphisagrias are mortified and deeply offended if they feel they have been insulted. This feeling is so strong, Staphisagrias can actually develop convulsions from feeling they have been wrongly accused or insulted. The problem with Staphisagrias is their sensitivity is out of proportion to the situation. If they have not allowed themselves to respond to all the other situations in which they have felt angry, it is understandable that they can overreact. It is important to point out that Staphisagrias can appear timid and gentle until they feel they are in a situation that is putting them down. The transformation is formidable. The rush of feelings and rage at these moments fill Staphisagrias with confusion and very real fear of losing control, and the loss of control is the usual outcome given the history of suppression.

The Emotional Challenge for Staphisagria in Relationships

Isabelle Huppert plays what would have to be the most absorbing picture of Staphisagria in the film *The Piano Teacher*, directed by Michael Haneke. This is the picture of the extreme unhealthy picture of Staphisagria. Even before the opening credits are finished, the suppressive relationship between the mother, played by actor Annie Girardot, and the daughter Erika Kohut, played by Huppert, is obvious. This is the more extreme unhealthy persona of Staphisagria and many people cannot comfortably cope with the abuse that is portrayed in this film. The suppression of Erika is quite severe in this film; we also see the self-abusive picture of Staphisagria. Not only is she in an abusive relationship with her mother, she also self-abuses her own body.

The portrayal of Erika's rigidity is faithfully depicted down to minute details.[87] Erika presents as wearing the plainest of clothes with no makeup and her hair tied tightly in a bun. Erika is repressed by her mother and is self-repressive as well. The opening argument with the mother has all the elements: abused, abuser, and remorseful abuser. The first fight we are witness to in the film is the mother ripping up a dress that she deems as unsuitable and risqué. The repression by the mother is fanatical; however, Erika is also abusive and violent in return toward her mother.

Erika presents as an exacting, classic, conservatory professor with a profound understanding and a highly refined, hypersensitive appreciation of the music of Schubert and Schumann. But she is also an overexacting teacher. The repression Erika inflicts upon her students is fanatical, and she is exacting to the point of being abusive.

It is when Erika falls in love with her student Walter Klemmer,[88] played by actor Benoît Magimel, that we see the degree to which she is trapped in the self-abusive, emotionally crippling distortions of her suppressive nature. The effect of the repression and suppression result in the distorted sexual aberrations Erika inflicts upon herself. Erika is emotionally crippled and unable to love without abuse and unable to receive love that is not abusive. Some very disturbing scenes in the film depict the result of the repressive upbringing she has suffered at the hands of her mother. Even though this is the more extreme presentation of Staphisagria, even in the presentation of a healthy Staphisagria there is still a struggle with psychological suppression.

Staphisagrias who are healthy are more able to allow themselves to acknowledge feelings of anger. They still might present as proud and controlled, but they will not allow themselves to fall into the trap of suppressing their feelings or being ashamed of themselves. The healthy presentation of Staphisagrias will still appear reserved and quiet, but instead of pride they will have more of an air of honor. Staphisagrias are proud of the fact that they are able to remain nice. Healthy Staphisagria will not feel like they can only be nice if they suppress their feelings of anger or rage. Vic,[89] the brother of Debbie in the television program *Queer As Folk,* is a healthy Staphisagria.

Vic has a strong need to be treated with respect and honor. He is not overtly proud but he wants to be perceived as dignified. He is quiet and reserved and he struggles with allowing himself to get angry, but he does not repress his anger to the degree he ends up suppressing and abusing himself. He also does not want to abuse or repress anyone else.

The challenge for the person in a relationship with Staphisagria, especially the more damaged presentation of Staphisagria, is not to fall into the trap of becoming the abuser. The challenge for Staphisagrias is to avoid getting into a relationship that does not allow them expression and free will. The challenge for Staphisagrias in life is to overcome feelings of shame. For Staphisagrias it is important to find someone who is sensitive to their feelings and is not going to abuse them or take advantage of their struggle with self-esteem. Most important, Staphisagrias need someone who is also not as righteous and judgmental of others as Staphisagrias can be toward themselves. The last thing that Staphisagrias need is to be controlled or suppressed any more than they already do themselves.

Staphisagria and Graphites

The Theme of Graphites

I use graphite, the mineral, in my front door security lock when the small metal cogs get jammed; the graphite helps to loosen the cogs so the key can move freely without friction. When you spill the mineral graphite on the floor it disintegrates into lots of fragments; the particles then appear to madly rush around trying to find other particles they can hang onto and then they form larger clumps. The same sort of frenetic experience is what happens to the Graphites constitution during emotional distress. Graphites can appear as fragmented as the mineral graphite and this is the psyche and theme of Graphites. They are easily upset and disturbed by unpredictability, and can appear as disturbed by disunity and disharmony as the particles of graphite rushing around on the floor. Most happy in a loving, secure relationship with no friction, Graphites people will be content to sit back and live their emotional life through their partner because they feel far too sensitive and easily upset on their own. The skill they bring to any conflict or to any family or relationship is that they do actually run around trying to gather all the fragmented pieces of the family together so it can form a harmonious whole.

The Needs of Graphites in Relationships

People who are Graphites love and support in a simple and uncomplicated way. Genuinely devoted to family and to the needs of their partner, Graphites people need to be needed. They come with built-in maternal instincts. Regardless of gender, Graphites is not career oriented; rather, this is a stay-at-home type. Debbie, the mother of Michael in the North American production of the television program *Queer As Folk*, is a wonderful portrayal of Graphites. Debbie works, but she is not motivated by career aspirations. Debbie works at the local café, which is frequented by her son and his friends. The café is an extension of her family home and a way of being with and surrounding herself with her extended gay community. Debbie also works in the café so she can financially provide the HIV medication for her brother Vic. The way Debbie frets and fusses around Michael and his friends is indicative of Graphites. She is sensitive to conflicts and worries if anyone in her brood is in trouble. Debbie is loud and boisterous and could initially be mistaken for a rebellious Nat-mur; however, she is too excitable and open for a Nat-mur constitution. Debbie is also too emotionally shy to be a Nat-mur; she does not possess her own emotional confidence, she lives for the harmony of the group, and needs to be surrounded by the group to validate and reinforce her role. Her protection and defense of her son Michael and her adopted son Justin is emotionally supportive like a Graphites "mother hen"; it is not defensive like a protective Nat-mur.

The character of Mrs. Jennings, played by actor Elizabeth Spriggs, in the film *Sense and Sensibility*, based on the novel by Jane Austen and directed by Ang Lee, is also a classic picture of Graphites. Mrs. Jennings is a down-to-earth woman who lives her life through her family. She rushes to the aid of the newly arrived Dashwood family, which has recently lost father, home, and family estate. She takes it upon herself to have the recently impoverished Dashwood daughters married and well-looked-after in no time at all. Mrs. Jennings is a highly excitable character who never stops talking and rushing around in the pursuit of finding out all the latest gossip concerning her brood. Her life is fulfilled by the intrigues of the people around her. She is also equally upset and concerned by the tragedies and misfortunes of the Dashwoods. Her desire for family harmony is reflective of the Graphites desire for harmony and stability. Her nature is also reflective of the theme of graphite the mineral, madly rushing around trying to clump all the particles together.

The Emotional Legacy for Graphites

A caring nature can sometimes be the Graphites constitution's downfall. They are so sensitive to suffering and are so aware of others' feelings they can become totally overwhelmed and distressed, especially when their own family is sick or suffering. Their fears and insecurities can totally incapacitate them, and they do not have confidence the situation will resolve itself. It is a simplification to say they are negative; they simply become so anxious, they are incapable of being decisive. Being so concerned with every little conflict or disharmony, a Graphites is likely to give in to keep the peace. Their nonconfrontational nature is a strong emotional defense mechanism[90] to distract themselves from their inner turmoil. They get so overwhelmed by feelings they actually feel better from letting go of themselves and disintegrating into tears.

Graphites is not a very complex or dynamic personality. These people often feel like they are overlooked by life and the skills and attributes they bring to a relationship are not often seen or valued by others. In these circumstances they will present with more of the timidity and lack of confidence associated with their personality. Unhealthier Graphites people are often quite anxious about all sorts of decisions. The image of the particles of graphite rushing around and trying to clump together is very reflective of the nature of a

Graphites who is alone, without a partner or family. They often fret and get very anxious if they are not surrounded by family. Graphites can be very needy for reassurance of love. If they spend too much time alone they think about their fear of losing the person they love.

Graphites wants and needs more than anything in life to be in a loving, supportive relationship. The emotionalism associated with the constitutional picture is in the background if they feel like they are in a secure relationship, and they will feel very sad if not joined together with a partner. Single Graphites will go to work and will be very responsible but will constantly crave a partner and the security of family. It is very confusing for them to come to terms with the lack of a partner because they know they are so supportive. The flip side of this is a strong knowing they cannot be in a relationship with a constitution that is too insensitive. In a secure, happy relationship or surrounded by family or community, like Debbie with Michael and his friends, Graphites is very happy.

Staphisagrias pride themselves on being the pillar of society. Debbie's brother Vic, whom she looks after and protects, is Staphisagria. In one episode of the program, Vic is wrongly accused of homosexually soliciting an undercover policeman. His struggle to be able to get angry enough to stand up and fight the charges is the struggle of Staphisagrias to defend their right not to be abused. His own shame and guilt over his disease, HIV/AIDS, is also reflective of the battle of Staphisagrias not to feel abusive and disgusted toward themselves. The struggle to come out and defend himself in court is the theme of Staphisagrias to stop their own self-abuse. Staphisagrias have so much pride about not appearing undignified that to be able to get angry enough to defend themselves is very difficult.

For Graphites, the most important goal in relationships is to avoid conflict. It is very unlikely that Staphisagria will lash out at Graphites. This is very true for the relationship between Debbie and her brother. Debbie and Vic are always there for each other to help resolve the conflicts that each one can become embroiled in. Graphites people actually want to resolve conflict and disharmony, and Staphisagrias struggle with acknowledging they have conflict and disharmony.

Graphites would be a perfect constitution for the suppressive Staphisagria to have a relationship with. Graphites will not confront or attack Staphisagria. They are sensitive enough to be aware of the painful history Staphisagrias bring with them into the relationship. Graphites' strength in life is an ability to express sympathy and empathy for the suffering of others. Staphisagrias need time in their life to heal their hurts and trauma, and their self-abusive suppression, and Graphites will be happy to be sensitive to every mood change Staphisagrias are experiencing.

The Strength of Graphites with Staphisagria

Graphites is an honest constitution in the sense that Graphites people do not give to receive love in return; they are happy simply to love and support. Staphisagrias need to spend time in their lives in relationships that are not going to reinforce their need to suppress their feelings. Graphites will not abuse Staphisagrias or threaten their pride and dignity by taking advantage of them. Because Staphisagrias are trapped by their own pride, they do not respond appropriately to being taken advantage of, and they often think that standing up for themselves, responding appropriately with anger, is somehow undignified. This trap, of course, becomes a self-fulfilling prophesy. The result of holding down so much rage means that when Staphisagrias do explode, it is usually undignified and out of proportion to the circumstances; this then sinks them into feelings of shame and remorse. The circuit of suppression will be stopped for Staphisagrias with Graphites. Graphites will not suppress or repress Staphisagria and Graphites will not manipulate or take advantage of Staphisagria's feelings of worthlessness. Graphites will not fall into the trap with self-abusive, unhealthier Staphisagrias of abusing them because Graphites has nothing in the constitutional picture that would be emotionally or sexually stimulated by the role of abuser. Given time and the effect of being in a relationship with Graphites, Staphisagria will break the pattern of feeling repressed. Graphites, in turn, will feel satisfied that resolution of the conflict inside has occurred. Graphites mirrors the behavior of graphite the mineral, and this is a case of the very nature of a constitution having a healing effect.

Staphisagria and Mercurius

The Theme of Mercurius

Mercury is the only metal that does not hold its atoms together in orderly, regular rows and columns of metallic lattice like other metals. Mercury lacks a stable form and is constantly changing shape and reforming. The fact that this is a metal that cannot retain structure is reflected in the psyche of the constitutional picture of Mercurius. Mercurius is able to adapt and change quickly but Mercurius is also constantly reacting and unable to maintain order over emotional reactions. The mind of Mercurius is equally weak and unstructured and as reactive as the emotional. This degree of damage and changeable sensitivity is the theme of Mercurius. Reactivity and changeability are also the strength of Mercurius, which brings about a unique sharp ability to quickly adapt to new circumstances.

The Emotional Legacy of Mercurius

Mercurius is also listed with Staphisagria under the remedies in the repertory for "egotism." It is the way each constitution responds that makes the study of constitutional homeopathy quite unique, and Mercurius is no exception to this. They fear being found out and they fear that the fact they are not stable or solid will be exposed. It is how they react to their ego that makes them distinctive from any other constitution. The grip they have on sanity is tenuous, and they do not want anyone else to find this out. They know they are reactive to the environment around them, and it is this reactivity that undermines their feeling of sanity. The most distinctive element of the psyche of Mercurius is the hypersensitivity and hypervigilance to contradiction. This is the egoism of Mercurius. They react impulsively and the underlying instability of Mercurius creates a persona that is dictatorial and violent in the need to protect themselves.

Mercurius constitutional types literally will want to kill or destroy anyone who contradicts or humiliates them. The degree to which feelings of rage manifest depends, of course, on where the person sits along the spectrum of healthy to unhealthy. Mercurius, even when healthy, does not like to be contradicted and will always perceive contradiction as an attack. With so much to protect, Mercurius will often appear as very guarded and closed. Nat-mur can also appear closed; the difference is that if you prompt Nat-mur you are always able to see right under the surface the emotionalism that Nat-mur is trying to hold in. Mercurius is closed with none of the emotionalism under the surface. Mercurius can also present as conservative as Nat-mur; the difference is that Mercurius needs order and conservatism to provide protection from the lack of order Mercurius can often feel inside. Nat-mur needs order to guard against being hurt emotionally. Nat-mur is soft underneath a closed, often very guarded exterior. The emotional guarding in Mercurius is there because of a need to protect a fragile, unstable reactivity. They are also guarded because they need to protect a fragile ego.

Conflict will bring out the difference between the two constitutions. The reactivity of Mercurius is distinctive. The first reaction to being contradicted for Nat-mur is hurt. The first response for Mercurius is to attack. Nat-mur will later plot revenge and fantasize about it, while Mercurius will be unable to restrain an egoistic, impulsive hatred at being contradicted and will carry out the revenge.

The Emotional History behind Mercurius

The need to remain in control and to dictatorially control their environment is there to protect the fact that as a constitution Mercurius is inherently unstable emotionally and physically. The character of the policeman Javert, played by actor John Malkovich, in the film *Les Misérables* (with actor Gerard Dépardieu as Jean Valjean) is a classic version of the persona of Mercurius. As a child he was betrayed and humiliated when his father, who was the victim of criminal deception, lost the family's wealth. The shame and humiliation of being left poor is the motivation behind his relentless pursuit of criminals. His entire life's purpose is to seek revenge to ease his initial humiliation and shame at having lost egoistic status in the world. Javert uses his mercurial skills to understand the criminal mind. His mercurial quickness and changeability enable him to always predict their next move. The Mercurius need to remain above or apart from the rest of the human mass is played out beautifully by the character Javert. Mercurius is often accused of not committing emotionally in relationships. Their need to remain separate reflects the nature of the mercury atom when it loses its structure. Mercurius can also not afford to get too close to others in case the instability within the persona is discovered. Javert always remains separate from the rest of humanity, and at no point is he willing to become one of the criminals he despises. When faced with the unimaginable dilemma of his crime in letting Jean Valjean go free, his grip on his own life is also automatically abandoned. At the point in the film Javert abandons his vengeance and revenge, and his duty and structure as a policeman, he has no choice but to also abandon his grip on his right to live. Underlying his arrogance is a very fragile ego; once he abandons his position of revenge and duty, he has nothing to hang onto. Javert walks calmly into the water and drowns himself.

The other side of the nature of Mercurius is that this constitutional picture is reactive and responsive to the emotional states of others. This does not mean, as in the case of the empathy of Nat-mur, that it is an attribute. Nat-mur is able to emotively understand others' grief and hurts. Phosphorus is also able to feel others' discomfort and respond with love and kindness. Causticum is able to take on the pains of others and fight for their causes. With Mercurius, however, the sensitivity has no positive side. Mercurius is as sensitive as the mercurial nature of a thermometer responding to the changes in temperature. They are so overreactive and so oversensitive they lose their own identity. The mind of Mercurius is not strong enough to resist the influences of the emotional states of others. This reactivity constantly undermines the physical and mental health of Mercurius. Mercurius is as sensitive to changes in temperature as changes in emotions. Instability results in a fanatic mania, and the more unstable they feel the more they try to overcompensate by impulsive hyperactivity. The reactivity of Mercurius is the underlying reason behind the hypervigilance. Their sensibilities are so easily upset they are often obsessive about all disturbances.

As a homeopathic remedy, *Mercurius* is used when there is a marked destruction[91] of tissue. Mercury destroys and the symptoms of poisoning by the substance mercury are evident in the destructiveness visible in the personality of Mercurius. If unhealthy, the mental and emotional states of Mercurius slowly deteriorate and become unstable. The most important aspect of this for the constitution is that in their relationships it is crucial they are not destroyed by their partner or they do not destroy their partner.

The Challenge for Mercurius in Relationships

The film *The Piano Teacher,* which I discussed in the description of the constitution Staphisagria, is a good example of the destruction and the destructiveness of the constitution Mercurius. The character of the student Walter Klemmer is Mercurius. In his first interactions with Erika he is stimulated and inspired by her. He possesses all the positive characteristics of Mercurius and he is quick to pick up on how to respond to her emotional state. In their first interactions at the musical evening, he is able to quickly change the piece of music he was going to play to the one piece he knows will have impact on her feelings. Mercurius is responsive and often able to absorb skills very quickly. Walter Klemmer is a self-taught musician. He has no real desire to study music and it is not until he beomes enthralled with the music teacher Erika Kohut that he even considers it necessary to study. His obsession with her compels him to become her student. The instability of the mercurial mind often means they become obsessive over whatever stimulates them. Just as Javert was unable to let go of a life dedicated to the destruction of criminals, Walter is not able to let go of his fascination with Erika.

The problem for Walter Klemmer in this situation is that Erika portrays the classic version of Staphisagria in its most extreme unhealthy side. The challenge for anyone in a relationship with a self-abuser is not to fall into the role of fulfilling their fantasies and becoming the abuser. The problem for Mercurius will be that Mercurius cannot resist restructuring by a stronger constitution. The positive aspect of this is the ability Mercurius has to pick up skills very quickly. The negative aspect is Mercurius is easily destroyed and manipulated by more destructive personalities.

Erika starts to play with Walter's emotions. There is a wonderful scene in the toilets at the music conservatorium, where their first sexual encounter takes place. Erika stimulates him sexually but does not let him achieve orgasm. Walter is clearly humiliated. The Achilles heel for Mercurius is being humiliated or undermined. In the process of Erika playing out her sexual fantasies and perversions, Walter feels he is being insulted and humiliated. The most important aspect of the abuse he eventually inflicts on her is his inability to resist the sadomasochistic relationship that the Staphisagria Erika wants and has successfully managed to manipulate him into. Mercurius does not have the strength of ego to resist a stronger constitution. By nature, Mercurius is responsive and reactive to others' emotions and controls. In their last interaction of the film, it is obvious that Walter feels he has destroyed Erika and he feels triumphant; however, he has also played the part that she as a Staphisagria has mapped out – he has become her abuser. The film ends painfully with Erika feeling ashamed and disgusted by herself and abused by him. The cycle is complete for Staphisagria as Erika then inflicts this shame and abuse on herself in the form of cutting herself. The cycle of abuser, and shame, and self-abuse then continues for Staphisagria, while Mercurius has fallen into being controlled by her and has in turn become the abuser.

Because Mercurius is unable to hold a solid form, Mercurius will always change dramatically in each relationship. In a relationship with a more solid, unchanging constitution like Nat-mur, Mercurius will be more stable. In a relationship with Staphisagria, Mercurius will have to work very hard not to fall into the trap of abusing or suppressing Staphisagria. Even if very healthy, Mercurius will have to work very hard at also not being abused.

Sulphur Partnerships

The Theme of Sulphur

In the wonderful comic strip *Peanuts*,™ Linus declares to the world that when he grows up he is going to be a doctor. He then says he is going to be even better than a doctor, he is going to be a "GREAT Doctor." The enthusiasm that Linus has grows from being a doctor to an even greater doctor and then grows to even loftier heights of being the learned doctor who writes a "syndicated medical column." The ultimate achievement of the Sulphur Linus was to be the accomplished publisher of a medical paper. In this one discourse by Linus, the entire Sulphur personality picture comes alive. Sulphurs have an amazing inspirational belief in their greatness. Sulphurs have such passionate enthusiasm for their pursuits in life it is infectious, and you can't help but be inspired. This belief in themselves can either be viewed as delusional, egoistic mania or creative genius, depending on how you look at it. Sulphurs are so enthralled with their own creative process they usually neglect the practical necessities of life. Linus is not going to be a doctor to help the sick or because it is a good career; what he wants to do with medicine is a far loftier ideal in his mind. Sulphurs are in pursuit of far greater ideals than the mundane and Sulphurs do not really care how the rest of the world views them. Sulphurs are enthralled by creative pursuits and the creative intellectual pursuit of knowledge.

There are, of course, many Sulphurs who are not recognized as geniuses or who are not even recognized as great by the rest of the world. The important point is that Sulphurs as a constitution have a powerful enough ego and belief in themselves that they see themselves as creative geniuses, whether they are or not. No matter what their pursuit is in life, their good opinion of themselves does not change. Lycopodiums, in contrast, will be able to boast and socially self-congratulate, and then will go home and doubt themselves. Sulphurs suffer no doubt about themselves.

One of the great desires of Sulphurs is to discover a new thought or theory. Sulphurs have optimism and hopefulness in life. They either inspire or frustrate others, who might view their beliefs as impractical philosophizing about life and basically a lot of hot air. Sulphurs have an explosive anger and passionate temperament that others will view either as flashes of visionary insight or just a bad temper. Sulphurs have a self-obsession with their own processes in life that could be viewed as the eccentricity of a genius or the pure selfishness of an egomaniac.

Sulphurs need the world to recognize and acknowledge their ideals. The visionary philosopher Samuel Johnson (definitely a Sulphur) wrote in 1766 about the inability of the world to understand his pursuits in life and the disdain with which he viewed the values of the worldly:

> My zeal for languages may seem, perhaps, rather over-heated, even to those by whom I desire to be well esteemed. To those who have nothing in their thoughts but trade or policy, present power, or present money, I should not think it necessary to defend my opinions.... Knowledge always desires increase; it is like fire, which must first be kindled by some external agent. (Boswell, p. 321)

The Challenge for Sulphur in Life

Sulphurs need the world to acknowledge their brilliance. If the world does not acknowledge them, it is the fault of everyone else in the world who lacks the insight into their quest for knowledge – it is never Sulphurs' fault. This drive for ego satisfaction can also be viewed as either inspirational genius or chauvinistic.[92] Hahnemann, the founder of homeopathy, was supposedly Sulphur. It is very probable that a lot of visionary founders were Sulphur, as it takes a certain amount of ego strength and unfaltering belief in your pursuit to be able to discover new thoughts, and Sulphurs definitely possess these qualities. Sulphurs have the strength of character to view themselves (as expressed by Johnson) as an agent to kindle the fire of knowledge for the rest of the world.

My other favorite Sulphur is the writer Balzac. The actor Gérard Depardieu plays a wonderful Balzac in the film *Balzac: A Life of Passion*. During Balzac's early career, the world did not recognize his genius as a great writer. He spent the majority of his life struggling with financial security and recognition. His long-suffering mother kept giving him money to fund his new pursuits but she did not see the genius in her son and wanted him to be a lawyer. Sulphurs have an overwhelming need to be recognized. The fact that his mother did not think highly of him caused Balzac enormous pain, and spurred a lot of the bad business choices he subsequently made. In the film, he sets up a printing shop to print his own books because other printing firms are not enlightened enough to see his genius. The venture, of course, loses a fortune because the general public do not read his books or recognize his brilliance. He is continually ending up in debtor's prison and is continually being financially bailed out by the friends who recognize his genius as a writer. At no point in this process is there any doubt or sign of guilt or embarrassment in Balzac's mind about his continual acceptance of their financial support. Balzac has an unfaltering belief in his genius. It is important not to assume that all Sulphurs are hopeless with money. The aspect that is important to emphasize is that Sulphurs will always be passionately blind to the practicalities surrounding the particular pursuit that interests them and they will always spend indiscriminately on whatever project inspires them. It might not necessarily equate that Sulphurs will be poor or frivolous with money, but if Sulphurs are inspired they will not do a financial[93] plan before they follow their dreams.

When Balzac does have money, he spends it on indulging either his senses by buying beautiful objects or by overindulging in good food and wine.[94] The need to be seen as a great and important person drives him to continually waste his money on showy furniture and *objets d'art*[95] to boost his social importance. The other reason Sulphurs need to be surrounded by beautiful objects is that they need the outer world to reflect their inner idealistic visions. One does not get the impression that Balzac ever feels compelled to pay back his mother or friends for their generosity. Rather, when he has money, he would also indulge in exuberant spending in the salons of Paris. The total accumulated debts from his failed businesses and ostentatious lifestyle left him owing 60,000 francs in the year 1828 (which for the times sounds like quite a substantial sum).

Balzac never gave up his dream or belief in his genius and was always hopeful of recognition; he was apparently well known for his egoistic boasting. Sulphurs have an amazing ability to block out or selectively forget adversity. It is as if they have been blessed with a selective vision of themselves. Sulphurs do not acknowledge their own faults or spend much time gazing at their navels. This is not to say that Balzac was not given to moments of melancholy, he was, but his depression, like that of all Sulphurs, was unique. Sulphurs definitely sink into hopeless despair and catatonic moroseness, but they never doubt themselves; instead, they despair over the injustice of life and the ignorance of the world to recognize their genius. Balzac, aside from wanting recognition from his mother, was not particularly interested in who she was or how she felt about her dwindling finances as a result of pulling him out of debt. He was only interested in fame and fortune or his mother's money because he needed both to pursue his writing. His love affairs with numerous rich, aristocratic women were also always a means to an end so that he could fund his writing. Balzac was not a man to waste his time on social niceties or placating his mother; the acquisition of her money was seen by him as a means to an end, to further pursuit of his creative ideals. Balzac's characters in his books are continually in conflict with the bourgeois values of the time, and Balzac himself by all accounts was not exactly conforming to the ideals of society. Sulphurs can be very disinterested in everything and everyone they find uninspiring. On the basis of this description, why would anyone wish to have a relationship or any sort of friendship with such a self-obsessed person?

The Sulphur Strength in Relationships

The homeopathic remedy *Sulphur* is derived from a dilution of the volcanic element sulfur. When a volcano explodes there is a strange magnetism and passion that draws you to it; the very nature of the passion and power behind the explosion is beautiful because it is alive and active, and it elicits wonder and fear in the spectator. Gérard Depardieu is such a good actor that he was able to portray the essence of why someone would fall in love with Sulphur. In one scene in the film *Balzac: A Life of Passion,* Balzac concentrates all his energy on seducing a woman. Admittedly, it is definitely in Balzac's financial interest to win her over and this is, of course, the inspiration behind his pursuit; however, it would have to be the most passionate love scene in any movie that I have ever seen. Sulphurs are very passionate about what inspires them; if inspired by a person, they could be quite irresistible to that person. Sulphurs might present as nonreflective of their own selfishness but they are expansive in trying to passionately and creatively inspire the world. Balzac's countess Eveline Hanska, who he eventually marries, abandons all her estates and wealth just so she can be with him. Her first husband, although providing financially well for her, was completely cold and emotionless, while Balzac the Sulphur, in contrast, is intensely passionate. She does not abandon all reason, however; she leaves Balzac's love letters with her daughter for future insurance against poverty. She rightly foresees that the depths of passion in his love letters will some day be recognized. Marriage to the countess meant that Balzac was able to clear all his debts. Aside from her obvious wealth, he was also enthralled that she believed in his genius — this is what inspires him the most. The reason for falling in love with her in the first place was that she wrote to him expressing her adoration of his writing. Even though he needs her money, he needs her adoration of his genius more.

Sulphurs give back to all relationships with their passion. The power of Sulphur is the passion and hopefulness that elicits possibilities and fires hopefulness and optimism. There is a crazy scene in the film where they are traveling to Paris in the snow; at every stop he buys her a present to remember him by. Sulphurs do not hold back from completely indulging in their experience of life, and this quality can be very attractive. When Sulphurs fall in love, they do so with such intensity that the object of that passion is seen as the most beautiful possession they own. This sort of passion is very attractive, and for Eveline Hanska it was well worth giving up her castle, inheritance, and position in Russian society. Sulphurs have a generosity that appears to be in opposition to their need for financial security. Sulphurs' need to surround themselves with *objets d'art*[96] and great opulence is also reflected in their lavish generosity toward loved ones and friends. (Quite often with Sulphurs, it is actually your money or the bank's that they are spending.) Financial security is only seen as a means to an end. The goal for Sulphurs is their aspiration to inspire.

The Emotional Legacy for Sulphur

Healthy Sulphurs are intensely passionate, intensely creative, and intensely inspirational. Unhealthy[97] Sulphurs are intensely depressed, intensely hopeless, intensely irritable, intensely withdrawn, and intensely cynical of the world. Sulphurs become unhealthy if they are not acknowledged or needed, and, most important, if they lose their freedom to do what they want in life. Sulphurs become unhealthy if they are not recognized all the time as great by the world. The psychodynamic force behind the Sulphur persona reflects the power and explosive nature of the element sulfur. Sulfur is only extracted from under the earth's surface with intense heat of 115° Celsius. Sulphurs sink into depression if they are not met with a worldly acknowledgment that is able to match how much they have struggled to come out from deep within the core of the earth's structure. It is a somatic experience for Sulphurs to be recognized. It is almost as if Sulphurs have conjured up so much force behind the exploding volcano that to not have it recognized is an insult. Sulphurs, if ignored, have an intense amount of irritable, sulphuric, corrosive angst.

The best portrayal of the depressed irritable genius who is waiting for the world to recognize his genius is the comic book caricature portrayal of the personality of Harvey Pekar in the film *American Splendor*. Directed and written by Robert Pulcini and Shari Springer Berman, *American Splendor* is a documentary-style film of a true living person who becomes a comic book personality. The film constantly smudges the lines between the real-life writer Harvey Pekar and the writer's interpretation of the comic book character Harvey Pekar, played by actor[98] Paul Giamatti. Harvey Pekar,[99] the superego of the comic book personality, is a larger-than-life caricature of the unhealthy Sulphur persona. He is constantly negative and depressed, and totally self-absorbed. He is a dismal failure in relationships and marriage. He feels irritable and unrecognized constantly. His job as a clerk in the basement of a hospital bores and depresses him. His flat is a domestic wasteland of rubbish and disorganization. He goes through life cynically destroying everyone and every interaction. Eventually his wry, caustic perspective of life inspires him to turn every boring interaction in his life into a comic strip. Harvey turns his introverted, irritable humor into genius inspiration and creates the comic book caricature of himself, Harvey Pekar.

Harvey slowly starts to become recognized by the underground comic book art scene. It is when the wider world starts to acknowledge him that the true nature of the Sulphur Harvey comes to the fore. When Harvey realizes that he is invited as a guest on a popular TV show so the host and audience can laugh at him, the Sulphur ego decides to defend with rage and anger. Like Balzac, Harvey does not waste his time on social niceties. Sulphurs have a need to be recognized but they will not be manipulated. Sulphurs have a very strong sense of their own ego and they are never wrong – it is always everyone else who is truly perverse. The very first scene in the film is of Harvey as a child getting angry with a woman at Halloween because she points out he is not in costume. For Harvey it is the woman who is crazy for expecting him to wear a Halloween costume; it does not occur to Harvey that in fact he is the one who has not conformed because he is not in costume like the other children. It is this sense of belief in themselves that fuels the Sulphur cynicism and ill humor with the world. Sulphurs have a cynical disinterest in everything and everyone they find uninspiring. His wife Joyce, played by actor Hope Davis, describes Harvey as having "delusions of grandeur." Sulphur is either a brilliant, inspired genius or suffers from delusions of grandeur; the interpretation is up to the beholder.

The Challenge for Sulphur in Relationships

A successful relationship for Sulphurs has to be with a partner who believes in their pursuits and passions in life and who believes in them. It is when this passion is not acknowledged that Sulphurs can become depressed and dejected. Sulphurs are listed in the eighteenth-century homeopathic *Materia medica* under "selfishness." With Sulphurs it is not selfishness in the sense of only caring about themselves; it is more a case of being totally absorbed by their own thoughts and creative processes. The difference is quite possibly a case of semantics, but it is crucial to understanding why Sulphurs will sink into hopelessness. The character Harvey in the film completely fell apart if he did not receive all the attention and notice he felt he deserved. Sulphurs are so passionate about how they feel that rejection can throw them into despair. Sulphurs will quickly sink into being ill-humored, peevish, and irritated by everything in the world if things are not going their way. The Achilles heel of Sulphurs, which can throw them into an unhealthy state, is rejection.[100]

It is important that a partner of Sulphur knows what to expect. Sulphurs will be off all the time pursuing their creative passions and their partner will be left with the practical necessities of life. There is a wonderful scene in *American Splendor* where Harvey invites Joyce back to his flat for the first time and the mess is unbelievable. His defense is that he did not want to delude her about the true nature of things by tidying up for her visit. Only Sulphurs would have such a caustic, cynical analysis to support their lack of domesticity. Balzac was equally recognized for his self-absorption. He supposedly wrote up to sixteen hours a day and consumed exorbitant amounts of coffee in the process. If he was not writing he was relaxing and indulging in his other passions – wine, women, and food. Sulphurs see they have a duty to altruistically stimulate the fire of creativity and thought in the belly of society, but they are not necessarily conventional in the methods they use.

Definitely, Sulphurs are considered to be one of the most self-absorbed constitutions. It is important in trying to determine your constitution that you ask yourself what the core motivation is behind all your actions. The egoistic selfishness of Sulphurs is distinctive. They are inspired by a sense of their own greatness and the need to inspire the rest of the world to see the beauty they see. The goal is as Linus expressed: the creative inspiration of others by publishing your thoughts for the rest of the world to read.

Sulphur and Lachesis

The Theme of Lachesis

The homeopathic remedy *Lachesis* is derived from a dilution of the poison of the Surukuku snake of South America, commonly known as the bushmaster snake. It has a reputation, when disturbed, of chasing its victim and attacking, and is known as one of the most vicious snakes because most snakes will choose to run rather than fight. Lachesis as a constitution carries an energy that is reflective of the hyper-vigilance of the bushmaster snake. Even when Lachesis is trying to charm and entice, Lachesis is continually aware of any sort of perceived competition or threat.

Sulphur and Lachesis Together in the Film *All About Eve*

The best example I have ever seen of Lachesis and Sulphur are in the film *All About Eve*, written and directed by Joseph L. Mankiewicz. Bette Davis plays the character Margo, who is Lachesis,[101] and Gary Merrill plays Margo's besotted lover Bill Simpson, who is Sulphur.

Margo is the venomous Lachesis – sharp-witted and sharp-tongued. She is envious, jealous, suspicious, and very possessive of Bill. She is also passionate and vividly expressive, intensely vibrant, attractive, exciting, and gorgeous – and Bill adores her. The venom of Lachesis is a powerful stimulant and Sulphur will be excited by the bitchiness of Lachesis. Many other constitutions would be devastated, but Sulphurs will be inspired by the aggressiveness of Lachesis. Sulphurs will feel they have found a partner who can match them in intensity and explosiveness. Sulphurs will be excited and stimulated by Lachesis and they will feel like their passion has been cut loose. Sulphurs, more than any other constitution (even Lycopodium), are the prime candidate to be attracted to Lachesis. Sulphurs will be drawn into the intensity, passion, and sexual magnetism of Lachesis, and the eternal philosopher within their nature will be enticed by the clever tongue and expansiveness of the Lachesis mind.

The sole purpose of the charm and venom of Lachesis is to entice and stun its intended victim so that Lachesis can feel secure that the territory is exclusively controlled by Lachesis. The creative pursuits of Sulphurs could consequently be seen as a restriction to Lachesis, and Lachesis is threatened by restrictions. Sulphurs' inherent belief in themselves will also be seen as a threat. Margo is very quick to point out how "conceited" Bill is. Jealous and envious, Lachesis will not allow Sulphur passion or freedom. All of the passion of Sulphurs' energy must be concentrated on Lachesis; no one must be more important than Lachesis.

It is not surprising in the film *All About Eve* that, when Bill is about to fly off to Hollywood to pursue his own career, Margo so aptly puts him in his place. There is a wonderful scene at the airport where Margo reminds him of his attributes just in case he might consider leaving her. Margo is very quick to tell him he is "conceited, thoughtless, and messy," and that there is no point to "get stuck on some glamour puss" because he really is not much of a catch or, as she states it, a "bargain." What is so ironic is that in comparison to the portrayal of Lachesis by Margo, the Sulphur Bill looks comparatively meek and mild and not at all conceited. When Bill returns from his trip, Margo immediately realizes that the "innocent Eve" is a threat to her territory. Lachesis the snake strikes, living up to the reputation that the bushmaster snake has over its territory. Margo is very quick to point out that she owns and manages "exclusive rights and privileges" over Bill. This Lachesis woman will fight her rival to the bitter end. She knows what belongs to her and will be passionately aggressive when fighting for it. A little later in the same scene, Margo (Bette Davis) comes out with her famous line, "Fasten your seatbelts, it is going to be a bumpy night."

The fact that Margo mentions Bill's messy nature is also wonderfully indicative of Sulphurs' love of chaos and disorder in their lives and in their surroundings. Sulphurs will also find the erratic, chaotic nature of Lachesis as stimulating and exciting as they find clutter and mess stimulating.

The Emotional Challenge for Lachesis in Relationships

This is where we see the downfall – the unhealthy Lachesis consumed with suspicion, paranoia, jealousy, and envy. Sulphur Bill stays passionately loyal; her suspicions of him are completely paranoiac. Margo has underestimated the depth of love and loyalty that her Sulphur has for her. All she sees at this point is her own rage and suspicious jealousy. Bill is passionate in his attempts to rescue her and he pleads with her to abandon her jealousy and "paranoiac tantrums." He sees she is not only hurting herself but him too. He declares his love for her and asks her to marry him. It doesn't surprise me that, in his attempts to rescue her from the hatred and jealousy that consume her, he walks into her territory even more, by asking her to marry him. Apparently in real life after the shooting of the film the actor Gary Merrill left his wife and married Bette Davis. They later separated and Bette Davis is reported to have said that letting him go was one of the great mistakes of her life. I am sure she would have been hard-pressed to find another man, unless he was also Sulphur, who would be so devoted to her. It is truly inspiring to see the depth of love that Bill has for Margo when he asks her to marry him. It is this passion and devotion that makes Sulphur attractive.

This is a relationship in which the delusional need of Sulphurs to surround themselves with showy possessions could be their downfall. Lachesis has the far more powerful ego. Lachesis will not allow Sulphur the freedom to pursue lofty ideals. Lachesis is the only pursuit that Sulphurs will be allowed to concentrate their passions on. The relationship for Lachesis with Sulphur is the ideal relationship for Lachesis. If Lachesis can move past the feelings of jealousy over Sulphur's creative passions, then this relationship is what Lachesis will need. Sulphur will always allow Lachesis freedom. The need for freedom is even more important to Lachesis than it is to Sulphur. With Sulphurs it is crucial to have freedom to be able to pursue their creative passions; with Lachesis, it is integral to feeling secure.

The flip side of this relationship, which in the case of Bette Davis was played out in real life, is that it is hard for a Lachesis to make a commitment to a relationship. The need to always be on guard in life results in an underlying insecurity about commitment to marriage. Marriage is interpreted as having lost control over territory. They have a knowing of the territory[102] that they own or guard, and if they are outside of their comfort zone it is interpreted as a threat to their life. Bill referred to her "paranoiac tantrums" for the very reason that Lachesis interprets threat as potentially life-threatening.

The Emotional Legacy for Lachesis

Lachesis is far happier in a relationship with the type of person who is happy to let Lachesis have control, space, and freedom. The price for Lachesis to lose that freedom is too high. When they feel threatened they move into the unhealthy, more restless,[103] uneasy state of Lachesis. They have the need to compete and destroy all competition when they feel threatened; the pursuit and destruction of Eve by Margo is a beautiful example of this.

Healthy Lachesis, in a relationship that does not bring up anxieties or threat, can present as opposite to the unhealthy. They are warm, charming, entertaining, and amusing. They entice with their speech – not to overwhelm, but to charm and stimulate. Sulphurs are an expansive constitution; they have a genuine need to inspire.

At no point will Sulphurs restrict, control, or restrain, and Lachesis will not feel under threat by Sulphurs. Sulphurs also have no great need to force Lachesis into making commitments in the form of an official marriage certificate. Sulphurs' allowing Lachesis space and freedom, and control over thoughts and feelings, will make Lachesis very happy. Sulphurs will be equally stimulated by Lachesis and will feel passionately excited and alive in the presence of such a powerful stimulant as the venom of Lachesis. The lesson for the jealous Lachesis is to allow Sulphurs to have their creative passion outside of the relationship.

Sulphur and Magnesium Carbonica

The Emotional History behind Mag-Carb

The homeopathic remedy *Mag-carb* is often the first remedy I would think of using for the anxieties of an orphaned or abandoned child. The same remedy can also be applicable for adults who feel like they were abandoned as a child. A child does not need to have physically lost its parents to experience abandonment. Children are spending long days in childcare or are being left at home with nannies, while their parents spend long days at work. Not every child will feel abandoned if left with a nanny or at childcare, but the child who does absorb this experience as an abandonment trauma[104] will often grow up to become the constitution Mag-carb. Mag-carbs experience a sense of underlying dread and apprehension of potential rejection and abandonment. This anxiety is reflected in the need that Mag-carbs have to protect themselves from conflict or disharmony.

Much of the trauma that Mag-carbs absorb into their psyche occurs during childhood. Many of their trauma-centered memories are not on the surface or able to be easily remembered because Mag-carbs have quite often repressed them. The pattern of repressing painful experiences continues and as adults they shut down emotionally and suffer from depression. Depression is one of the main reasons a Mag-carb adult will consult me for treatment. The habit of denying or repressing painful experiences is a hard pattern for Mag-carbs to break; rather than allowing themselves to get in touch with these feelings, Mag-carbs continue the habit of repression into adulthood. Mag-carbs have a switched-off emotional façade of controlled calmness. The calm exterior is flat, monotone, and slightly unfriendly — often reminiscent of a person on antidepressant medication. Mag-carbs are sitting on years of suppressed experiences and they have a very definite desire not to feel any more pain, so it is understandable that Mag-carbs would hate any sort of fights or disagreements, particularly within their family or home.

The other defense mechanism that Mag-carbs can have is to deny that they have any need for people at all. They convince themselves they do not even need to talk[105] to others and this isolated repression is then able to protect them from any potential upsets. It is also quite common to see Mag-carbs suffering from no experience of apprehension or depression, but rather from dreadful, unexplainable, shifting muscle aches and pains[106] that come about for no reason. Years of holding onto feelings also has the effect of suppressing their physical energy. Every step they take has the appearance of exhausting them.

The Emotional Needs of Mag-Carb in Relationships

The fact that Mag-carbs are not in touch with what they are feeling leaves them with a constant generalized feeling of apprehension and indecision[107] — it is much harder for Mag-carbs to make decisions than it is for anyone else. This is a constitution that needs constant reassurance of love. Mag-carbs look toward a secure stable home[108] to ease their anxiety. A relationship with a partner who is loyal and sure is crucial to the health of Mag-carbs. Mag-carbs have strong fears they will be abandoned by their partner in the same way their parents abandoned them. Mag-carbs are the constitution who will work to hold the family together in adversity, because they need the security of home and family to provide them with comfort and strength.

Based on my knowledge of Sulphur it would appear on first impression to be an unlikely relationship for Sulphurs to enter into because Sulphurs are not noted for their love of responsibility. Sulphurs do not like responsibility, nor do they like being backed into a corner, or made to feel like they have to do something they do not want to do. Sulphurs will, however, find an enormous amount of ego satisfaction from this relationship and will see that being needed is a worthy ideal. Sulphur's ego and potency in this world is based on being needed and recognized; Mag-carbs by their very nature of needing nourishment, care, and stability will constantly reinforce in Sulphurs how much they are needed. Sulphurs will also use the security obsessions of Mag-carbs to pursue their ideals.

Is Co-Dependency Always Unhealthy?

Traditional psychology has always said co-dependent relationships are unhealthy for both partners. If both constitutions choose a partner who enables them to remain healthy, it makes sense to assess this relationship combination, from a homeopathic standpoint, as being successful even if it falls into the classic definition of co-dependency. Mag-carbs will often set up co-dependent relationships with people. Mag-carbs not only need the other person, they also like to make sure the other person needs them. If the other person in a relationship with Mag-carb wants to withdraw support, then Mag-carbs can be very manipulative and needy. There are not too many constitutions that have the strength of personality or ego to be able to walk away from, or stand up to, the neediness of Mag-carb. There are also not too many constitutions that will not harbor feelings of resentment or anger at being manipulated. Sulphurs have the strength of ego to walk away from Mag-carbs when they need some space. They are also encompassing and expansive enough in their love that they will not hold onto feelings of resentment at being manipulated.

Except for matters to do with money, it is very hard to manipulate Sulphur. Sulphurs are able to be manipulated because they do not know how to be practical with money management.[109] Mag-carbs are aware of their need for security and will be very practical and careful with money. The carbonica side to their nature means they hoard money, holding onto everything and not letting go, and the magnesium side to their nature means they will make sure they work hard in life to secure a solid financial base. What is interesting about Sulphurs is they also set up co-dependent relationships. Sulphurs will feel important and potent because they will be needed by Mag-carbs and, in trade, Sulphurs will want to be looked after. What Sulphurs need is to be able to pursue their altruistic dreams; to do this, Sulphurs need financial support. The most important thing to remember with Sulphurs is they are motivated by idealistic beliefs in a better society. Sulphurs believe their purpose in life is to altruistically inspire and stimulate creative thought. It is the sulphuric fantasies about their creative projects and goals that will entice and hold Sulphurs to Mag-carbs. Sulphurs are aware of their co-dependent need for financial support from Mag-carbs, but this will not concern them in the least.

I recently asked a Sulphur man what his occupation in life was. His answer was a textbook case of Sulphur. He replied, "I like to meet people for lunch or breakfast. I am a great philosophizer. I like to share my insights, get to know what others think about life, then I like to go down to my property and dig the earth with my hands." This is such a beautiful Sulphur answer; what other constitution would respond that way to the question of what he did for a living?[110] It's easy to see from this answer why this Sulphur man would need the practical money skills of a Mag-carb.

The exchange for Mag-carbs comes in the security of knowing that Sulphurs will not leave, and this feeling of security allows Mag-carbs to be healthy. Sulphurs are an expansive and inspiring constitution, and they love to feel they have inspired others. In exchange for support of their creative ideals and pursuits, Sulphurs will be eternally grateful and adoring. When they love, Sulphurs throw their whole being into the passion of loving. The most important thing in life for Sulphurs is to be able to pursue their passion. Balzac knew what he needed in life was support[111] for his writing. Mag-carbs will be content with the dependency that Sulphurs will have on them and Sulphurs will be delighted that they have been able to find a partner willing to support them in their pursuits. Sulphurs will pursue their ideals and then come back when they are ready; meanwhile, Mag-carbs will not be upset or insecure because they know Sulphur will return. Mag-carbs know that the exchange rate is equal and fair in this relationship.

Mag-carbs will be quite happy to create dependency[112] in their loved ones but they do not often acknowledge it to themselves. Just as they shut down or push their feelings inside, they often set up the same sort of convoluted process in relationships because to concentrate on their feelings of insecurity is a little too close to home. Every constitution is motivated by different emotional needs. A Nat-mur in a relationship with Sulphur could easily be hurt by Sulphur's selfish pursuit of goals, and many constitutions in a relationship with Mag-carb could tire of Mag-carb's constant neediness. This is why it is so important to understand and accept each other's constitutional needs. Mag-carbs will react very differently to Nat-murs. Mag-carbs know that Sulphurs are never going to leave them, so they actually feel very secure and content with this arrangement. Mag-carbs interpret all of life through their own emotional needs and insecurities.

The film *Her Majesty Mrs. Brown,* directed by John Madden, has a wonderful example of a Mag-carb in the character of Queen Victoria and a Sulphur in the character of Mr. Brown. The portrayal of Queen Victoria by actor Judy Dench is a Mag-carb in a grieving state after having lost her adored husband Albert. The exhaustive length of time she has been grieving, her suppressive nature of grieving, and her apprehensiveness about letting go of the grief are Mag-carb. It is obvious that, without the support of her beloved Albert, she is struggling with feelings of insecurity and needs desperately to hold onto the memory of him by grieving for an interminable amount of time. This is the nature of Mag-carbs when they feel abandoned. The character of Queen Victoria and her devotion to family and harmony is also revealed as the film progresses.

Mr. Brown is brought to court in the hope he will be able to encourage the Queen to leave the castle and go riding again. Mr. Brown, played by actor Billy Connolly, is a headstrong Scottish Highlander who takes his service to his Queen very seriously and passionately.

His sulphuric passion for life is able to compel her to abandon her long-lasting grief and start to live again. The Queen becomes more and more dependent and happy in Mr. Brown's company, and they both grow to need each other. Queen Victoria feels she can return to the demanding role of head of state if she has Mr. Brown to depend upon. He in turn believes he is important to her, and he passionately believes he is the only one who can protect her. Sulphurs need to be seen as important in life. This relationship is based on the fulfillment of mutual co-dependency. The story is unfortunately of unrequited love because such a relationship between a servant and the Queen would have been viewed as a potential threat to the monarchy and government.

Sulphur and Mag-Carb Together in the Film
American Splendor

The personality and relationship between the two comic book characters in the film *American Splendor* are Mag-carb and Sulphur. *American Splendor* is a documentary-style exposé of the life of Harvey Pekar. The film switches between the real-life Harvey Pekar and the comic book character and the film's caricature of Harvey, played by actor Paul Giamatti. Harvey Pekar the caricature is the classic cynical and irritable, caustic Sulphur who is totally depressed and downtrodden with his life. Harvey is inspired to make a comic book exposé of his wry, cynical perceptions of his social interactions in everyday life. Because Harvey is Sulphur, most of the comic book is self-involved grumbling about how the actions and feelings of everyone in the world either annoy him or inconvenience him. His partner Joyce,[113] played by actor Hope Davis, is also exposed and dissected in the comic book with the same degree of cynical dismemberment.

Joyce the comic book caricature, as revealed through the eyes of Harvey, is Mag-carb. Consequently, the depression that Joyce[114] experiences is also revealed in terms of how it inconveniences Harvey. Joyce is portrayed as the more extreme, unhealthy presentation of Mag-carb. In the comic book caricature presentation, Joyce is filled with depressive gloom and fatalism. He also describes her as so depressed she is never able to lift her body off the futon.[115] Joyce moved to a new city and gave up her career and security to move in with Harvey, and for Mag-carb this would have the effect of being extremely upsetting. The fact she sinks into chronic depression and is unable to get out of bed after also hearing that Harvey is not prepared to have his vasectomy reversed is also conveniently glossed over. Joyce craves a normal functioning family and wants to have children and a sense of belonging. These are the normal desires and needs of Mag-carb. Harvey does not want children[116] and Joyce sinks into a classic Mag-carb depressive abandonment. Harvey's frustration with her is always described and assessed on the basis of his own needs in the relationship. His irritation is solely based on the fact she is not there to meet his needs, and he is forced to look after her. The line he throws her does not have too much slack in the sense that there is not a lot of time for understanding her depression and grief.

The fact that Harvey also needs her to look after him is not mentioned until he can use her absence to his emotional advantage in the telling of the story of "who is there for whom." Joyce rarely gets to tell her side of the story. Harvey continually dismisses her observations and talks over the top of her. Harvey only concentrates on allocating blame, and it is because Joyce goes off to Israel to save orphaned children that he sinks into decay and disarray. Because she is not there to care for him, his life starts to disintegrate. The fact that his life was like that before she entered it is conveniently not mentioned. The fact that she feels disemboweled and useless in her life and relationship with him is also not acknowledged, and all her attempts to tidy up the apartment or create any space for herself being actively sabotaged by him are also conveniently not acknowledged. Harvey only emphasizes that Joyce has this need to go off and look after abandoned children. This is a perfect description of Sulphurs in their most unhealthy, self-absorbed, self-involved state. His discovery of a cancerous lump in his testes happens when she is away, and that makes matters even worse. The one thing that Sulphurs fear is illness. His inability to acknowledge or deal with the lump until she comes home is also a classic portrayal of the unhealthy side of Sulphurs when they try to avoid responsibility.

Sulphurs will also set up co-dependency relationships[117] in life and be equally as comfortable as Mag-carbs with the dynamic that results. Harvey needs Joyce as much as she needs to be with him. The symbiotic co-dependency between them is wonderful, yet both of them have a frustration and irritation with the need and love they have for each other. This film is a wonderful portrayal of the need and dependency and fulfillment that they are able to bring to each other as Sulphur and Mag-carb.

Bibliography

Bailey, Philip, M, M.D. *Homeopathic Psychology,* Berkeley, California, North Atlantic Books, 1995.

Bell, Gail, *The Poison Principle.* Sydney, Australia, Picador, Pan Macmillan Publishing, 2001.

Bohjalian, Chris, *The Law of Similars.* New York, Harmony Books, 1999.

Boswell, James, *The Life of Samuel Johnson.* London, Everymans, 1994.

Coulter, Catherine, *Portraits of Homoeopathic Medicines.* Berkeley Springs, West Virginia, Ninth House Publishing, 2002.

Dickens, Charles, *David Copperfield.* New York, Macmillan, 1962.

Hahnemann, Dr. Samuel, *The Chronic Diseases.* New Delhi, B. Jain Publishers, 1995.

Høeg, Peter, *Miss Smillas's Feeling for Snow.* London, Flamingo Publishing, 1994.

Sankaran, Rajan, *The Soul of Remedies.* Santa Cruz, Bombay, Homoeopathic Medical Publishers, 1997.

Schulz, Charles M., *Slide Charlie Brown Slide, Peanuts.*™ London, Coronet Books, 1960.

The Concise Oxford Dictionary. New York, Oxford University Press, 1982.

Brewer's™ *Concise Phrase & Fable.* London, Cassell & Co. Publishing, 2000.

Mankiewicz, Joseph L., *All About Eve.* Twentieth Century Fox.

About the Author

Liz Lalor has been working as a natural therapist in the alternative health industry for twenty-four years. She read her first *Materia medica* from cover to cover in 1989 when her son was diagnosed with a rare disease. Through her successful treatment of his illness, she was able to form an unfaltering belief in the unique healing ability of homeopathy. The same enthusiasm and drive that helped her son is evident in this book. Liz Lalor is dedicated to finding a vehicle in which to introduce homeopathy to the lay person. Everyone is interested in their relationships, and a book on homeopathy and relationships is seen by Lalor as an inspirational avenue through which she can introduce homeopathy to the general public.

Lalor has published an extract of her original thesis, "Choosing the Right Partner," in the Australian homeopathic magazine *Similia*. The chapters on Carcinosin, and on Carcinosin and Ignatia, have been published in the renowned homeopathic magazine *Links*. Lalor has a busy and varied homeopathic practice that is concerned with all aspects of health. She has also published an article on her successful treatment of infertility in *Similia*. Her interest in and successful treatment of infertility has introduced homeopathy to people who would never previously have thought of consulting a homeopath.

Liz Lalor can be contacted by email: lalor@ozonline.com.au

Acknowledgments

I am indebted to the following people; without their support this book would never have become a reality.

To Dana Ullman of Homeopathic Educational Services, for his faith and belief in this book.

To Dr. Rajan Sankaran, for his endorsement and interest in my book. Dr. Sankaran's book *The Soul of Remedies* is one of the first homeopathic books that has delved into the psychodynamic crisis within each constitutional picture and has been a great inspiration for me.

To Dr. Philip Bailey for his support in writing the foreword. Dr. Bailey's book *Homeopathic Psychology* is also one of the first books that considered the emotional nature of each constitution and has also been an important influence on forming my ideas.

To the homeopathic magazine and staff of *Links* for publishing "Carcinosin" and "Ignatia."

To Emily Boyd and Winn Kalmon from North Atlantic Books for their invaluable finishing touches to the final editing of this book.

To Paula Grunbaum, Glennis Pitches, and Philippa Youngs, who have helped me with editing and encouragement to pursue my dream of publishing.

To Paula Grunbaum for the inspiration of Silicea.

To homeopath Catherine Bullard for the inspiration of Lachesis.

To Maynard Ellis for all the help with computer advice.

This book was originally written as a final-year thesis. The original inspiration came from my homeopathic lecturer Dr. Isaac Golden. Isaac's inspiration has resulted in a book that is able to introduce homeopathy to everyone who is interested in understanding themselves and finding their ideal partner.

Finally, my deepest thanks go to my Sulphur partner for his inspiration and belief in my being able to write this book.

Index of Film and
Literature References

Carcinosin
    Personal Velocity, directed by Rebecca Miller
    The Joy Luck Club, directed by Wayne Wang
Carcinosin and Ignatia
    Respiro, directed by Emanuele Crialese
    I Capture the Castle, directed by Tim Fywell
Carcinosin and Mercurius
    High Fidelity, directed by Stephan Frears
    The Way I Killed My Father, directed by Anne Fontaine
Carcinosin and Silicea
    Intermezzo, directed by Gregory Ratoff
Lycopodium
    The Apartment, directed by Billy Wilder
    Shoah, directed by Claude Lauzmann
    Nowhere in Africa, directed by Caroline Link
    Une Affaire de Femmes, directed by Claude Chabrol
Lycopodium and Calc-carb
    David Copperfield, by Charles Dickens
    Persuasion, directed by Roger Michell
Lycopodium and Lachesis
    A Touch of Class, directed by Melvin Frank
Lycopodium and Nat-mur
    Full Moon in Paris, directed by Eric Rohmer
Lycopodium and Pulsatilla
    David Copperfield, by Charles Dickens
    Canada-based North American TV series *Queer As Folk*
    Husbands and Wives, directed by Woody Allen
    Hannah and Her Sisters, directed by Woody Allen

Lycopodium and Silicea
>   *Rebecca*, directed by Alfred Hitchcock
>   *Far from Heaven*, directed by Todd Haynes
>   *Adam and Evelyne*, directed by Harold French

Nat-mur
>   Canada-based North American TV series *Queer As Folk*
>   *Kramer vs. Kramer*, directed by Robert Benton
>   *It All Starts Today (Ca Commence Aujourd'Hui)*, directed by Bertrand Tav-
>   ernier

Nat-mur and Arsenicum
>   *The Law of Similars*, by Chris Bohjalian
>   *Hannah and Her Sisters*, directed by Woody Allen
>   *Husbands and Wives*, directed by Woody Allen
>   *The Joy Luck Club*, directed by Wayne Wang

Nat-mur and Causticum
>   *Gandhi*, directed by David Attenborough
>   *The Blues Brothers*, directed by John Landis
>   *The African Queen*, directed by John Huston

Nat mur and Nat-mur
>   *Go Fish*, directed by Rose Troche
>   *Bedrooms and Hallways*, directed by Rose Troche

Nat-mur and Phosphorus
>   *Life Is Beautiful*, directed by Roberto Benigni
>   Canada-based North American TV series *Queer As Folk*
>   *I Capture the Castle*, directed by Tim Fywell
>   *Sense and Sensibility*, directed by Ang Lee

Nat-mur and Sepia
>   *Kramer vs. Kramer*, directed by Robert Benton
>   *Une Liaison Pornographique (A Pornographic Affair)*, directed by Frederic
>   Fonteyne

Sepia
>   *The Hours*, directed by Stephan Daldry
>   *Une Liaison Pornographique (A Pornographic Affair)*, directed by Frederic
>   Fonteyne
>   *The French Lieutenant's Woman*, directed by Karel Reisz

Sepia and Lycopodium
>   *Venus Talking*, directed by Rudolf Thome

Sepia and Medorrhinum
>   Canada-based North American TV series *Queer As Folk*
>   *Miss Smillas's Feeling for Snow*, by Peter Høeg
>   *Loulou*, directed by Maurice Pialat

Carrington, directed by Christopher Hampton

Sunday Bloody Sunday, directed by John Schlesinger

Sepia and Nux vomica

Howards End, directed by James Ivory

Network, directed by Sidney Lumet

Casablanca, directed by Michael Curtiz

Staphisagria

A Man & Two Women, directed by Valerie Stroh

The Piano Teacher, directed by Michael Haneke

Canada-based North American TV series *Queer As Folk*

Staphisagria and Graphites

Canada-based North American TV series *Queer As Folk*

Sense and Sensibility, directed by Ang Lee

Staphisagria and Mercurius

The Piano Teacher, directed by Michael Haneke

Les Misérables, TV mini-series directed by Josée Dayan and Dedier Decoin

Sulphur

The Life of Samuel Johnson, by Boswell

Slide Charlie Brown Slide, by Charles M. Schulz

Balzac: A Life of Passion, directed by Josée Dayan

American Splendor, directed by Robert Pulcini and Shari Springer Berman

Sulphur and Lachesis

All About Eve, directed by Joseph L. Mankiewicz

Sulphur and Mag-carb

Her Majesty Mrs. Brown, directed by John Madden

American Splendor, directed by Robert Pulcini and Shari Springer Berman

Endnotes

1. The article is in Volume 172, issue 2316, November 10, 2001, page 4. The article is written by Andy Coglan and is titled "Is this the trick that proves homeopathy isn't hokum?"

2. Three constitutions — Calc-carb, Pulsatilla, and Silicea — feel emotionally insecure. The distinguishing differences are Calc-carbs feel secure when they know their home and family are secure, Pulsatillas feel secure when they have the total attention of their partner, Siliceas feel secure when they are in harmony with their own morals. Calc-carbs do not have inner security and protection. Calc-carbs appear obstinate and stubborn, but in fact, it is more the case that they are too scared to move or change. Calc-carbs need family to feel secure.

3. Both Carcinosins and Mag-carbs share the feeling of abandonment in childhood. Mag-carbs are different to Carcinosins, in that they respond to their anxieties by trying to build family security around themselves. The distinguishing characteristic of Carcinosin is the need to push and expand horizons. Medorrhinums also have the same need to expand and push boundaries, but Medorrhinums do not necessarily want to know who they are; they are happy moving between extremes. Carcinosins have a pressing need to find definition of self.

4. Diabetes is a marker indicating an inherited history of breakdown of the body. The significance of this characteristic within the theme of Carcinosin is the body working against itself.

5. This is another important distinction from Mag-carbs, who are chilly.

6. This is also a physical peculiarity of the constitution Medorrhinum. The emotional themes differentiate the two constitutions. Carcinosin has a similar need to explore boundaries as Medorrhinum, but Carcinosin is motivated by a strong sense of duty and responsibility, while Medorrhinum is not.

7. Iridology often interprets this as an indication of a possible breakdown of the immune system.

8. Carcinosins have a strong need to experience sensations. This characteristic is evident in their urgent need to explore the boundaries of their own body through their love of dance and adventure. Masturbation is simply a reflection of this need.

9. I say this very liberally. An acceptable mourning period can only be assessed after first taking into consideration cultural differences.

10. Nat-mur in comparison to Causticum will hang on much longer. Nat-mur is motivated by revenge; Causticum is motivated by principles. Causticum can move on to a new cause, and this ability also distinguishes Causticum from Nat-mur.

11. The homeopathic remedy *Causticum* is also often used for the lack of progression of labor.

12. Because potassium deficiency deals with the balance of fluids, a lot of the skin conditions do not heal well. Causticums are prone to anal fissures or tears from constipation that take a long time to heal. The homeopathic remedy is also used for slow-healing burns and for the emotional trauma of being burned. *Causticum* is especially relevant for the patient who is unable to let go of the trauma.

13. Non-metals do not make good conductors of heat. The mineral graphite is the exception because it has a special structure that allows it to conduct heat. The conductive theme of graphite is reflected in Graphites' emotive sensibility.

14. Nat-mur also remembers hurt. The difference is that Graphites is genuinely confused as to why someone was so cruel, while Nat-mur holds painful memories to fuel revenge or as an excuse for never opening up again. Conversely, Graphites becomes more timid and sensitive as a result of these experiences.

15. *Aggravated* is a homeopathic term that is also understood as "made worse by."

16. This is a common experience associated with unresolved grief.

17. The homeopathic remedy *Lachesis* is often considered for patients who can't trust again after disappointment in love. Trust is an important Achilles heel with Lachesis, and with Nat-mur hurt is the most important Achilles heel.

18. This fear is reflective of the physical effect of snake poisoning on the heart muscle.

19. This symptom can mirror the fear of being strangulated by a snake.

20. *Lachesis* is often a good remedy for the adverse symptoms of menopause. Because Lachesis the constitution is aggravated by the delay or restriction of menses, the use of the homeopathic remedy *Lachesis* is often indicated as one of the best remedies to consider. The physical characteristics of *Lachesis* the remedy match the hot flushes and excessive sweating that are a problem for a lot of women. It is also an important remedy to consider for hypertension during menopause.

21. This is applicable to both women and men.

22. For the homeopathic student it should be noted that the carbonate aspect of the remedy is the aspect that contributes to the level of fear and anxiety that is particular to Mag-carbs.

23. In my clinical practice, I have used *Mag-carb* for children who are not able to digest their mother's milk. The use of *Mag-carb* in this instance is a very clear example of the emotional theme of anxiety matching the physical theme of a sensitive stomach. It is also one of the main remedies to consider in cases of "failure to thrive" (FTT) and for orphaned or rejected babies.

24. Homeopathy assumes a person can move into a particular constitutional state as a result of contracting a disease, in this case gonorrhea. The assumption is that it is then possible to lift that state by giving the person the homeopathic remedy *Medorrhinum*. This is seen more commonly in homeopathic practice in the use of *Nat-mur*. A dose of the homeopathic remedy *Nat-mur*, if it is indicated, has the ability to lift someone out of a long-lasting grief.

25. The homeopathic remedy *Mercurius* is a good remedy to use in gastroenteritis if the person feels that the diarrhea will never end.

26. For the homeopathic student reading this book, please note that all Natrum constitutions are predominantly closed. When the muriaticum is added to Nat-mur then the emphasis is strongly centered on issues to do with being hurt and avoiding hurting others. Nat-murs will consequently have more issues to do with recovering from past hurts in relationships than, for example, a Natrum phosphoricum. Nat-murs overgive to avoid hurting; consequently, they have issues to do with martyrdom. The reason I have chosen to concentrate on Nat-murs is that in my clinical experience they are the most common constitution needing help with love and relationships.

27. This might seem bizarre, but it is an amazingly common complaint. An obsession with robbers reflects the degree to which Nat-murs struggle with vulnerability. This is highlighted by their vulnerability in bed.

28. Strychnine was also used in Victorian times as an aphrodisiac. The need to be stimulated on all levels is still evident in the energy of Nux vomica.

29. Siliceas have a strong fear of needles; they are particularly sensitive to, and aggravated by, vaccination. The remedy is often used to expel foreign objects like splinters. The Silicea need to expel foreign objects is also mirrored on the emotional and mental sphere in Siliceas' need to expel foreign thoughts or feelings that are not compatible with their own.

30. Siliceas will also become sick if they try to suppress emotions or feelings that are upsetting them, or if they worry excessively about a particular function or event.

31. Pedanius Dioscorides (born c.AD 40, Anazarbus, Cilicia, died c.90), Greek physician and pharmacologist whose work *De materia medica* was the classical botanical pharmacological text.

32. Staphisagria children are easy targets for sexual abuse. They pride themselves on never expressing any "bad feelings," so consequently they struggle with finding enough anger to stand up to the abuser. They are quiet and sensitive, and this makes them an easy target.

33. Staphisagrias are drawn to meditation and Eastern religions as a way of controlling their feelings. "Enlightened" Staphisagrias are proud they are able to control anger. In a constitutional Staphisagria, meditation can be suppressive unless the person also works on accepting anger.

34. *Staphisagria* is also a good remedy to use for the sensitivity and pain of shingles.

35. The homeopathic remedy *Staphisagria* is still used for infections associated with head lice; this use reflects its herbal history.

36. The tendency to swallow is particularly noticeable if Staphisagrias are starting to share feelings or emotions they do not want to acknowledge or admit. The poison is noted for the excessive production of saliva.

37. Forced yawning is a good somatic psychotherapy technique to help the person let go of suppressed feelings or tension.

38. Sulfur is also obtained from natural gas impurities and from sulfur-containing chemicals.

39. One of the most distinguishing features of Carcinosins is that they often have a stunned, emotionless look. Carcinosins are so conditioned to expanding inside, they are unable to express or show emotion. The course that the disease cancer takes is to expand into surrounding tissue and organs, and this is a process that often takes place without cancer sufferers even knowing they have the disease. Often cancer victims will only discover they have cancer because the size of their tumor has become large enough to push against surrounding organs. The same process is evident in the constitution Carcinosin. In my clinical experience it is quite common to see Carcinosins at the point that they do not know who they are and are no longer able to function. This is important to understand because it is at this time that they need a lot of help and support, to be able to undo the emotional pathology and find out who they are. Carcinosin can also get healing from many other forms of therapy. A large percentage of my patients who are Carcinosins come to me for somatic body work and massage, which can also help in defining a physical and emotional sense of boundary and self. It is also not unusual to find that Carcinosins often pursue themselves through dance, yoga, or meditation. All these therapies help in the exploration and definition of self.

40. The *Concise Oxford Dictionary* describes hysteria as "psychoneurosis with anaesthesia, convulsions, etc., and usu. with disturbance of moral and intellectual faculties; uncontrolled or morbid excitement."

41. Ignatias are also unpredictable in how they deal with physical complaints.

42. *Nat-mur* is the complementary remedy of *Ignatia*. Ignatias will often need the homeopathic remedy *Nat-mur*, to help unblock how stuck they have become in their grief. Both *Nat-mur* and *Ignatia* are used for grief – *Nat-mur* for controlled grief held within, and *Ignatia* for hysterical grief.

43. The mercurial vulnerability of Rob is particularly evident in the last scene of the film. The eccentric Barry, played by actor Jack Black, who works in his record shop is going to sing at the launch of Rob's new band. The fear of being humiliated in public because Barry is wacky is terrifying to Rob.

44. Lycopodiums will always assess situations on the basis of survival. If it is a life-or-death situation, Lycopodiums will do what it takes to survive, but they also will make sure that they will never be in that situation again. If it is not crucial to survival they will maintain their position and walk away.

45. Arsenicums also fear death but they will be the first to call a doctor; in fact, if they could have a doctor "in residence" they would be very happy.

46. It is not unusual in my clinical experience for Lycopodium patients to spend the entire consultation telling you they don't need you. In the second consultation they tell you they are feeling better, but they were already feeling good in the first place, which confirms they did not need to come!

47. Lycopodiums will demand more attention and mothering when they are sick than any of the children in a family.

48. Lycopodiums have the ability to survive the most horrendous of situations. I realized after writing this chapter on Lycopodium that in Claude Lauzmann's film *Shoah*, the majority of the survivors of the concentration camps he interviewed appeared to me to be Lycopodiums. Lycopodiums have the ability to assess how to survive in a concentration camp – who to bribe, what job to secure, and so on – to make sure they come out on top and survive. The other constitution that would also have an advantage in the survival stakes would of course be Nux vomica. It is blatantly obvious from survivor's stories that survival depended on luck, "mazel." The other thing that was needed was skillful assessment of what it was going to take to survive. Lycopodiums do not emotionally react; rather, they intellectually assess. By saying this I am not saying that Lycopodiums do not feel – they do, but they will not be overcome or crippled by their emotions. Only people who are not overcome by the depth of their emotional responses could have an advantage in the death camps. Nat-murs, for example, would be so overcome by empathy they would take on the suffering around them. To discuss this concept in depth is obviously not the aim of this book, but it is a revelation that I wanted to share to help in the understanding of Lycopodium. In one interview in *Shoah*, a survivor talks about the last traumatic moments he spent with his wife and children. His job was to cut their hair before they went to the gas chambers. In the film the survivor reveals the painful thinking processes he went through at the time. If he

were to reveal their fate the guards would know what he had done, and his own life would also be lost. Nat-murs or Carcinosins would be so empathic they would surrender their own lives. The Lycopodium state of mind is to continue to cut their hair and to ultimately survive. It is not that he did not care or feel intensely his pain or their potential anguish – he did, but the main issue for him was to survive. This interpretation of this story and my assessment of the constitution being Lycopodium are not based on fact, but entirely on my interpretation. I have no knowledge that in real life this particular man is Lycopodium. The thinking process of this particular man could quite possibly be different to how I have interpreted it. In stark contrast to this film, the portrayal of the personality of the Holocaust survivor Wladyslaw Szpilman in the film *The Pianist*, directed by Roman Polanski, is not the nature of Lycopodium. Szpilman survived because he was, first, lucky, but most important, he was helped because he was famous among Poles. The Lycopodium mind would all the time be calculating every move and every advantage point. Lycopodium would be driven to join the Jewish Police, not sitting down like he did, and deciding he didn't like the principles of such a move. At every point he survived because he was assimilated enough into Polish society and he had friends to help him. He was pushed off the transport by the Jewish Police because he was a genius. The German soldier at the end of the film helped him to survive because he was talented; he would not have been helped if he had been an ordinary Jew who was unassimilated into Polish society. I have used this film to point out the stark difference between the two stories of survival. This analysis is entirely my interpretation of how the actor portrayed the character and I do not base my interpretation on the real-life person Wladyslaw Szpilman.

It is important to explain that from a homeopathic point of view it is possible, through trauma, to move into the emotional phase of a constitution and not actually be that personality picture or constitution. This is of course the most probable explanation of the type of survival trauma that Holocaust victims would have had to endure. This would also explain the high proportion of Lycopodiums in the film *Shoah*. The majority of survivors of the Holocaust also continue to play out the theme of Lycopodium long after their lives in the camps. The psyche of survival is also being passed on to the following generations in the form of the need to accumulate more and more wealth and power so they will never as a race be so vulnerable to annihilation again. This is the psyche of Lycopodiums' need for survival.

49. Lycopodiums suffer loss of hair and graying before others. The stress of potential failure also has a direct effect on their gut, where they hold their anxiety. They suffer from heartburn, bloating, and digestion problems. Sleep is often difficult because they have so much to control and churn over, it is hard to let go

enough to sleep. If they do get to sleep, they often wake worrying about the day or the past or future. They hang on and retain their urine so much during the day from anxiety; then they wake all night to go to the toilet. By four in the afternoon the exhaustion of competing in the world takes over and they are obsessed with the need for "sugar hits" to get through the rest of the day. All their worry overworks their liver. The homeopathic remedy is often one of the first remedies I consider using with chronic fatigue sufferers, precisely because the mental and emotional fatigue also matches the picture of Lycopodium.

50. The French state guillotined her more for the deaths of the unborn French citizens who were needed to rebuild France after the war, than for the death of the woman.

51. The homeopathic *Materia medica* is written in the language of the eighteenth century. Calc-carb is listed in the repertory as having a "desire to be magnetized." For Calc-carbs this literally means they need their partner to protect them and take control.

52. *Balebo'ste* is a Yiddish word that describes a woman who is a good homemaker. It is a great compliment to call someone a "balebo'ste" because she is a good housewife who also knows how to keep house without making you poor! This is Calc-carb.

53. Calc-carb has a unique physical symptom that reflects this. Calc-carbs feel better when constipated; they have no physical urging to move their bowels and will feel exhausted after a bowel movement.

54. I have discussed Lachesis from a female perspective because it is poignant to the traps that a Lycopodium man will fall into with a female Lachesis. The two examples of Lachesis I use from films in this book are both female; however, in my clinical practice I have statistically far more men than women. A Lachesis man can equally present as alluring and seductive as the Lachesis woman. The Lachesis need to seduce often results in a warm and effeminate voice, and charming personality in the male Lachesis. This softness quickly disappears if you step on their toes. The aggressive, jealous side of Lachesis is seen equally in the male or female Lachesis. It is always important to ask Lachesis about friends. They will always have in their closet many broken friendships that are the end result of friends or lovers assuming too much. Lachesis has a very clear idea of territorial boundaries.

55. Lachesis is listed in the homeopathic *Materia medica* as having "clairvoyance." Rather than viewing this as spiritual clairvoyance, I interpret clairvoyance as part of the instinctive nature of the bushmaster snake to guard its territory.

56. If they hold back sexual passion they feel repressed physically, and suffer from all sorts of fluid congestion problems such as high blood pressure.

57. The ability to charm and control the conversation with clever talk is also

indicative of the power of the venom that the homeopath Hering was so over-come by.

58. Within homeopathic circles there are often very strong gender biases. This example of Lycopodium demonstrates that a Lycopodium woman can "play the field" just as much as a Lycopodium man.

59. It is important to emphasize that the typical Parisian views the suburbs as passé. Lycopodiums need to have their life match their illusion of importance.

60. Ironically she clears the debt on her apartment in Paris so she can set it up for her affairs.

61. A female Pulsatilla is particularly vulnerable to hormonal changes and is likely to be more weepy and critical at these times than usual.

62. Pulsatillas are also very likely not to sleep if they are overexcited. Pulsatillas have such a sympathetic, responsive nature they are easily influenced by emo-tion, regardless of whether the emotion is happiness or sadness.

63. It has been noted that the first time Pulsatilla suffers from serious health prob-lems coincides with the onset of puberty. This has often been interpreted as a physical ailment; however, I interpret this as a difficult time emotionally. Puberty is the first time as a child you are required to move away from the security of family and it is assumed at this time you should become independent. Pul-satillas would find puberty very stressful emotionally because they are happy being dependent. It is not surprising that all the Pulsatilla teenagers I have seen in clinical practice start relationships very early because they need the atten-tion of a lover. Pulsatilla children who do not have the full attention of their mother or father will also get sick a lot. Pulsatilla children involved in divorce will also suffer because they feel abandoned emotionally.

64. Pulsatillas will be far stronger in all business ventures if they are in a business partnership and not on their own. It is important to understand that this does not relate to their having a weak personality or being incompetent. Pulsatillas need emotionally to be with others; this is true for business relationships as well as love relationships.

65. Hahnemann, in his writings on the proving of *Lycopodium*, suggests a dose of *Pulsatilla* to calm the feverish physical states of Lycopodium. Emotionally the same can be also said: Not only do Pulsatillas have the ability to calm Lycopodi-ums, they also have the ability to stimulate Lycopodiums.

66. Adolescence is the time Siliceas start to formulate their opinions. Siliceas never give an inch; they hold onto what they believe and are never flexible or able to be negotiated with. Combine this with the usual dynamics of being a teenager, and the parents of Siliceas are in for fun and games.

67. "Healing" is a process that can take many forms, but with Nat-murs it has to involve some form of talking therapy. It is not enough to just give a Nat-mur a homeopathic potency of the remedy *Nat-mur*. A Nat-mur dwells on self-

blame, hurt, and revenge that must be talked out. Nat-murs also take failure in relationships to heart, and if this is not sorted out, Nat-murs will spend the rest of their lives alone, because it is much easier than having to confront their pain or hurt. The other consequence of Nat-murs not working out past hurts is that they will avoid commitment in their future relationships.

68. I discuss this relationship more fully from a Pulsatilla point of view in the chapter on Lycopodium and Pulsatilla.

69. My comments are based on the characters that Woody Allen plays and this is entirely my interpretation. I have no claims to knowing whether Woody Allen is in fact an Arsenicum constitution.

70. Arsenicums are generally arrogant about their opinions. Arsenicums do not like to delegate responsibility in the workplace or even to any workman at home because they are convinced that the job will never be done properly by anyone else. Arsenicums will work ten times harder than anyone else in an office or corporation to make sure they do not make mistakes. Arsenicums will never win the "most-popular-person-at-work" award, but they will have the satisfaction that they are right and this is what genuinely makes them feel needed and secure in the world. They will also not necessarily be able to take risks in business, but if you employ any Arsenicums in your business you can be sure they will be obsessively careful.

71. Causticums can obsessively stick to a belief system so rigidly they are not able to be flexible to changing circumstances or embrace different views. In 1938 Gandhi wrote an article on his pacifist solution for the Jews in Nazi Germany. His pacifist solution for India was obviously inappropriate and not applicable for the Jews in Nazi Germany. It does not matter whether Gandhi's beliefs were right or wrong; the point of this discussion is that Causticums can become fossilized and inflexible, unable to adapt or change their views. It can also be said that Gandhi was equally rigid in his views of the right to religious differences between Muslims and Hindus in his own country. I am not offering an opinion on either of these views. The important point in this discussion is Causticums can be viewed as either enlightened pacifists or terrorists, and they can be either. The theme of Causticums is inflexibility.

72. The analysis of Causticum is based purely on my interpretation of Causticum and is based on the presentation of the character role the actor Ray Charles has in the film *The Blues Brothers*. I make no claim to any knowledge whether he is in fact a Causticum constitution. It is not possible to predict any celebrity's constitution until you sit down with that person and get to know him or her. It is for this reason I have continually referred to characters in films or literature for examples of particular constitutions.

73. Even though Dora's name was not on the list for the transport train, and she would not have been sent by the Italian Fascists, she insists on going to the

camp to share the fate of her son and Guido. The film does not explore the personality of Dora enough for me to be sure of her constitution, but her dedication, loyalty, and support of Guido at a very delicate time in history for a gentile to support a Jew are noteworthy, distinguishing characteristics. I suspect her empathic nature, determinism, or martyrdom (depending on individual interpretation) could quite possibly be the constitution Carcinosin.

74. It just so happened that the horse had earlier been painted green with graffiti on it, declaring it was a Jewish horse, a wonderful humorous twist that makes the scene even more poignant.

75. Phosphorus enthusiastically can often appear and act like a child. It is this quality that makes them so attractive and unique. Guido plays the role of a child and playmate to his son Joshua and this is portrayed in a wonderful scene in which Guido drops off Dora in the town square so she can go to work; all three are on the bike with Guido peddling like a maniac.

76. If Dora was indeed a Carcinosin it would add weight to the depth of Guido's love for her and her excitement about him. Carcinosins, in comparison to Nat-murs, are far more expansive and emotive.

77. The film is concerned with a time in English history when women had no control over inheritance. The tight controls of society at that time have to be taken into consideration when analyzing the film and the constitutions portrayed in the film. The story is set after the death of their beloved father, so the context of loss and grief must also be taken into consideration. Not only have they lost their father, they are also losing their house and status in society. I have analyzed Elinor as Nat-mur. Nat-mur is a constitutional picture that can be present after the loss or death of a loved one – the person might not truly be the constitution Nat-mur. It is possible after grief to move into another state and to stay in that homeopathic constitution for a long time. This is particularly evident in the case of Nat-mur.

78. The film *Kramer vs. Kramer,* directed by Robert Benton with Dustin Hoffman and Meryl Streep, deals mainly with the painful ending of a marriage and bitter court struggle over custody of a child. The character Ted is Nat-mur and his wife Joanna is Sepia. A Sepia woman, if ungrounded, will feel as if she has to flee to restore her space and grounding, while Nat-murs, when abandoned and hurt, will react by seeking revenge. This is the exact scenario played out in their marriage breakdown and custody battle.

79. The portrayal of the woman in the film *Respiro,* directed by Emanuele Crialese, has aspects that cross over into the constitutional portrayal of Sepia. Grazia, played by actor Valeria Golino, is a free spirit who is seen as crazy by a stifling, small, rural Italian community. Grazia is not Sepia but Ignatia and, although she is trapped, her need to escape is not the motivation of Sepia. Igna-

tias are motivated by the need to have freedom to express themselves emotionally, while Sepias actually need freedom just to find themselves.

80. The presentation of sexual strutting is no different between the female Lycopodium and the male Lycopodium.

81. If left untreated, gonorrhea can cause a systemic disease called disseminated gonococcal infection, or DGI.

82. Brian is continually irritated by the character Ted, who is the Calc-carb in the series. Calc-carbs are motivated by the need to remain stable and secure; they have no drive to push into the unknown.

83. Nat-mur, who is usually renowned for revenge, pales into insignificance in comparison to Medorrhinum.

84. Napoleon was famous for getting his men to march on no sleep because he needed none. Nux vomicas have an unusual physical characteristic: brief naps make them feel better. Napoleon supposedly only slept for 20 minutes at a time. Nux vomicas suffer from sleep problems due to having an overstimulated mind; consequently, they can only sleep for short periods.

85. *Nux vomica* and *Sepia* are referred to as complementary remedies. A complementary remedy is often prescribed on the basis that the person has moved into the complementary phase of the other remedy picture. Unhealthy Sepias are often very muddled and disorganized and will often go into manic cleaning sessions. Sepias also get disconnected and trapped in this mania, which consequently makes them feel more disconnected. The manic phase of Sepia is matched and is "like" the picture of Nux vomica.

86. Note that this symptom mirrors the effects of the poison causing excess salivation.

87. Staphisagrias have a strong physical sensitivity and reactivity to match the sensitivity on the emotional side; this mirrors the nature of the poison the remedy was derived from. There is a wonderful scene in the film where Erika is walking through a shopping center. A man brushes her arm. The trembling and distain she shows as a result of being touched is a beautiful portrayal of the physical as well as emotional hypersensitivity of Staphisagria.

88. This abusive relationship is discuss further in the chapter on Staphisagria and Mercurius.

89. Vic as a personality is discussed more fully in the chapter on Staphisagria and Graphites.

90. Graphites people also experience the same sorts of issues with health. They often feel like they lack inner structure. Often having very sluggish nutrition and circulation, they are often overweight and have a tendency to put on soft fat. But it is important to note that Graphites is not particularly disturbed by being fat. One of the most common excuses used by fat people is they feel emotionally

secure underneath their layers of fat. For Graphites this excuse is true. For other constitutions like Nat-murs, Calc-carbs, or Mag-carbs, their use of the same excuse is not completely true; these constitutions have other strengths in their personalities to fall back on in times of stress. Graphites does not have these strengths. If it is a particularly stressful time, with worries about the security of family, Graphites will tend to need more body layers. Graphites people do not just need the comfort of food; they need the security of fat because this is their defense mechanism against the turmoil of the world.

91. The old blood pressure machines that contain mercury are no longer recommended for use in hospitals and medical practice because it was discovered that the mercury was leaking and was potentially destructive to the health of the practitioners using the machines. Mercury is destructive because it has the ability to corrode tissue. When ingested, it can burn the stomach lining, which then causes intestinal inflammation and bleeding. Mercury can affect not only the digestive system but also the kidneys and the nervous system. Chronic mercury poisoning occurs when small amounts are ingested over long periods. This intoxication causes irreversible damage to the brain, liver, and kidneys. The most famous case of this occurred in Minata Bay, Japan, where a factory dumped waste containing dangerously high levels of mercury into the surrounding sea. The fish, which were the staple food of the island, became contaminated with dangerously high levels of thiomethyl-mercury, a by-product of mercury.

92. I have not been gender-specific with Sulphur. In referring to Sulphur as chauvinist, I am applying this to female as well as male. Female Sulphurs are equally as chauvinist as male Sulphurs. The *Concise Oxford Dictionary* defines *chauvinist* as "bellicose patriot; fervent supporter of a cause."

93. The most common reason Sulphurs are good with money and are able to plan ahead is a desire to retire early so they can indulge in other creative pursuits.

94. Sulphurs are often noted for their obsession with their health. Balzac gave a very good portrayal of why this is the case. Sulphurs suffer from continual digestion problems caused by overeating. Sulphurs will complain of feeling faint if they have not eaten in the last hour! Hahnemann listed more than 300 different symptoms of types of digestive complaints experienced by Sulphurs. I know from treating Sulphurs in my own practice that it is inconceivable and viewed as preposterous that they even consider the benefits of not eating so much. The fact they overeat and indulge in too much alcohol is never considered the answer to health problems; it must be that irritable bowel syndrome or even cancer is causing their indigestion. The inference is that it is my fault as their practitioner, for not knowing what ails them, and that I should be able to restore their health so they can go back to eating properly. Balzac, after being

put on a bland diet by his doctor friend, expressed that life is simply not worth living if he could not have his wine and coffee and his large helpings of very rich food.

95. The following is quoted from Catherine Coulter's book, *Portraits of Homoeo-pathic Medicines*. I could not resist including it as it enhances my image of Balzac: "The museum-like décor of his home is rivaled only by that of an Arsenicum, but Sulphur's rooms will be crowded with objects, while the Arsenicum connoisseur is more select. Both types share a specific form of mate-rialism, wanting to own whatever they appreciate. If it were possible, some Sulphur or Arsenicum would by now have purchased Versailles or the Taj Mahal." (Coulter, Vol. 1, p.158)

96. Even in the height of passion, when Balzac leaves Russia with his countess, Balzac takes along several of the art objects from her estate in the coach. Iron-ically, the weight of all these possessions subsequently causes them to be stuck in the snow.

97. Boswell describes the depression of his friend Samuel Johnson in the following quote. It clearly portrays the depression and melancholy that inflict Sulphur: "The 'morbid melancholy,' which was lurking in his constitution and to which we may ascribe those particularities and that aversion to regular life, which, at a very early period, marked his character, gathered such strength in his twen-tieth year, as to afflict him in a dreadful manner. While he was at Lichfield, in the college vacation of the year 1729, he felt himself overwhelmed with a hor-rible hypochondria, with perpetual irritation, fretfulness and impatience; and with a dejection, gloom and despair, which made existence misery ... John-son, who was blest with all the powers of genius and understanding in a degree far above the ordinary state of human nature, was at the same time visited with a disorder so afflictive, that they who know it by dire experience, will not envy his exalted endowments.... But let not little men triumph upon knowing that Johnson was an HYPOCHONDRIACK." (Boswell, p. 31)

98. The portrayal of Harvey in the film *American Splendor* also reflected the phys-ical characteristics of a Sulphur constitution. Just the way Harvey walked along the street with his shoulders stooped and the fact that he kept itching were very humorous. Sulphurs feel like their back is unable to hold them so they often have stooped shoulders and they also suffer from various itching skin irrita-tions.

99. My interpretation of Harvey Pekar as Sulphur is based entirely on my inter-pretation of Harvey Pekar the comic book caricature, and not on the presen-tation of the real Harvey Pekar, who was interviewed in person in the film *American Splendor*. I have no proof or knowledge that Harvey Pekar, the real-life person, is the constitution Sulphur.

100. When rejected, Sulphurs will quickly sink into depression. When Sulphurs are depressed they can become obsessed with any potential threat to their existence. Sulphurs at this time will reflect the typical hypochondria that Samuel Johnson suffered.

101. The character of Mrs. Cotton, played by actor Sinéad Cosack in the film *I Capture the Castle*, directed by Tim Fywell, is also Lachesis. The way she reacts to her territory being invaded by a potential "gold-digging" daughter-in-law is classic of the sharp-tongued quality of Lachesis.

102. Lachesis will also not be able to stay in a job or occupation that does not allow freedom and control of territory or domain.

103. Their ability to entice and charm and stun is the ultimate control for Lachesis. When they are unhealthy, their speech becomes nervous and loquacious and they can often move into delusional rambling. Lachesis can move into fearful paranoia when feeling hemmed in. At this time it is even hard for them to work because the need to escape often pushes them to the brink of paranoia. Lachesis people in these states also find it difficult to sleep without drugs to slow them down. The worst thing is that they feel overly burdened with responsibility or hemmed in. This struggle with responsibility can be so intense that it is quite common to see Lachesis becoming obsessed with religion – the lure being that God can protect them from any potential perceived threats, and that God can deal with the responsibility of making decisions.

104. Mag-carbs can also easily interpret their parents' divorce as a rejection or abandonment.

105. It is also important to note that Mag-carbs have a very rich dream life. Often their dreams give them incredible insights into how they are feeling. The emotional security of their bed allows them to get in touch with their innermost feelings and thoughts, which they cannot allow themselves to go near during the day. It is also not surprising to find that in the morning when they wake up, Mag-carbs are the most indisposed to talk and emotionally shut down. The idea of having to get out of bed and go out into the world creates a lot of anxiety. Ironically, although Mag-carbs feel secure and emotionally better in bed at night they often suffer physically from neuralgic pains that force them to get up and move about. Mag-carbs during the day also suffer from physical exhaustion and the restlessness at night is the complete opposite to the physical heaviness they experience during the day.

106. Mag-carbs can suffer from violent neuralgic pains along the course of nerves, especially in the legs and feet; the pain can be so intense they feel it is only better when they are constantly moving. Conversely, they also feel their feet are too heavy and too tired to move. The other leading physical symptom of Mag-carbs is extreme sensitivity to being touched when they have experienced any sort of mental or emotional distress. They are so sensitive in their body at these

times that even cold air can cause them to feel like they are being bruised.

107. This feeling of inactivity crosses over to the physical. Mag-carbs often suffer from constipation. I have noticed in my Mag-carb patients that they often suffer extreme constipation and total inactivity of their bowels, with absolutely no urge to pass a stool when they are avoiding making decisions. The opposite of this is also experienced. Mag-carbs suffer from watery stools that float on the surface. I have observed that diarrhea coincides with difficult dilemmas or conflicts or difficult emotions they are trying to avoid, or emotional traumas they have had to endure.

108. What is particular to the apprehensiveness they suffer is that, although they can have anxiety all day, at night in bed it goes away. Home and the security of being in bed are very important for Mag-carbs. It is this peculiarity that reveals what lies underneath the insecurity and apprehensiveness of Mag-carbs. Mag-carbs feel like they have been abandoned from the security of family. Home and their bed are consequently very comforting.

109. It is important to quantify what I mean by Sulphurs being not very practical with money. The aspect to emphasize is that Sulphurs will always be passionately blind to seeing the practicalities of a particular pursuit that interests them. Sulphurs lack financial discrimination. Sulphurs will not stop, like Calc-carbs, and work on a financial plan. Mr. Brown (see the text discussion of the film *Her Majesty Mrs. Brown*) has no family or plans for the future – he is truly inspired by service and devotion. Balzac (as portrayed in the film *Balzac: A Life of Passion*) was inspired by his writing. Sulphurs are not interested in working or planning for anything that does not fit into their particular pursuit in life. If Sulphurs are good with money, it is likely there is a very strong partner who is controlling the overall finances and keeping them in check.

110. This is definitely the partner that Samuel Johnson needed at twenty. I'm sure his hypochondria and melancholy came on at the same time he had to face the practicalities of life in terms of earning money and not just being able to live his life writing.

111. Balzac knew he needed to marry someone wealthy enough to support his writing. He had the choice of several wealthy women, but the fact his countess also thought he was a genius was the crucial ingredient needed to make him choose her. Sulphurs might be willing to trade their passion and love, but they will not prostitute themselves. The exchange rate or negotiated price of Sulphurs' support for Mag-carbs is that Mag-carbs have to believe in Sulphurs' ideals. Sulphurs will not tolerate anyone who does not share their vision. If Mag-carbs want to keep Sulphurs, they have to believe in Sulphurs.

112. Mag-carbs, because they have such a strong need for support, will put a lot of effort into creating a co-dependent extended family unit. Because Mag-carbs struggle with feelings of being abandoned or orphaned, large close families

ease their feelings of not being needed or wanted. This will also appeal to Sulphurs, as the greater the family the more important they will feel.

113. My interpretation of Joyce as Mag-carb is based entirely upon my homeopathic analysis of the caricature comic book personality as presented in the film *American Splendor,* and not on the real-life person.

114. The real-life Joyce is only interviewed in the film once and in that interview she states that she sees Harvey's interpretation of her as negative. I interpret the presentation of Joyce by the Sulphur Harvey as Mag-carb. In real life she may not in fact suffer as intensely from depression as cynically portrayed by Harvey.

115. Mag-carbs will often suffer from anxiety during the day and will feel a lot safer at home in bed. Often when depressed they will also feel emotionally secure by going to bed. Harvey also portrays Joyce as being chronically hypersensitive to food and having either extreme food allergies or a very dysfunctional attitude about eating. Often the effort of dealing with anxiety and holding down their feelings of apprehensiveness and depression can totally exhaust Mag-carbs. Mag-carbs suffer from sensitive digestion problems that also emotionally coincide with difficult dilemmas or conflicts. Mag-carbs have a characteristic physical theme: When sick, they suffer from sour perspiration, sour diarrhea, sour vomit, and a sour temper. The types of physical complaints that Mag-carbs suffer come on with the stress of emotional disharmony or discord, especially within the family and relationships. It is impossible to ever reject the emotional cause when considering the physical complaints of Mag-carbs.

116. Harvey will not have children because the world does not live up to his Sulphuric ideals.

117. *American Splendor* is a documentary-style film of a film within a film and Harvey Pekar is a real-life person making a caricature of his own personality. My comments are to be taken in the context that it is entirely my interpretation that the personality of the two comic book caricatures as presented in the film *American Splendor* are Sulphur and Mag-carb. My comments on their relationship are also based on the film's comic book caricature portrayal only; I make no claims that they have a co-dependent relationship in real life.

Index

A

Adam and Evelyne, 144–45
Une Affaire de Femmes, 118–19
The African Queen, 166–67
All About Eve, 11, 127, 234–37
Allen, Woody, 135, 137, 157, 158–59,
    160
Allium cepa, 9
American Splendor, 232–33, 243–45
The Apartment, 112–14
arsenic, 16, 155
Arsenicum album (constitution)
    Carcinosin and, 161
    emotional legacy of, 157–62
    examples of, 92, 137, 139, 156–59,
        160, 161
    mental and emotional
        characteristics of, 17
    Nat-mur and, 159–62
    physical characteristics of, 18
    Pulsatilla and, 137, 139, 158–59
    theme of, 16–17, 155–57
Arsenicum album (remedy)
    origins of, 16, 156
    uses for, 157, 158
Attenborough, David, 163
Austen, Jane, 121, 178, 217
Avogadro's number, 8

B

Balzac: A Life of Passion, 228–31,
    233–34
Bedrooms and Hallways, 168–70
Benigni, Roberto, 172
The Blues Brothers, 163–64
Bohjalian, Chris, 156
Brewer's Concise Phrase & Fable, 148
bushmaster snake, 36, 124, 234

C

Ça Commence Aujourd'Hui, 154–55
Calc-carb (constitution)
    challenge for, 120–21
    emotional legacy of, 123–24
    examples of, 30, 120, 121–23
    Graphites vs., 30–31
    Lycopodium and, 119–24
    mental and emotional
        characteristics of, 20
    physical characteristics of, 20–22
    theme of, 12, 19, 119–20
Calc-carb (remedy)
    origins of, 19, 20, 119
    uses for, 21, 22
calcium, 20–21
cancer, 23–24, 25–26, 84
Carcinosin (constitution)

Arsenicum and, 161
challenge for, 88–89, 98–99, 104
emotional history behind, 85–86
emotional legacy of, 86–88
examples of, 90–92, 96–108, 161, 174
Ignatia and, 96–98
mental and emotional characteristics of, 24–25
Mercurius and, 98–104
physical characteristics of, 25–26
Silicea and, 104–8
theme of, 23–24, 84–85
Carcinosin (remedy)
origins of, 23, 84
uses for, 26
Carrington, 196–97
Casablanca, 207–8
Causticum (constitution)
examples of, 163–64, 166–67
mental and emotional characteristics of, 28
Nat-mur and, 164–67
Phosphorus vs., 162–63
physical characteristics of, 28–29
theme of, 27–28, 162–63
Causticum (remedy)
origins of, 27, 162
uses for, 27, 28, 29
Christie, Agatha, 155
A Christmas Carol, 161
Cinchona officinalis, 7–8, 9
codependency, 240–43
Comment J'ai Tué Mon Père, 101–4
complementary remedies, 120
constitutions. *See also individual constitutions*
definition of, 4, 10–11, 47
determining your, 11–12
theme of, 4–5, 12

consultations, 3
cuttlefish, 68, 69, 70

D
David Copperfield, 120, 134
Delphinium staphisagria, 75, 77
Dickens, Charles, 120, 134, 161
Dioscorides, 75
Du Maurier, Daphne, 141

F
Far from Heaven, 142–43
The Female Eunuch, 126
Flaubert, Gustave, 16
Forster, E. M., 204
The French Lieutenant's Woman, 186–87
Full Moon in Paris, 128–32
Fywell, Tim, 94

G
Gandhi, 163
Go Fish, 168
gonorrhea, 47–48, 192
graphite, 30–31, 216
Graphites (constitution)
Calc-carb vs., 30–31
emotional legacy of, 218–20
examples of, 30, 217–18
mental and emotional characteristics of, 31
needs of, 217–18
physical characteristics of, 31–32
Staphisagria and, 219–20
theme of, 30–31, 216–17
Graphites (remedy), 30
Greer, Germaine, 126

H
Hahnemann, Samuel, 7–8, 40, 227–28

Hannah and Her Sisters, 137–38, 157–58, 160

Haynes, Todd, 142

Hering, Constantine, 36, 38

Her Majesty Mrs. Brown, 242–43

High Fidelity, 99–101

Høeg, Peter, 194–95

Holroyd, Michael, 196

homeopathy. *See also* constitutions; consultations; remedies
    evidence for, 8–9
    founding of, 7
    popularity of, 2
    principles of, 6, 7, 12
    provings in, 9
    repertory for, 9

The Hours, 185

Howards End, 204–6

Husbands and Wives, 135–39, 158–59, 160

I

I Capture the Castle, 94, 96–98, 174–75, 178

Ignatia (constitution)
    Carcinosin and, 96–98
    challenge for, 93–96
    examples of, 93–94, 96–98
    mental and emotional characteristics of, 33–34
    Nux vomica vs., 33, 92, 94–95
    physical characteristics of, 34–35
    theme of, 33, 92–93

Ignatia (remedy), 33, 92–93

Intermezzo, 105–8

It All Starts Today, 154–55

J

Johnson, Samuel, 227, 228

Josephine, 203–4

The Joy Luck Club, 91–92, 161

K

Kramer vs. Kramer, 153, 185–86

L

Lachesis (constitution)
    challenge for, 236–37
    emotional legacy of, 237–38
    examples of, 11, 97, 125–28, 234–37
    Lycopodium and, 124–28
    mental and emotional characteristics of, 37
    physical characteristics of, 38–39
    Sulphur and, 234–38
    theme of, 36, 124, 234

Lachesis (remedy)
    origins of, 36, 124, 234
    uses for, 11, 38

The Law of Similars, 156–57

Lessing, Doris, 211

Une Liaison Pornographique, 179–82, 186, 188

Life Is Beautiful, 172–73

Loulou, 195–96

Lycopodium (constitution)
    Calc-carb and, 119–24
    challenge for, 114–19, 128–30
    emotional history behind, 110–12
    emotional legacy of, 124–25
    examples of, 112–14, 116–19, 121–23, 125–32, 137–38, 144–45, 168, 169, 178
    Lachesis and, 124–28
    Lycopodium and, 116–18
    mental and emotional characteristics of, 41–42
    Nat-mur and, 128–32
    Nat-mur vs., 110, 112
    Nux vomica vs., 60, 79, 190–91

physical characteristics of, 42–43
Pulsatilla and, 137–40
Sepia and, 188–92
Silicea and, 140–41, 143–47
Sulphur vs., 79
theme of, 40–41, 109–10, 112
Lycopodium (remedy)
origins of, 40
uses for, 40–41, 126, 210

M

Madam Bovary, 16
Mag-carb (constitution)
codependency and, 240–43
emotional history behind, 238–39
emotional needs of, 239–40
examples of, 242–45
mental and emotional
characteristics of, 45
physical characteristics of, 46
Sulphur and, 239–45
theme of, 44
Mag-carb (remedy), 44, 238
magnesium, 44
A Man & Two Women, 211–12
Mankiewicz, Joseph L., 234
Matthew, book of, 149
Medorrhinum (constitution)
emotional legacy of, 193–95,
198–99
examples of, 48, 151–52, 193–201
mental and emotional
characteristics of, 48–49
Nat-mur and, 151–52
physical characteristics of, 49–50
theme of, 47–48, 192–93, 195–98
Medorrhinum (remedy), 47, 192
Mercurius (constitution)
Carcinosin and, 98–104
challenge for, 98–99, 224–25

emotional history behind, 222–24
emotional legacy of, 221–22
examples of, 99–104, 222–25
mental and emotional
characteristics of, 52–53
Nat-mur vs., 222
physical characteristics of, 53–54
Staphisagria and, 224–25
theme of, 51–52, 99–101, 221
Mercurius (remedy)
origins of, 51
uses for, 53, 221, 224
mercury, 51, 53, 221, 224
The Merry Wives of Windsor, 148
Miller, Rebecca, 90
Les Misêrables, 222–23
Miss Smilla's Feeling for Snow, 194–95

N

Napoleon, 203–4
Nat-mur (constitution)
Arsenicum and, 159–62
Causticum and, 164–67
challenge for, 128–30, 167–68,
170–72
emotional depth of, 154–55
emotional legacy of, 151–54,
159–62, 168–70
examples of, 117, 128–32, 134,
151–55, 166–70, 174–75,
179–82, 204–6
Lycopodium and, 128–32
Lycopodium vs., 110, 112
Medorrhinum and, 151–52
mental and emotional
characteristics of, 56–57
Mercurius vs., 222
Nat-mur and, 134, 167–72
Nux vomica and, 204–6
Phosphorus and, 173–79

physical characteristics of, 57–58
Pulsatilla and, 134
Sepia and, 153, 179–83
Staphisagria vs., 75–76
Sulphur and, 242
theme of, 55–56, 148–51
Nat-mur (remedy)
origins of, 55, 148
uses for, 149, 178
Network, 206–7
"never-well-since" symptom, 3
Nowhere in Africa, 116–18
Nux vomica (constitution)
challenge for, 201–2
emotional legacy of, 206–8
emotional need of, for power and
devotion, 203–4
examples of, 203–8
Ignatia vs., 33, 92, 94–95
Lycopodium vs., 60, 79, 190–91
mental and emotional
characteristics of, 60
Nat-mur and, 204–6
physical characteristics of, 60–61
Sepia and, 201–2, 204–6, 208
Sulphur vs., 79
theme of, 59–60, 201
Nux vomica (remedy)
origins of, 33, 59, 201
uses for, 210

O
Othello, 148

P
Peanuts, 226
Pekar, Harvey, 232–33, 243–45
Personal Velocity, 90–91
Persuasion, 121–23
Phosphorus (constitution)

Causticum vs., 162–63
challenge for, 175–79
examples of, 121, 172–75, 178–79
mental and emotional
characteristics of, 63
Nat-mur and, 173–79
physical characteristics of, 63–64
theme of, 62–63, 172
phosphorus (mineral), 62, 172, 177
Phosphorus (remedy)
origins of, 62
uses for, 177, 179
The Piano Teacher, 214–15, 224–25
A Pornographic Affair, 179–82, 186, 188
potassium, 27, 162–63
potentizing, 8
provings, 9
Pulsatilla (constitution)
Arsenicum and, 137, 139, 158–59
emotional fragility and needs of,
133–35
examples of, 134, 135–39, 158–59
Lycopodium and, 137–40
mental and emotional
characteristics of, 66
Nat-mur and, 134
physical characteristics of, 66–67
theme of, 65, 132–33, 134
Pulsatilla (remedy), 65, 132–33

Q
Queer As Folk, 30, 48, 121, 135, 151–52,
173, 193–94, 215–16, 217

R
Rebecca, 141–42
remedies. *See also individual remedies*
choosing the right, 12–13, 23
complementary, 120
diluting and potentizing, 7–8

sources of, 10, 47
repertory, 9
Respiro, 93–94

S
salt, 55, 148–51
Sankaran, Rajan, 109, 111
Sense and Sensibility, 178–79, 217–18
Sepia (constitution)
    challenge for, 187–88, 191–92,
        201–2
    emotional legacy of, 184–85,
        198–99
    examples of, 153, 179–82, 185–87,
        199–201, 204–6
    freedom and, 184, 187–88
    Lycopodium and, 188–92
    Medorrhinum and, 193, 197–201
    mental and emotional
        characteristics of, 69–70
    Nat-mur and, 153, 179–83
    Nux vomica and, 201–2, 204–6, 208
    physical characteristics of, 70–71
    theme of, 68–69
Sepia (remedy), 68, 70
Shakespeare, William, 148–49
silica, 72, 140
Silicea (constitution)
    Carcinosin and, 104–8
    challenge for, 104, 145–46
    emotional legacy of, 141–43
    examples of, 105–8, 141–43, 144–45
    mental and emotional
        characteristics of, 73–74
    physical characteristics of, 74
    theme of, 72–73, 104, 140–41
Silicea (remedy), 72, 140
Staphisagria (constitution)
    challenge for, 211–12, 214–16
    emotional history behind, 212–14

emotional legacy of, 210–11
examples of, 211–12, 214–16, 224–25
Graphites and, 219–20
mental and emotional
    characteristics of, 76–77
Mercurius and, 224–25
Nat-mur vs., 75–76
physical characteristics of, 77–78
theme of, 75–76, 209
Staphisagria (remedy)
    origins of, 75
    uses for, 77, 210, 213, 221
A Story of Women, 118–19
Strachey, Lytton, 196
strychnine, 33, 34, 59, 60, 75, 92, 201
sulfur (element), 79–80, 81, 230, 231
Sulphur (constitution)
    challenge for, 227–30, 233–34
    emotional legacy of, 231–33
    examples of, 226, 227–30, 232–33,
        234–37, 242–45
    Lachesis and, 234–38
    Lycopodium vs., 79
    Mag-carb and, 239–45
    mental and emotional
        characteristics of, 80–81
    Nat-mur and, 242
    Nux vomica vs., 79
    physical characteristics of, 81–82
    strength of, in relationships, 230–31
    theme of, 79–80, 226–27
Sulphur (remedy)
    origins of, 79, 230
    uses for, 210
Sunday Bloody Sunday, 199–201

T
Tan, Amy, 92, 161
A Touch of Class, 125–28

V
Venus Talking, 189–91
Victoria, Queen, 242–43
La Vita é Bella, 172–73

W
The Way I Killed My Father, 101–4
wind flower, 65, 132–33